GOD is
with US

Myron K. Loss (signature)

BY
MYRON K. LOSS

GOD IS WITH US

Cover art by Myron Loss

ISBN: 978-1-4951-3811-9

Published by Encouragement Ministries
3408 NE 23rd Ave.
Ocala, FL 34479
encmin@gmail.com
570-765-2352

Additional copies available for $15.00 which includes shipping to US addresses. Write for costs for overseas shipping.

40% discount to everyone on purchases of ten or more, and 40% discount to bona fide bookstores on purchases of three or more.

Other titles available from Encouragement Ministries:

Culture Shock – Dealing with Stress in Cross-cultural Living - by Myron Loss - 175 pages $12.00
(A time-proven standard for preparing missionaries and other workers for the transition from one culture to another)

The Reward of the Righteous – by Myron Loss – 71 pages $8.00
(A study of the rewards that God is preparing for those who are in Christ)
All prices include shipping to US add.

Available in 2015:
Letters from Heaven by Myron Loss – 101 pages
(Anthony Moyer dies and goes to Heaven and finds a way to write letters to his niece and other friends back on earth)

The World is Up-side-down by Myron Loss – 400 pages
(A serious study in the contrasts between the values of the world and the values in the Kingdom of Heaven.)

Impreso en Colombia - Printed in Colombia

Table of Contents

About the author   7
Introduction   9

Section one
God and his work   17

1. God, a very present help   19
2. Does God have feelings?   41
3. God's purpose and plan in creation   63
4. Can God answer prayer?   73
5. The process of salvation   91
6. Where does faith come from?   123
7. Sons of God   145
8. What does it mean to be "in Christ?"   163
9. Jesus, a man just like us with one exception   177
10. Does God change his mind?   201
11. Foreknowledge, fore–ordination, omniscience
    and the sovereignty of God   213
12. What is predestination?   235
13. Does time affect God?   239
14. The problem of the origin of evil   243
15. Examining some of the "proof texts" used to support
    belief in the absolute foreknowledge of God   249
16. The questionable legacy of Augustine and
    the sixteenth century reformers   257
17. Conclusion   273

Section two
Biblical evidence for skeptics   277

18. Overwhelming biblical evidence that the
    future has not all been determined   283
19. More overwhelming evidence   311
20. Still more evidence   347
21. New Testament evidence   379

Appendix A, A critique of Frame's "No Other God"   391

About the author

Myron Loss is a retired missionary who served 35 years in Bolivia, Paraguay and Uruguay with Andes Evangelical Mission and SIM. Prior to that, he was a pilot in the USAF and served one year in Viet Nam.

His ministries have been varied including evangelism, discipleship, missionary aviation, Marriage Encounters and marriage counseling, church–planting, radio, construction, candidate recruitment, literature distribution, hospitality, teaching, writing, and administration.

He has an industrial engineering degree from Penn State University, an aeronautical rating from the USAF, a diploma in Advanced Bible Studies from Moody Bible Institute, a Master of Arts in Cross-cultural Communication degree from Columbia Graduate School of Bible and Missions, and a Master of Divinity degree from Columbia Biblical Seminary.

He has authored three other books including, "Culture Shock – Dealing with Stress in Cross-cultural Living," The Reward of the Righteous," and "The World is Up–side–down."

He presently resides in Ocala, Florida with his wife Alice. They are members of Center Point Presbyterian Church (PCA), and also minister in a Hispanic church.

Introduction

Over my years in full-time ministry for the Lord, I have visited many churches in many different countries, and often noticed a great degree of theological confusion. Sincere believers are often ignorant of who God is and how God interacts with them. There are some errant beliefs about God that are very common and that hinder God's work and his outreach through the church. I have often felt deeply saddened at seeing the distortion of sound doctrine and the resulting practices that come out of it.

I am writing this book because I feel the necessity that someone explain certain truths about God's nature and eternal purpose as revealed in the Holy Scriptures. I see error in many churches and it is hard to find one that comes close to a practical theology as revealed in the Bible. Almost all churches have perversions of God's teaching locked up in their thinking and their practices. Satan has a definite monopoly on lies and error, but he has a lot of unwitting collaborators in the established church.

Over the years in Bible School and seminary, as I studied the pre-packaged theology courses (which are often not the "study of God," but the study of "what others have said about God:" i.e. theology–ology), I saw the lack of logic of some of the doctrines, particularly the one about God's foreknowledge of all things future. I couldn't reconcile it with reason or with the Scriptures. I was told to just accept it because it had to be so. I have kept the issue of its authenticity simmering on the back burner for nearly fifty years, often meditating and questioning some of the standard interpretations in mainline Christianity. So, finally, in my retirement from active missionary work, I have dedicated the time necessary to investigate these truths profoundly, examining everything I could in the Bible to see what God has said about these subjects.

Early on, I read a few other books and articles on these themes, but later decided to limit nearly all of my research to the Scriptures, and ignore the controversies exhibited in other people's writings. God has said enough in his Word to make his purposes clear if we are willing to accept his truth.

This is my offering as a primer of practical theology as I understand it from God's Word. It doesn't fit some of our approved and accepted doctrines, but I believe with all my heart that it is rooted and grounded in the Bible and nothing else. My purpose is to help the church to have a clearer understanding of God, his purposes, and his workings.

I have been concerned that so many Christians have errant views of who God is and what he wants to do for them. Many accepted doctrines if taken to their logical conclusions make it impossible for God to lift a finger to help anyone. If God knows all the future, there is no reason whatsoever to pray to him or ask him to do anything. If God knows all the future, there is no incentive whatsoever to tell others about Christ because it won't make one iota of difference in the end. If God knows all the future, he is an inveterate liar, or at best a sinister actor, because he would be telling people things that are far from the truth. (One of the most neglected attributes of God is his veracity – he always says what is true and is incapable of lying or deceiving.) If God knows all the future, you cannot have an intimate personal relationship with him, because a relationship is a two way street, and he can do nothing besides what is already determined by his foreknowledge. The more I studied the Bible on these topics, the more I became angry about the hoaxes perpetrated on the church by Satan and his minions.

Many historians paint George Washington and the founding fathers of the USA as deists. It is true that there were several professing deists in the total (like Jefferson and Franklin), but the vast majority were not. They were people who believed that God still acted in the affairs of human beings, and responded to the pleas of his people. A deist believes that God made the world, and then distanced himself from it to watch how it all turns out. He wound the clock and is letting it run down naturally without any intervention on his part. A deist believes that man is on his own, and that God isn't going to do anything to help him. A deist would have no incentive to pray to God since he believes that he would not or could not respond.

I want to try to help you see God as he has revealed himself in the Scriptures to his prophets and servants. As you read, throw away your colored theological glasses. Don't come into this study with pre-conceived conclusions and distort the Scripture to support them. Take a new look at the old Book with a heart and mind willing to know the true God. It is risky business because you have to sacrifice your theological comfort zone, but I assure you that this is necessary in order to grow in your relationship with him.

Some years ago, we were visiting my sister–in–law and her husband in New Port Ritchey, Florida. They had a large aquarium in their living room with several fish and one crab. While we were there, the crab decided it was time to molt, or detach itself from its old shell. It went through all kinds of contortions until it was finally free and the shell was lying on the bottom of the tank. Now, the crab was a lot more vulnerable to predators (of which in this tank there were none). If out in free water, he would have taken a big risk by removing his protective shell, but he had to do it because it was the only way he could grow. Either he took the risk or remained a pigmy crab the rest of his life.

If it can be shown that the Bible teaches a certain truth, then we should be willing to let go of errant past beliefs when necessary in order to move closer to reality. No man has perfect doctrine, but I have met many people who thought they did, and yet very few of them would agree with each other on many points. We must humbly come to God with the desire to know him better realizing that we still have so much to learn.

All of our doctrines and traditions are subject to fine tuning in the light of God's word, and some of the commonly accepted ones need a complete overhaul. All doctrine must stand the scrutiny of the Scriptures and that which is contrary must be put to the theological knife. If a land surveyor starts off with the wrong coordinates, then all of his conclusions will be wrong except by accident. Most Christians believe what they are told to believe without really knowing why. This creates a real shallowness and makes them an easy target for unprincipled people to take these ignorant sheep captive. Not everyone can be what we consider a Bible scholar, but everyone should, to the best of his capacity, examine the Scriptures to see what is true. Evangelicals and Protestants have long criticized the

Roman Catholic hierarchy for saying that only the clergy may interpret the Scriptures. Let us not make the same mistake and say that the average Christian has no business wrestling to find doctrinal answers in the Word of God.

In these pages, especially in Section Two, you will find hundreds of Bible references and quotations. Please don't let it dissuade you from reading or distract you from the basic principles: I have put them there to show you the exceedingly overwhelming evidence for what I am saying. I am presenting my case by calling on hundreds and hundreds of witnesses. You can decide what to believe as you see the Scriptures, and decide if what I am teaching is true or not.

> *The people in Berea were more open–minded than those in Thessalonica. They were so glad to hear the message Paul told them. They studied the Scriptures every day to make sure that what they heard was really true.*
> Acts 17:11

I challenge you to take the risk. Shake off your old theological straightjacket and go with me on an odyssey of learning. We will be safe so long as we recognize that the Bible is God's inerrant, fully inspired Word, and that we can trust it and the Holy Spirit to guide us on our journey. The Bible trumps all other books, theological confessions, or doctrinal statements ever made by man. No matter how high a regard we have for the Westminster Confession, or the Council of Nicaea, or the catechisms of our church, or any other doctrinal statement, they all must stand correction when God's Word is measured against them and they are found wanting.

Many errors are generated in our beliefs when we distort what God has said. Far too often we manipulate what God has said in order to make it say something entirely different. Someone aptly has commented, "If God doesn't mean what he says, then why doesn't he say what he means?" The problem is not that he hasn't said what he means; the problem is that we don't like what he said, and so we try to change it. We often shape our image of God based on what we want him to be, and not on what he says about himself.

Some say that there are many things in the Bible we can never understand, but God didn't give us the Bible to be understood on the other side of glory where we will keep saying "Aha! So that's what he meant." He gave us the Bible for the here and now so that we could understand and apply what it means and live accordingly. Otherwise, there would be no purpose in his giving it to us, other than to laugh at us later for being so stupid.

My desire is for my readers to come to grow in understanding and practical application of God's truth.

> *I want them to be strengthened and joined together with love and to have the full confidence that comes from understanding. I want them to know completely the secret truth that God has made known. That truth is Christ himself. In him all the treasures of wisdom and knowledge are kept safe.*   Colossians 2:2-3

Paul thought it was possible to reach profound understanding. All the treasures of knowledge and wisdom are found in Christ. He is the center and focus of all of the work of God in creation and in salvation. There is no truth outside of him. There is no love extended to humans except through his hands. There is no true hope offered that does not come as the result of his work. All creation and all of history will someday be placed at his feet, and every knee will bow and every tongue will confess that Jesus is Lord, to the glory of God the Father.

The test of fellowship with another Christian should not be our sworn allegiance to a doctrinal statement, but whether or not we know Christ, and bear the fruit of the Spirit in our lives. The Pharisees were orthodox, but they had none of the fruit of the Spirit of God, and Christ condemned them for their lack of godliness. They had signed the intellectual pledge of sound doctrine, but that was of absolutely no value to them spiritually.

I have written this book mostly for people who have a sincere desire to learn more about God, and a hunger to know and understand him.

This is my offering to you. It is based on fifty–six years of being a Christian, of pondering and studying the Bible (not as a full time occupation, but as an on–going, practical desire to walk with God), and of trying to find a reasonable understanding of what God has revealed to us.

God wants us to understand. *These mysteries were hidden in times past, but now have been revealed.*

We shouldn't throw up our hands and say "It's not understandable."

> *We received the Spirit that is from God, not the spirit of the world. We received God's Spirit so that <u>we can know all that God has given us</u>.*   1 Corinthians 2:12

I hope that you find liberation from some false beliefs and enter into a deeper relationship with God who loves you with all his heart.

This is my prayer for you: that your love will grow more and more; that you will have knowledge and understanding with your love; that you will see the difference between what is important and what is not and choose what is important; that you will be pure and blameless for the coming of Christ; that your life will be full of the many good works that are produced by Jesus Christ to bring glory and praise to God.   Philippians 1:9-11

Section one

God and his work

This first part has the purpose of helping you understand who God is and how he works with his creation. It shows that God loves you so very much, and wants to be your affectionate loving Daddy who walks hand in hand with you through life.

He is always present, feels what you feel, and tries to help you in your every challenge. He wants you to ask him for things you need, and wants to hear your expressions of love in prayer and worship. He rejoices at your successes, and weeps when you do wrong. He wants to have an intimate two-way relationship with you, and bring you to spiritual maturity.

God wanted people to look for him, and perhaps in searching all around for him, they would find him. But he is not far from any of us. It is through him that we are able to live, to do what we do, and to be who we are. As your own poets have said, 'We all come from him.' Acts 17:27-28

You will see something of the amazing wonder of God's plan for your salvation. You will see how he made it possible to forgive a person and change his destiny, because he is united with Christ. You will see how God sent his Son the "Word" to become a human like you so that he could die in your place and give you his righteousness in exchange for your sin.

You will see how much God respects you because he gave you a free will to choose to accept his affections or to turn away. He does not dictate the outcome of your life nor overwhelm you with his will. He loves you, respects you, is cheering for you, and only wants the very best for you both now and in eternity.

God has taken many first steps to woo your affections and is hoping that you will love him in return. How you respond will determine your future.

1. God, a very present help

What are some of the things that God does for his creation and particularly the human race? What is his attitude towards us? Can we trust him to really want the best for us, or is he a self-centered ogre who only cares about himself? Is he easily angered and quick to punish or take revenge on people who hurt or defy him? What is God really like?

A. God wants to help us and bless us with good things

> God is our refuge and strength, an <u>ever-present</u> help in trouble. Therefore we will not fear, though the earth give way and the mountains fall into the heart of the sea, though its waters roar and foam and the mountains quake with their surging. Psalm 46:1-3 NIV

The meaning of the word translated "ever-present" is very emphatic: "he is found an 'exceeding' or 'superlative' help in difficulties."

The Sovereign LORD is my strength; he <u>makes</u> my feet like the feet of a deer, he <u>enables</u> me to go on the heights.
                                                    Habakkuk 3:19 NIV

But God was always there doing the good things that prove he is real. He gives you rain from heaven and good harvests at the right times. He gives you plenty of food and fills your hearts with joy.   Acts 14:17

This was Paul's statement to a group of unbelieving Gentiles in Asia Minor. The good blessings and provision of God extend to all of his creatures, not only those who have put their faith in him.

Look at the birds. They don't plant, harvest, or save food in barns, but your heavenly <u>Father feeds them.</u> Don't you know you are worth much more than they are?
                                                    Matthew 6:26

B. God is a loving, caring, affectionate Father for all his children

See what great love the Father has lavished on us, that we should be called <u>children</u> of God! And that is what we are! The reason the world does not know us is that it did not know him. Dear friends, now we are <u>children</u> of God, and what we will be has not yet been made known. But we know that when Christ appears, we shall be like him, for we shall see him as he is.   1 John 3:1-2 NIV

We Christians are not fully grown, matured sons of God, but rather we are toddlers walking hand in hand with our Daddy. He is on our right side (Isaiah 41:13), and our older brother Jesus is on the other side, holding our other hand.

My sheep listen to my voice. I know them, and they follow me. I give my sheep eternal life. They will never die, and no one can take them out of my hand. My Father is the one who gave them to me, and he is greater than all. No one can steal my sheep out of his hand.

John 10:27-29

We don't have to stand up to the enemies in the world with our own strength. We don't have to pretend to be fully grown and able to defend ourselves. Our Lord Jesus and our Daddy can fight all the battles for us if we will only learn to trust in their care and be at peace. Throughout the whole Bible, God is saying, "Trust me." It's not like the promise made by John Wayne in one of his movies: "Don't worry little girl. We're not going to let anything happen to you." Men make promises they cannot keep, but God always keeps his promises, and also will overflow his blessings to us when we sincerely trust him.

C. God is the most compassionate person who ever existed

Then the LORD came down to him in a cloud, stood there with Moses, and spoke his own name. That is, the LORD passed in front of Moses and said, "YAHWEH, the LORD, is a kind and merciful God. He is slow to become angry. He is full of great love. He can be trusted. He shows his faithful love to thousands of people. He forgives people for the wrong things they do, but he does not forget to punish guilty people.

Exodus 34:5-7a

(See also 2 Chronicles 30:9; Nehemiah 9:17; Psalm 86:15; Joel 2:13; Jonah 4:2)

He is more compassionate than the most loving mother could ever be.

> *"Can a mother forget the baby at her breast and have no compassion on the child she has borne? Though she may forget, I will not forget you!*
> Isaiah 49:15 NIV

> *I will comfort you like a mother comforting her child. You will be comforted in Jerusalem.*
> Isaiah 66:13

> *From far away, the LORD will appear to his people. The Lord says, "I love you people with a love that continues forever. That is why I have continued showing you kindness.*
> Jeremiah 31:3

Those of us who believe in God and all he has said are very proud of our Dad. We aren't ashamed to be seen with him in public. We don't try to hide the fact that we are his children. We acknowledge our dependence on him. We don't hesitate to call, "Dad, Dad!" And he doesn't hesitate to answer, "Yes son. What is it?" And we say, "Could I have a drink of water?" "I can't sleep," etc. A child who loves and trusts his father has a free line of communication with him. He doesn't have to schedule a meeting at a certain time each day to talk things over – it is spontaneous.

It is often said that the best time in the life of a parent is when his children are little and fully dependent on him. Could that also be what God our Heavenly Father enjoys the most – when we are totally dependent on him and trusting him for our every need?

God desires and loves to show mercy. He punishes out of necessity, not out of taking pleasure in it.

D. Here are some of the things that God does for us: The first ones are unconditional and have nothing to do with what we do

1. The most important thing God does for us is to love us

We are his creation, we are made in his image, and we have been given his breath of life. In all of his creation, there is nothing more highly prized than a human being. Even after the fall of man into rebellion against God's authority, he still loved us and worked to save us.

> John 3:16-17 (NIV), tells us: *For God so loved the world that he gave his one and only Son, that whoever believes in him shall not perish but have eternal life. For God did not send his Son into the world to condemn the world, but to save the world through him.*

> *Your faithful love is higher than the highest clouds in the sky!*   Psalm 57:10

> *Your faithful love is better than life, so my lips praise you.*
>   Psalm 63:3

God's purpose is to rescue man from his dire predicament and coming isolation and suffering. He and the Son paid an extremely high price to ransom us. They have done everything they can to achieve that purpose, and now the outcome for each person depends on his individual response to God's initiative.

2. He respects us as persons and honors our freedom to choose

He is not a control freak who micromanages every detail of our lives. He allows us to make choices, some very good, some very bad, and many of little consequence. Although he has the power to control the whole universe to the most finite detail, he has given some freedom to the living creatures, especially to man, the acme of his creation. He gives man the ability and freedom to follow his Creator's wisdom and purpose, or to reject his supremacy over us. He wants to have an intimate, personal, one–to–one relationship with each of us. He wants us as his friends, not as his slaves.

> *I no longer call you servants, because a servant does not know his master's business. Instead, I have called you friends, for everything that I learned from my Father I have made known to you.*   John 15:15 NIV

3. He wants to be in a love relationship with us and is actively trying to be reconciled with us

He is not standing idly by waiting to see what happens, but is proactive in trying to persuade us to be reconciled to him. He offers to forgive us all our sins. He paid the penalty for our transgressions through the blood of his Son Jesus on the cross. In the past, he sent out multitudes of messengers called prophets to communicate his message to mankind, and today he sends out millions of evangelists to proclaim the good news of his offer of forgiveness and redemption.

All this is from God. Through Christ, God made peace between himself and us. And God gave us the work of bringing people into peace with him. I mean that God was in Christ, making peace between the world and himself. In Christ, God did not hold people guilty for their sins. And he gave us this message of peace to tell people. So we have been sent to speak for Christ. It is like God is calling to people through us. We speak for Christ when we beg you to be at peace with God.   2 Corinthians 5:18-20

4. He provides food for all the creatures, and provides for life's on-going needs

We are told that he causes it to rain on both the good and the evil. He provides seed for the sower and bread for the hungry. Every good gift comes down from above, and God is working steadily as a provider and sustainer of all his creation. He has not made the world and left it to fare for itself, but he is here constantly maintaining his masterpiece. God is not a clock-maker who wound the clock and went away like the deists believe. He never calls in sick or takes a vacation.

In his defense Jesus said to them, "My Father is always at his work to this very day, and I too am working."
John 5:17 NIV

Though God rested on the seventh day from all his creation, he has not rested from doing the maintenance and providing for its continued welfare.

Abraham gave God the name, "Jehovah Jireh" – The Lord will provide: *Then Abraham noticed a ram whose horns were caught in a bush. So Abraham went and took the ram. He offered it, instead of his son, as a sacrifice to God. So Abraham gave that*

place a name, "The LORD Provides." Even today people say, "On the mountain of the LORD, he will give us what we need."
                                        Genesis 22:13-14

> *God is the one who gives seed to those who plant, and he gives bread for food. And God will give you spiritual seed and make that seed grow. He will produce a great harvest from your goodness. God will make you rich in every way so that you can always give freely. And your giving through us will make people give thanks to God.*
>   2 Corinthians 9:10-11

> *"So don't be afraid of those people. Everything that is hidden will be shown. Everything that is secret will be made known. I tell you all this secretly, but I want you to tell it publicly. Whatever I tell you privately, you should shout for everyone to hear. "Don't be afraid of people. They can kill the body, but they cannot kill the soul. The only one you should fear is God, the one who can send the body and the soul to be destroyed in hell. When birds are sold, two small birds cost only a penny. But not even one of those little birds can die without your Father knowing it. God even knows how many hairs are on your head. So don't be afraid. You are worth more than a whole flock of birds.*   Matthew 10:26-31

The Greek wording really implies that a sparrow cannot fall to the ground "without God being present." He attends the funeral of every bird.

5. He delights to show mercy

> *For the LORD your God is a compassionate God; He will not fail you nor destroy you nor forget the covenant*

with your fathers which He swore to them.
Deuteronomy 4:31NASB

"But you are so kind! You didn't completely destroy them. You didn't leave them. You are such a kind and merciful God! But in your great mercy you did not put an end to them or abandon them, for you are a gracious and merciful God.   Nehemiah 9:31

God will forgive his people who survive. He will not stay angry with them forever, because he enjoys being kind.
Micah 7:18

Let us then approach the throne of grace with confidence, so that we may receive mercy and find grace to help us in our time of need.   Hebrews 4:16 NIV

Because Your lovingkindness is better than life, My lips will praise You.   Psalm 63:3 NASB

The following things he does are conditional, based on whether we believe God and how we act

1. He can make you his child and give you his life

He came to the world that was his own. And his own people did not accept him. But some people did accept him. They believed in him, and he gave them the right to become children of God. They became God's children, but not in the way babies are usually born. It was not

because of any human desire or plan. They were born
from God himself.   John 1:11-13

Praise be to the God and Father of our Lord Jesus Christ.
God has great mercy, and because of his mercy he gave us
a new life. This new life brings us a living hope through
Jesus Christ's resurrection from death. Now we wait
to receive the blessings God has for his children. These
blessings are kept for you in heaven. They cannot be
ruined or be destroyed or lose their beauty. God's power
protects you through your faith, and it keeps you safe
until your salvation comes. That salvation is ready to be
given to you at the end of time.   1 Peter 1:3-5

See how very much our Father loves us, for He calls us
His children, and that is what we are! But the people who
belong to this world don't recognize that we are God's
children because they don't know Him. Dear friends, we
are already God's children, but He has not yet shown
us what we will be like when Christ appears. But we do
know that we will be like Him, for we will see Him as
He really is.   1 John 3:1-2 NLT

Everything good comes from God. Every perfect gift is
from him. These good gifts come down from the Father
who made all the lights in the sky. But God never changes
like the shadows from those lights. He is always the same.
God decided to give us life through the true message he
sent to us. He wanted us to be the most important of all
that he created.   James 1:17-18

Every other conditional blessing depends on becoming his child.
He has obligations and affections for his children that he doesn't
have for those who are not.

2. He can forgive you

> *So now anyone who is in Christ Jesus is not judged guilty.*
> *That is because in Christ Jesus the law of the Spirit that*
> *brings life made you free. It made you free from the law*
> *that brings sin and death.*   Romans 8:1-2

> *At one time you were separated from God. You were*
> *his enemies in your minds, because the evil you did was*
> *against him. But now he has made you his friends again.*
> *He did this by the death Christ suffered while he was in*
> *his body. He did it so that he could present you to himself*
> *as people who are holy, blameless, and without anything*
> *that would make you guilty before him.*
>   Colossians1:21-22

> *In him we have redemption through his blood, the*
> *forgiveness of sins, in accordance with the riches of*
> *God's grace that he lavished on us. With all wisdom*
> *and understanding.*   Ephesians 1:7-8 NIV

This forgiveness depends on our repentance and belief in Jesus, God's eternal Son.

3. He can answer your prayers

When you call on God by faith and with humility, God will always give you what you ask for or something better. He cannot always answer "yes" because we often don't know what to ask for or have the wrong motives in our asking. Also, God cannot violate his nature, his morality, or his promises. He will not give anyone something that is not in his power to give.

*You do not have because you do not ask God. When
you ask, you do not receive, because you ask with wrong
motives, that you may spend what you get on your
pleasures.*   James 4:2b-3 NIV

*". . . if my people, who are called by my name, will humble
themselves and pray and seek my face and turn from their
wicked ways, then I will hear from heaven, and I will
forgive their sin and will heal their land.*
                          2 Chronicles 7:14 NIV

*And if you ask for anything in my name, I will do it for
you. Then the Father's glory will be shown through the
Son. If you ask me for anything in my name, I will do it.*
                          John 14:13-14

*In that day you will not have to ask me about anything.
And I assure you, my Father will give you anything
you ask him for in my name. You have never asked for
anything in this way before. But ask in my name, and you
will receive. And you will have the fullest joy possible.*
                          John 16:23-24

*Elijah was a person just like us. He prayed that it would
not rain. And it did not rain on the land for three and a
half years! Then Elijah prayed that it would rain. And the
rain came down from the sky, and the land grew crops
again.*   James 5:17-18

4. He can give you hope

Yes, my soul, find rest in God; my hope comes from him.
                          Psalm 62:5 NIV

Remember your word to your servant, for you have given
me hope.   Psalm 119:49 NIV

"I say this because I know the plans that I have for you."
This message is from the LORD. "I have good plans for
you. I don't plan to hurt you. I plan to give you hope and
a good future."   Jeremiah 29:11

No one who hopes in you will ever be put to shame, but
shame will come on those who are treacherous without
cause. Show me your ways, LORD, teach me your paths.
Guide me in your truth and teach me, for you are God
my Savior, and my hope is in you all day long.
                        Psalm 25:3-5 NIV

I pray that the God who gives hope will fill you with
much joy and peace as you trust in him. Then you will
have more and more hope, and it will flow out of you by
the power of the Holy Spirit.   Romans 15:13

God is the giver of and the object of our hope. Aside from God,
there is no other hope that will lead to receiving what we hope
for. Hope in anything but the true God and his promises will
eventually lead to frustration and disappointment.

5. He can take away your worries

Give your worries to the LORD, and he will care for
you. He will never let those who are good be defeated.
                        Psalm 55:22

So be humble under God's powerful hand. Then he will lift
you up when the right time comes. Give all your worries
to him, because he cares for you. 1 Peter 5:6-7

*The Lord is good, a refuge in times of trouble. <u>He cares</u>
for those who trust in him.*   Nahum 1:7 NIV

We are admonished to turn our cares, worries, and anxieties over
to him. He will take charge of the worrying department. A toddler
does not need to worry about where his next meal is coming from
or whether his clothes will get washed. Neither does a child of
God need to worry about the provision of his daily needs.

*"And why do you worry about clothes? Look at the
wildflowers in the field. See how they grow. They don't
work or make clothes for themselves. But I tell you that
even Solomon, the great and rich king, was not dressed
as beautifully as one of these flowers. If God makes what
grows in the field so beautiful, what do you think he will
do for you? It's just grass—one day it's alive, and the next
day someone throws it into a fire. But God cares enough
to make it beautiful. Surely he will do much more for
you. Your faith is so small! "Don't worry and say, 'What
will we eat?' or 'What will we drink?' or 'What will we
wear?' That's what those people who don't know God
are always thinking about. Don't worry, because your
Father in heaven knows that you need all these things.
What you should want most is God's kingdom and doing
what he wants you to do. Then he will give you all these
other things you need. So don't worry about tomorrow.
Each day has enough trouble of its own. Tomorrow will
have its own worries.*   Matthew 6:28-34

6. He will help you

*"I tell you the truth, anyone who believes in Me will do
the same works I have done, and even greater works,*

*because I am going to be with the Father. You can ask
for anything in My name, and I will do it, so that the Son
can bring glory to the Father. Yes, ask Me for anything
in My name, and I will do it!*   John 14:12-14 NLT

*Do not be afraid or discouraged, for the LORD will
personally go ahead of you. He will be with you; He
will neither fail you nor abandon you.*

Deuteronomy 31:8 NLT

*Jesus, our high priest, is able to understand our weaknesses.
When Jesus lived on earth, he was tempted in every way.
He was tempted in the same ways we are tempted, but he
never sinned. With Jesus as our high priest, we can feel
free to come before God's throne where there is grace.
There we receive mercy and kindness to help us when we
need it.*   Hebrews 4:15-16

7. He can guide you and protect you

*. . . Even there your hand will guide me; your right hand
will hold me fast.*   Psalm 139:10 NIV

God continually works to guide and protect us.

8. He can comfort you

*Praise be to the God and Father of our Lord Jesus
Christ, the Father of compassion and the God of all
comfort, who comforts us in all our troubles, so that
we can comfort those in any trouble with the comfort
we ourselves receive from God.*

2 Corinthians 1:3-4 NIV

*I have seen their ways, but I will heal them; I will guide
them and restore comfort to Israel's mourners.*

Isaiah 57:18 NIV

*Do not let your hearts be troubled. You believe in God;
believe also in me. My Father's house has many rooms;
if that were not so, would I have told you that I am
going there to prepare a place for you?*

John 14:1-2 NIV

9. He can give you confidence

*We can come to God with no doubts. This means that
when we ask God for things (and those things agree with
what God wants for us), God cares about what we say.
He listens to us every time we ask him. So we know that
he gives us whatever we ask from him.*

1 John 5:14-15

*So we can feel sure and say, "The Lord is my helper; I
will not be afraid. People can do nothing to me."*

Hebrews 13:6

10. He can give you victory over your enemies

*Do not be fainthearted or afraid; do not panic or be
terrified by them. For the LORD your God is the one
who goes with you to fight for you against your enemies
to give you victory.*   Deuteronomy 20:3b-4 NIV

*I do not trust in my bow, my sword does not bring me
victory; but you give us victory over our enemies, you
put our adversaries to shame.*   Psalm 44:6-7 NIV

This does not mean that he will destroy anyone we don't like, or anyone we want to overcome. He is not our attack dog who we can sic on anyone we are at odds with. Instead, he is committed to defend those who are his and put their trust in him. Anyone who comes against us because we are allied with the Lord will sooner or later be destroyed. Every human being has enemies. The first is Satan, who wants to destroy everything that is good and all that God made. Also, since hate is prevalent in the world, most everyone is hated by someone. Those of us who have been re-born into God's family are the natural enemies of those who are still in the family of Satan.

"The Lord is on our side, whom shall I fear?"; this does not mean that he does everything that we want, but that he does <u>everything he wants</u> to defend the orphan, the widow, the helpless, and especially those who are his own children. When we cry out to him with a legitimate need, he rescues us in an appropriate way and at an appropriate time.

> *"If the world hates you, remember that they hated me first. If you belonged to the world, the world would love you as it loves its own people. But I have chosen you to be different from those in the world. So you don't belong to the world, and that is why the world hates you.*
> John 15:18

11. He will reward you according to your faith and deeds

> *. . . and with you, Lord, is unfailing love"; and, "You reward everyone according to what they have done."*
> Psalm 62:12 NIV

But I, the LORD, search all hearts and examine secret motives. I give all people their due rewards, according to what their actions deserve.   Jeremiah 17:10 NLT

The Son of Man will come again with his Father's glory and with his angels. And he will reward everyone for what they have done.   Matthew 16:27

Anyone who builds on that foundation may use a variety of materials—gold, silver, jewels, wood, hay, or straw. But on the judgment day, fire will reveal what kind of work each builder has done. The fire will show if a person's work has any value. If the work survives, that builder will receive a reward.   1 Corinthians 3:12-14 NLT

12. He will take all of his children to live with him for eternity

"Father, I want these people you have given me to be with me in every place I am. I want them to see my glory—the glory you gave me because you loved me before the world was made.   John 17:24

We know that our body—the tent we live in here on earth—will be destroyed. But when that happens, God will have a home for us to live in. It will not be the kind of home people build here. It will be a home in heaven that will continue forever.   2 Corinthians 5:1

But the government that rules us is in heaven. We are waiting for our Savior, the Lord Jesus Christ, to come from there. He will change our humble bodies and make them like his own glorious body. Christ can do this by his power, with which he is able to rule everything.   Philippians 3:20-21

Martin Luther, who some call the Father of the Reformation, had learned to trust in God, not in the church or in his own strength, and so he wrote this great hymn.

A mighty fortress is our God, a bulwark never failing;
Our helper He, amid the flood of mortal ills prevailing:
For still our ancient foe doth seek to work us woe;
His craft and power are great, and, armed with cruel hate, On earth is not his equal.

Did we in our own strength confide,
our striving would be losing;
Were not the right Man on our side,
the Man of God's own choosing:
Dost ask who that may be? Christ Jesus, it is He;
Lord Sabaoth, His Name, from age to age the same,
And He must win the battle.

And though this world, with devils filled,
should threaten to undo us,
We will not fear, for God hath willed
His truth to triumph through us:
The Prince of Darkness grim, we tremble not for him;
His rage we can endure, for lo, his doom is sure,
One little word shall fell him.

That word above all earthly powers,
no thanks to them, abideth;
The Spirit and the gifts are ours through
Him Who with us sideth:
Let goods and kindred go, this mortal life also;
The body they may kill: God's truth abideth still,
His kingdom is forever.

The God of the deist is **there** (at a distance), but the God of the trusting Christian is **here** (nearby). God is ever present with us at our side. He is not a God who is far away and out of reach. He is present and a more than able help in trouble.

God is watching my life develop according to his guidance. He is my loving Father, my friend, my supporter, my confidante, my deliverer, and relates to me and helps me in lots of other ways. It means that I am dependent on a living, "breathing" person with whom I have a love relationship. I am not locked into a computer program where no one, including God can intervene.

I look up to the hills, but where will my help really come from? My help will come from the LORD, the Creator of heaven and earth. He will not let you fall. Your Protector will not fall asleep. Israel's Protector does not get tired. He never sleeps. The LORD is your Protector. The LORD stands by your side, shading and protecting you. The sun cannot harm you during the day, and the moon cannot harm you at night. The LORD will protect you from every danger. He will protect your soul. The LORD will protect you as you come and go, both now and forever!
Psalm 121:1-8

Unless the LORD had given me help, I would soon have dwelt in the silence of death. When I said, "My foot is slipping," your unfailing love, LORD, supported me. When anxiety was great within me, your consolation brought me joy.   Psalm 94:17-19 NIV

It is a great blessing for people to have the God of Jacob to help them. They depend on the LORD their God. He made heaven and earth. He made the sea and everything

in it. He can be trusted to do what he says. He does what is right for those who have been hurt. He gives food to the hungry. The LORD frees people locked up in prison. The LORD makes the blind see again. The LORD helps those who are in trouble. The LORD loves those who do right. The LORD protects strangers in our country. He cares for widows and orphans, but he destroys the wicked.
Psalm 146:5-9

I am the LORD your God, who holds your right hand. And I tell you, 'Don't be afraid! I will help you.' People of Israel, descendants of Jacob, you may be weak and worthless, but do not be afraid. I myself will help you." This is what the LORD himself says. "I am the Holy One of Israel, the one who saves you.   Isaiah 41:13

The challenge of faith

Will you trust God and his promises? Men believe what they believe not based on an intellectual analysis of the evidence, but rather on a decision of the will. Our emotions may nudge us to make decisions, but our emotions do not make our decisions for us. In Marriage Encounter ministries, we often used the term, "Love is a decision." Believing in God and Christ the Son of God is a decision of the will. Will you believe, or will you keep on rejecting God's control in your life and rebelling against him?

There is overwhelming evidence in our world showing God's existence and his wonderful nature. However, many men choose to ignore the evidence. They make a decision, not based on the evidence they see, but rather based on what they will to do.

Other men look at the same evidence, and make the decision to believe in God and what he has revealed to them. It is not the evidence that proves something beyond a doubt. It is the decision of the will of the person whether he wants to believe or not. You cannot prove the existence of a nose to a person who refuses to believe that he has one. We may say, "It's as plain as the nose on your face" but if he doesn't want to believe, he <u>will</u> not believe regardless of any amount of evidence.

It is the same with belief in God. His existence is so plain and so obvious that a person can't miss it, but he can <u>choose</u> to ignore it. If he chooses to ignore it, he will contrive all kinds of weird explanations to deny God's existence. You cannot convince him by giving him more evidence or appealing to his reason. It is a choice he has made, and only he can choose to change it.

The Bible shows us a wonderful God who created us, but who didn't abandon us when we rebelled against him. He has done everything possible to rescue us and guide us to the path that leads to eternal life. Even if we continue to reject him, he patiently woos us trying to get us to believe in him and trust him so that he can deliver us from coming condemnation and judgment. God is on your side. He lovingly, deep from his heart, desires all the best for you and is saddened if you do not believe in him.

If you do believe in him and accept his Son Jesus, then you have no better friend in all existence. Not only has he forgiven you, but he is preparing a banquet, a home, and a paradise for you.

2. Does God have feelings?

This old hymn from the 1800s by Walter C. Smith describes the average Christian's view of what God is like:

Immortal, invisible, God only wise,
In light inaccessible hid from our eyes,
Most blessed, most glorious, the Ancient of Days,
Almighty, victorious, Thy great Name we praise.
Unresting, unhasting, and silent as light,
Nor wanting, nor wasting, Thou rulest in might;
Thy justice, like mountains, high soaring above
Thy clouds, which are fountains of goodness and love.
To all, life Thou givest, to both great and small;
In all life Thou livest, the true life of all;
We blossom and flourish as leaves on the tree,
And wither and perish—but <u>naught changeth Thee</u>.
Great Father of glory, pure Father of light,
Thine angels adore Thee, all veiling their sight;
But of all Thy rich graces this grace, Lord, impart
Take the veil from our faces, the vile from our heart.

All laud we would render; O help us to see
'Tis only the splendor of light hideth Thee,
And so let Thy glory, Almighty, impart,
Through Christ in His story, Thy Christ to the heart.

This hymn is true and exalts the power and the superiority of God. But by only presenting one aspect of the God revealed in the Bible, it distorts our understanding of who God is. It would appear from this hymn that God has no feelings and is impervious to our needs and our cries to him. It is partly because of hymns like this that most people do not know God very well, if at all. This hymn is typical of the view of God that believes him to be unmovable, insensitive, unconcerned, and without feelings for the suffering of his creatures.

I pray that through this study at least part of the prayer in this hymn will be answered: "Take the veil from our faces."

Most people form their image of God based on people they have known. If a person has had cruel and unloving parents, their image of God is usually that he is a tyrant who doesn't care about the welfare of his creatures. It is very difficult to correct this mistaken image. Suffice it to say that you can sum up all the good you have ever seen in persons you have known and it won't be more than a drop in the proverbial bucket compared to the goodness of God. Add up the wonderful light of a thousand candles, but it is nothing compared to the light of the sun at noonday.

We should worship God for his character, not just for his abilities. What he does is a direct product of who he is. We usually fear God for his great power, but we ought to worship him for his innate goodness. When we emphasize and exalt mainly his power and great ability, we make him seem like a sterile, unfeeling God. When we emphasize his compassion, mercy, love, patience and other character virtues, we see God as a loving family member and a person who feels and identifies with our weakness.

God has moral purity and selflessness. This is far more important than his omnipotence. With Jonah and the Ninevites, God preferred to show his mercy rather than his power. He could easily have destroyed them all and they deserved it. But he chose to show his mercy because that is who he is.

God is a very feeling God. He created us in his image with intellect, emotions and will. We have emotions because God has emotions. We can only love because God loves. Star Trek presented us with two characters that could feel no emotions: Spock and Data. One episode has Data working on and trying out his emotions chip, and as a result crying for the first time. Many theologians believe that God is like these two Star Trek characters and can feel nothing. Sometimes theologians get it right and sometimes they get it wrong — this is one of the latter. God has emotions and they are not the same every day and in every situation. Though his character and moral virtue never change, his emotions do, as I am sure Walter C. Smith, the writer of the above hymn, discovered when he reached the throne of God.

1. Some of God's feelings as revealed in Scripture:

A. God is a compassionate God

Literally, this means that he shares the feelings of other people.

Compassion — *feeling or showing sympathy and concern for others. –synonyms: sympathetic, empathetic, understanding, caring, solicitous, sensitive, warm, loving compassion is the feeling of empathy for others. Compassion is the emotion that we feel in response to the suffering of others and that motivates a desire to help.*

As stated, some theologians want to have a God who loves, but who doesn't feel. They describe a God who cannot be moved by the plight or the petitions of men. This kind of God would be no better than a plaster saint sitting on your mantle.

When the Bible describes God and his nature it almost invariably says that he is compassionate.

> *"If you loan money to any of my people, that is, the poor among you, don't be like a moneylender and charge them interest. You might take their cloak to make sure they pay the money back, but you must give that cloak back to them before sunset. That cloak might be their only protection against the cold when they lie down to sleep. If they call to me for help, I will listen because I am kind (compassionate).*   Exodus 22:25-27

> *And he passed in front of Moses, proclaiming, "The LORD, the LORD, the* <u>compassionate</u> *and gracious God, slow to anger, abounding in love and faithfulness, maintaining love to thousands, and forgiving wickedness, rebellion and sin.*   Exodus 34:6 NIV

> *If you return to the LORD, then your brothers and your children will be shown compassion by their captors and will come back to this land, for the LORD your God is*

gracious and <u>compassionate</u>. He will not turn his face from you if you return to him.   2 Chronicles 30:9 NIV

They refused to listen, and did not remember Your wondrous deeds which You had performed among them; So they became stubborn and appointed a leader to return to their slavery in Egypt. But You are a God of forgiveness, gracious and compassionate, Slow to anger and abounding in lovingkindness; And You did not forsake them.
Nehemiah 9:16-17 NASB

But you, O Lord, are a <u>compassionate</u> and gracious God, slow to anger, abounding in love and faithfulness.
Psalm 86:15 NIV

The LORD is <u>compassionate</u> and gracious, slow to anger, abounding in love.   Psalm 103:8 NIV

He has caused his wonders to be remembered; the LORD is gracious and compassionate.   Psalm 111:4 NIV

The LORD is merciful and compassionate, slow to get angry and filled with unfailing love.
Psalm 145:8 NLT

Tear your hearts, not your clothes. Come back to the LORD your God. He is kind and merciful. He does not become angry quickly. He has great love. Maybe he will change his mind about the bad punishment he planned.
Joel 2:13

But Jonah was greatly displeased and became angry. He prayed to the LORD, "O LORD, is this not what I said

when I was still at home? That is why I was so quick to flee to Tarshish. I knew that you are a gracious and <u>compassionate God</u>, slow to anger and abounding in love, a God who relents from sending calamity.
Jonah 4:1-2 NIV

The next day Jesus and his followers went to a town called Nain. A big crowd was traveling with them. When Jesus came near the town gate, he saw some people carrying a dead body. It was the only son of a woman who was a widow. Walking with her were many other people from the town. When the Lord saw the woman, he felt very sorry for her and said, "Don't cry."
Luke 7:11-13
NLT – *His heart overflowed <u>with compassion</u>, and he said, "Don't cry."*

Praise be to the God and Father of our Lord Jesus Christ, <u>the Father of compassion</u> and the God of all comfort, who comforts us in all our troubles, so that we can comfort those in any trouble with the comfort we ourselves have received from God.
2 Corinthians 1:3-4 NIV

We often study the different names for God, like "El Shaddai," the Mighty One; or "Jehovah Jireh," the God who provides. But this passage is telling us that our God is also the God who not only has compassion, but who gave it birth. He is also the God who is the origin of all comfort. There would be no compassion nor comfort of any kind on the earth or in Heaven if it had not originated in God himself. After reading these descriptions of God's character, how could anyone say that God is not moved by his feelings for us?

B. In the above verses we also saw that God was gracious

Definition of grace:
1. Characterized by kindness and warm courtesy.
2. Characterized by tact and propriety: "He responded to the insult with gracious humor."
3. Of a merciful or compassionate nature.
4. Condescendingly courteous; indulgent.
5. Characterized by charm or beauty; graceful.
6. Characterized by elegance and good taste: gracious living.

C. Also the Bible describes God as a person committed to loving relationships

Definition of Love:
1. An intense feeling of deep affection. "Babies fill parents with intense feelings of love."
2. A person or thing that one loves. "She was the love of his life."

So remember that the LORD your God is the only God, and you can trust him! He keeps his agreement. He shows his love and kindness to all people who love him and obey his commands. He continues to show his love and kindness through a thousand generations, . . .
Deuteronomy 7:9

"If you listen to these laws, and if you are careful to obey them, the LORD your God will keep his agreement of love with you. He promised this to your ancestors. He will love you and bless you. He will make your nation

grow. He will bless your children. He will bless your fields with good crops and will give you grain, new wine, and oil. He will bless your cows with calves and your sheep with lambs. You will have all these blessings in the land that he promised your ancestors to give you.
                                          Deuteronomy 7:12-13

Then Solomon stood before the altar of the LORD in front of the whole assembly of Israel, spread out his hands toward heaven and said: "O LORD, God of Israel, there is no God like you in heaven above or on earth below–you who keep your covenant of love with your servants who continue wholeheartedly in your way.
                                          1 Kings 8:22-23 NIV

Praise God, who did not ignore my prayer or withdraw His unfailing love from me.   Psalm 66:20 NLT

As for me, LORD, this is my prayer to you: Please accept me! God, I want you to answer me with love. I know I can trust you to save me.   Psalm 69:13

Yes, God loved the world so much that he gave his only Son, so that everyone who believes in him would not be lost but have eternal life.   John 3:16

And this hope will never disappoint us. We know this because God has poured out his love to fill our hearts through the Holy Spirit he gave us.   Romans 5:5

But in all these troubles we have complete victory through God, who has shown his love for us. Yes, I am sure that

nothing can separate us from God's love—not death, life, angels, or ruling spirits. I am sure that nothing now, nothing in the future, no powers, nothing above us or nothing below us—nothing in the whole created world—will ever be able to separate us from the love God has shown us in Christ Jesus our Lord.   Romans 8:37-39

But God is so rich in mercy, and He loved us so much, that even though we were dead because of our sins, He gave us life when He raised Christ from the dead. (It is only by God's grace that you have been saved!)
                                                              Ephesians 2:4-5 NLT

I pray that Christ will live in your hearts because of your faith. I pray that your life will be strong in love and be built on love. And I pray that you and all God's holy people will have the power to understand the greatness of Christ's love—how wide, how long, how high, and how deep that love is. Christ's love is greater than anyone can ever know, but I pray that you will be able to know that love.   Ephesians 3:17-19

You are God's dear children, so try to be like him. Live a life of love. Love others just as Christ loved us. He gave himself for us—a sweet-smelling offering and sacrifice to God.   Ephesians 5:1-2

How great is the love the Father has lavished on us, that we should be called children of God! And that is what we are!   1 John 3:1 NIV

Dear friends, we should love each other, because love comes from God. Everyone who loves has become God's

child. And so everyone who loves knows God. Anyone who does not love does not know God, because God is love. This is how God showed his love to us: He sent his only Son into the world to give us life through him. True love is God's love for us, not our love for God. He sent his Son as the way to take away our sins. That is how much God loved us, dear friends! So we also must love each other. No one has ever seen God. But if we love each other, God lives in us. If we love each other, God's love has reached its goal—it is made perfect in us.

1 John 4:7-12

So we know the love that God has for us, and we trust that love. God is love. Everyone who lives in love lives in God, and God lives in them. If God's love is made perfect in us, we can be without fear on the day when God judges the world. We will be without fear, because in this world we are like Jesus. Where God's love is, there is no fear, because God's perfect love takes away fear. It is his punishment that makes a person fear. So his love is not made perfect in the one who has fear.

1 John 4:16-18

Love is not only an emotion, but it certainly involves the emotions. God's love is not a sterile, emotionless, unaffected concern for us. His love originates in his heart and his heart is full of intense feelings.

How much does God love his children? Jesus said in John 17:23 that the Father loves us just as much as he loved him. *May they experience such perfect unity that the world will know that you sent me and that <u>you love them as much as you love me</u>* (NIV).

D. God is often grieved by man's behavior

To grieve:
1. to cause (someone) to feel sad or unhappy
2. to feel or show grief or sadness

The LORD saw how great man's wickedness on the earth had become, and that every inclination of the thoughts of his heart was only evil all the time. The LORD was grieved that he had made man on the earth, and his heart was filled with pain. So the LORD said, "I will wipe mankind, whom I have created, from the face of the earth–men and animals, and creatures that move along the ground, and birds of the air–for I am grieved that I have made them." Genesis 6:5-7 NIV

So the LORD sent a plague on Israel, and seventy thousand men of Israel fell dead. And God sent an angel to destroy Jerusalem. But as the angel was doing so, the LORD saw it and <u>was grieved</u> because of the calamity and said to the angel who was destroying the people, "Enough! Withdraw your hand." 1 Chronicles 21:14-15 NIV

Then the word of the LORD came to Samuel: "<u>I am grieved</u> that I have made Saul king, because he has turned away from me and has not carried out my instructions." 1 Samuel 15:10-11 NIV

Then Samuel left for Ramah, but Saul went up to his home in Gibeah of Saul. Until the day Samuel died, he did not go to see Saul again, though Samuel mourned for him. <u>And the LORD was grieved</u> that he had made Saul king over Israel. 1 Samuel 15:34-35 NIV

Oh, they caused him so much trouble in the desert! They made him so sad.   Psalm 78:40

But I will spare some, for some of you will escape the sword when you are scattered among the lands and nations. Then in the nations where they have been carried captive, those who escape will remember me—how I have been grieved by their adulterous hearts, which have turned away from me, and by their eyes, which have lusted after their idols. They will loathe themselves for the evil they have done and for all their detestable practices. And they will know that I am the LORD; I did not threaten in vain to bring this calamity on them.
Ezekiel 6:8-10NIV

Time after time, God was very sad to the point of a broken heart because his creatures rebelled against all his good influence and had not turned out like he had hoped.

When you talk, don't say anything bad. But say the good things that people need—whatever will help them grow stronger. Then what you say will be a blessing to those who hear you. And don't make the Holy Spirit sad. God gave you his Spirit as proof that you belong to him and that he will keep you safe until the day he makes you free.
Ephesians 4:29-30

E. God rejoices when his children do what is right

Your children will commit themselves to you, O Jerusalem, just as a young man commits himself to his bride. Then God will rejoice over you as a bridegroom rejoices over his bride.   Isaiah 62:5 NLT

"The LORD your God is in your midst, A victorious warrior. He will exult over you with joy, He will be quiet in His love, He will rejoice over you with shouts of joy.
Zephaniah 3:17 NASB

F. God is pleased and displeased

Moses said to the LORD, "You told me to lead these people, but you did not say who you would send with me. You said to me, 'I know you very well, and I am pleased with you.' Moses said to the LORD, If I have really pleased you, then teach me your ways. I want to know you. Then I can <u>continue to please you</u>. Remember that these people are your nation."
Exodus 33:12-13

Then the LORD said to Moses, "I will do what you ask. I will do this because <u>I am pleased with you</u> and because I know you very well."
Exodus 33:17

It is a land filled with many good things. If the LORD <u>is pleased with us</u>, he will lead us into that land. And he will give that land to us.
Numbers 14:8

"I wish one of you would close the Temple doors to stop the lighting of useless fires on my altar. I am not pleased with you. I will not accept your gifts." This is what the LORD All-Powerful said.
Malachi 1:10

Do not be afraid, little flock, for your Father <u>has been pleased</u> to give you the kingdom. (NIV)
Luke 12:32
NLT — *It gives your Father great happiness to give you the kingdom.*

> But God *was not pleased* with most of those people, so
> they were killed in the desert.   1 Corinthians 10:5

> But my righteous one will live by faith. And if he shrinks
> back, I *will not be pleased* with him.
>   Hebrews 10:38 NIV

> Enoch was carried away from this earth, so he never died.
> The Scriptures tell us that before he was carried off, he
> was a *man who pleased God*. Later, no one knew where
> he was, because God had taken Enoch to be with him.
> This all happened because he had faith.
>   Hebrews 11:5

> Through Jesus, therefore, let us continually offer to God a
> sacrifice of praise–the fruit of lips that confess his name. And
> do not forget to do good and to share *with others, for with
> such sacrifices God is pleased*.   Hebrews 13:15-16 NIV

Being pleased or not pleased means a feeling of satisfaction or
dissatisfaction on the part of God. He is sensitive to what men
do and say. God observes and responds to the actions of human
beings and their actions provoke responses.

G. God gets angry

> But Moses begged the LORD his God, "LORD, don't
> let your anger destroy your people. You brought them
> out of Egypt with your great power and strength."
>   Exodus 32:11

> You will live in the country a long time. You will have
> children and grandchildren there. After all that time, be

sure that you do not then ruin your lives by making any kind of idol! That is something the LORD your God considers evil, and it would <u>make him very angry</u>!
Deuteronomy 4:25

The LORD your God is always with you, and he hates for his people to worship other gods! So if you follow those other gods, the Lord <u>will become very angry with you</u>. He will destroy you from the face of the earth.
Deuteronomy 6:15

Remember this and never forget how you <u>provoked the LORD your God to anger</u> in the desert.
Deuteronomy 9:7 NIV

If you break the covenant of the LORD your God by worshiping and serving other gods, <u>His anger</u> will burn against you, and you will quickly vanish from the good land He has given you. Joshua 23:16 NLT

It was the LORD, the God their ancestors worshiped, who had brought the Israelites out of Egypt. But they stopped following him and began to worship the false gods of the people living around them. <u>This made the LORD angry</u>. Judges 2:12-13

And the anger of the LORD burned against Uzzah, and God struck him down there for his irreverence; and he died there by the ark of God. 2 Samuel 6:7 NASB

. . . because of all the sins Baasha and his son Elah had committed and had caused Israel to commit, so that <u>they provoked the LORD</u>, the God of Israel, <u>to anger</u> by their worthless idols. 1 Kings 16:13 NIV

See also: 1 Kings 22:53; 1 Chronicles 13:10; 1 Chronicles 15:13; 2 Chronicles 24:18; 2 Chronicles 28:25; 2 Chronicles 29:10; 2 Chronicles 30:8; Ezra 8:22; Ezra 10:14; Nehemiah 9:17; Job 4:9; Job 9:13; Job 16:9; Job 20:23; Job 21:17; Psalm 7:6; Psalm 27:9; Psalm 56:7; Psalm 74:1; Psalm 77:9; Psalm 80:4; Psalm 86:15; Jeremiah 42:18; Hosea 11:9; Joel 2:13; Jonah 3:9; Jonah 4:2; Hebrews 4:3

H. God hates wickedness

> *The LORD examines those who are good and those who are wicked; he hates those who enjoy hurting others.*
>
> Psalm 11:5

I.   God is a jealous God

Jealousy is often viewed as a negative trait in a person. However, when a person is jealous over something that is unjust, it is a positive thing. It is righteous indignation. God has every right to be jealous about those who should love him because he is their Creator and Sustainer, and to be angry over their betrayal for other lovers.

> *You must not bow down to them or worship them, for I, the LORD your God, am a jealous God who will not tolerate your affection for any other gods. I lay the sins of the parents upon their children; the entire family is affected—even children in the third and fourth generations of those who reject Me.*   Exodus 20:5 NLT

> *Do not worship any other god, for the LORD, whose name is Jealous, is a jealous God.*
>
> Exodus 34:14

> *Joshua said to the people, "You are not able to serve the*
> *LORD. He is a holy God; <u>he is a jealous God</u>. He will*
> *not forgive your rebellion and your sins. If you forsake*
> *the LORD and serve foreign gods, he will turn and bring*
> *disaster on you and make an end of you, after he has been*
> *good to you."*   Joshua 24:19-20

God deeply desires our affections for him. He has every right
to them and is insulted and hurt when we turn away from him.

2. Jesus, the revelation of God's character

As the Son of God in this world, Jesus was not an emotionless
automaton. He felt what we feel, weeping with those who wept
(John 11:35), feeling compassion for the multitudes (Mark 6:34).

> *Jesus saw the huge crowd as He stepped from the boat,*
> *and <u>He had compassion</u> on them because they were like*
> *sheep without a shepherd. So He began teaching them*
> *many things.*   Mark 6:34 NLT

> *He told Peter and the two sons of Zebedee to come with*
> *him. Then he began to be very <u>sad and troubled</u>. Jesus*
> *said to Peter and the two sons of Zebedee, "My heart is*
> *so <u>heavy with grief</u>, I feel as if I am dying. Wait here and*
> *stay awake with me."*   Matthew 26:37-38

Jesus, God in human form, revealed the nature of the Father
to us (John 14:9). When we see the feelings of Jesus, we are
seeing the feelings of the Father also.

> *Jesus answered, "Philip, I have been with you for a long*
> *time. So you should know me. Anyone who has seen me*

has seen the Father too. So why do you say, 'Show us the Father'? Don't you believe that I am in the Father and the Father is in me? The things I have told you don't come from me. The Father lives in me, and he is doing his own work.   John 14:9-10

Jesus wept. So the Jews were saying, "See how He loved him!"   John 11:35-36 NASB

No one can see God, but the Son is exactly like God. He rules over everything that has been made.
                    Colossians 1:15,19

Before the Passover celebration, Jesus knew that His hour had come to leave this world and return to His Father. He had loved His disciples during His ministry on earth, and now He loved them to the very end.
                    John 13:1 NLT

Jesus replied, "All who love Me will do what I say. My Father will love them, and We will come and make Our home with each of them.   John 14:23 NLT

Jesus is telling us that there is no difference between his feelings and the feelings of the Father. He was the exact revelation of the nature and feelings of God; Father, Son and Holy Spirit. There is nothing that the human mind and heart can know about God that was not revealed fully in Jesus. There is much more to know about God, but we cannot comprehend it until we are transferred out of this life and into the heavenly realm and are made like the Lord.

"So he returned home to his father. And while he was still a long way off, his father saw him coming. Filled with

*love and compassion, he ran to his son, embraced him,
and kissed him.*   Luke 15:20 NLT

The father in this parable represents God the Father and
demonstrates God's deep, intense feelings toward his children.

3. Errant images of God

A. God who cannot be moved by man's pleadings

*Reformed theology (classical theology) followed medieval
traditions about God, traditions that often were derived
more from Greek philosophers like Aristotle than from
the Bible. Aristotle said that "God is the Unmoved Mover
who moves everything, but who is himself not affected
or moved by anything.*

*The emphasis in that theology is that God is totally
different from us and that he certainly does not have
feelings like us. So, when we read in the Bible about God
being angry or jealous or envious, classical theology says,
"We must take that as figurative language. That is just a
human way of talking about God, but God is not human."
We should be deeply troubled by the obvious fact that
what classical Christian theology says about God and
what the Bible says about God are so blatantly different.*

*In classical theology, feelings are regarded as weakness.
Again, the theologians got that more from human society
than from the Bible. In human society, there has always
been the perception that thinking is a masculine, strong
trait, and feeling is a feminine, weak trait. Thus, we*

admire great thinkers: from Plato and Aristotle to Albert Einstein and Stephen Hawking. We do not admire those who feel deeply. We regard them as weak and ineffectual people.

Classical theology defines "love" in such a way that it is not an emotion. That is a devious trick of this theology. If you don't like something, you just redefine it into something you do like. A definition of love that I was taught in seminary was: "a willingness to act for the benefit of others." That definition does not imply any feelings at all. That definition says that God will act for our benefit, but God does not share either our sorrows or our joys. God is up there and we are down here, and never the twain shall meet, at least not on any emotional level. Thus, classical theology took a perfectly good word like "love," a word loaded with emotion and feelings, and stripped it down and twisted it around so that it ceased to be have any emotion attached to it.

That is why it hurt so much when Israel rejected God. God is a lover and when his love rejected him, he writhed with agony and pain. God is the rejected lover and he hurts. We are not dealing with Aristotle's Unmoved Mover here. We are dealing with a God who loves infinitely well and grieves infinitely deeply when the beloved discards him.

A God of love never wants any person to be lost. But God has created us with free will and made us responsible for the exercise of our free will—which implies that the only person who is responsible for me going to heaven or to hell is me. Let me say that again. The only person who can send you to heaven or hell is you.

Does God have Feelings? From a sermon
by Tony Grant (Sermoncentral.com)

Charles Finney said, "*God enters fully into all the relations between himself and his creatures. I mean that he enters into these relations with all his heart and all his soul. He is feelingly alive to them all. It should ever be remembered that he is not a mere abstraction, an intellect without volition, emotion or sympathy. But his feelings are infinitely intense, so that every object in the universe, every creature, every want, every woe, every sorrow, and every joy, enkindle in the mind of God that same feeling. In Jesus, we find the feelings of God most perfectly expressed.*"

Again, Finney says, the "*one great design of the incarnation was to create a sympathy between God and men. Christ showed God's feelings for us. Christ taught us that God has the feelings and heart of a father. A guilty child knows that a father's heart can be moved to forgiveness. Even so, we know that however guilty we are in our sins, our father in heaven yearns over us and longs to forgive us and save us from hell. All that we have to do is to accept God's forgiveness and accept his love.*"

(from the Oberlin Evangelist lectures,
October 9, 1839, Lecture XVIII)

B. God's Impassibility (changelessness)

God's nature and moral character never change, and his purpose never changes. However, his methods of achieving his purpose can change according to need.

When classical theology describes God, its proponents are describing an object like a computer, not a person. But the true God is not like a computer that has no feelings or personal relationships with its contacts. Classical theology's god is a wooden god, no less an idol than the ones carved from wood and stone. Its god cannot weep, nor answer a prayer, nor lift a hand to help the needy. I reject that god as an aberration and an abomination that stinks to high Heaven.

4. Who God really is

The true God weeps at our sins, rejoices at our successes, cheers us on in our challenges, holds our hand in his tender grip, and only wants the very best for us. He loves us more than any mother ever loved her child, and he is more proud of his children than any earthly father ever could be. He is a loving Daddy to all those who put their trust in Jesus, and an advocate for salvation for all those who are still lost. He wants all humanity to be reconciled to him and to find the fullness of his love.

Someone has aptly said, "You can die without being saved, but you can't die without having been loved." If you are not saved from the judgment and condemnation to come, it is not God's fault. There is no more he can do to save you. You will never find a person who has more feelings than God.

3. | God's purpose and plan in creation

A. God wants a people/family of his own

God's plan was to make a family for himself and have many children who are like him. He doesn't want them so that he can manipulate them. He wants to have children to bless them and give them his abundant life.

Healthy couples have a desire to reproduce themselves and have a relationship with their offspring. They do it for the children's good as well as for their own. They desire offspring who will look like them, and have their life within them. It is pure, healthy love that motivates someone to give his life to others. God wanted to give life to others. He wants to create offspring in his image.

> Lord GOD, *this is why you are so great! There is no one like you. There is no god except you! We know that because of what we ourselves have heard about what you did. And there is no nation on earth like your people,*

Israel. They are a special people. They were slaves, but you took them out of Egypt and made them free. You made them your people. You did great and wonderful things for the Israelites and for your land. <u>You made the people of Israel your very own people forever</u>, and LORD, you became their God.   2 Samuel 7:22-24

All the people kept silent, and they were listening to Barnabas and Paul as they were relating what signs and wonders God had done through them among the Gentiles. After they had stopped speaking, James answered, saying, "Brethren, listen to me. Simeon has related how God first concerned Himself about <u>taking from among the Gentiles a people for His name</u>."   Acts 15:12-14 NASB

He gave His life to free us from every kind of sin, to cleanse us, and <u>to make us His very own people</u>, totally committed to doing good deeds.   Titus 2:14 NLT

B. God wants to make children with his nature

Then God said, "Now let's make humans <u>who will be like us</u>. They will rule over all the fish in the sea and the birds in the air. They will rule over all the large animals and all the little things that crawl on the earth." So God created humans in his own image. <u>He created them to be like himself</u>. He created them male and female.
                    Genesis 1:26-27

If anyone takes a human life, that person's life will also be taken by human hands. For God made human beings <u>in His own image</u>.   Genesis 9:6 NLT

*Imitate God, therefore, in everything <u>you do, because
you are His dear children</u>.*   Ephesians 5:1 NLT

*Through these he has given us his very great and precious
promises, so that through them you may <u>participate in
the divine nature</u> and escape the corruption in the world
caused by evil desires.*   2 Peter 1:4 NIV

C. We can see with what high esteem God holds man

*And furthermore, it is not angels who will control the
future world we are talking about. For in one place the
Scriptures say, "What are mere mortals that You should
think about them, or a son of man that You should care
for him? Yet You made them only a little lower than the
angels and crowned them with glory and honor. [You
gave them charge of everything You made.] You gave
them authority over all things." Now when it says "all
things," it means nothing is left out. But we have not yet
seen all things put under their authority.*

Hebrews 2:5-8 NLT

*. . . and from Jesus Christ. Jesus is the faithful witness.
He is first among all who will be raised from death. He
is the ruler of the kings of the earth. Jesus is the one who
loves us and has made us free from our sins with his blood
sacrifice. <u>He made us his kingdom and priests</u> who serve
God his Father. To Jesus be glory and power forever and
ever! Amen.*   Revelation 1:5-6

*Therefore, angels are only servants—spirits sent to care for
people who will inherit salvation.   Hebrews 1:14 NLT*

The purpose and job of angels is to help in the whole process of the birthing and revealing of God's children. They are not God's children now, nor ever will become his children. They do not inherit salvation. We might say that angels are "mid–wives" for the children of God.

> *I tell you that in the same way there will be more rejoicing in heaven over one sinner who repents than over ninety-nine righteous persons who do not need to repent . . . In the same way, I tell you, there is rejoicing in the presence of the angels of God over one sinner who repents."*
>
> Luke 15:7, 10 NIV

D. The Father wants a bride for his son

> *And they sang a new song: "You are worthy to take the scroll and to open its seals, because you were slain, and with your blood you purchased men for God from every tribe and language and people and nation.*
>
> Revelation 5:9 NIV

> *Let us rejoice and be happy and give God glory! Give God glory, because the wedding of the Lamb has come. And the Lamb's bride has made herself ready. Fine linen was given to the bride for her to wear. The linen was bright and clean." (The fine linen means the good things that God's holy people did.)*   Revelation 19:7-8

> *Then I saw a new heaven and a new earth, for the first heaven and the first earth had passed away, and there was no longer any sea. I saw the Holy City, the New Jerusalem, coming down out of heaven from God, prepared as a*

bride beautifully dressed for her husband. And I heard a loud voice from the throne saying, "Now the dwelling of God is with men, and he will live with them. They will be his people, and God himself will be with them and be their God.   Revelation 21:1-3 NIV

E. God wants a healthy offspring not tainted by disease

Humans don't know what it is to be healthy. Because our race began with two rebellious sinners, we were born with a congenital defect. Since everyone is born that way, we don't realize that we are sick, or have any idea what it means to be well. Someday those who have been reborn with God's nature will experience true health when all the damage to the tissue (old body) is taken away. Jesus was a healthy man in a sick world. He gave his untainted blood as a sacrifice to heal all people who receive it.

Jesus said, "Believe me when I say that you must eat the body of the Son of Man, and you must drink his blood. If you don't do this, you have no real life. Those who eat my body and drink my blood have eternal life. I will raise them up on the last day. My body is true food, and my blood is true drink. Those who eat my body and drink my blood live in me, and I live in them. "The Father sent me. He lives, and I live because of him. So everyone who eats me will live because of me. I am not like the bread that your ancestors ate. They ate that bread, but they still died. I am the bread that came down from heaven. Whoever eats this bread will live forever."
                                            John 6:53-58

> *And He took a cup of wine and gave thanks to God for it. He gave it to them and said, "Each of you drink from it, for this is My blood, which confirms the covenant between God and His people. It is poured out as a sacrifice to forgive the sins of many.*   Matthew 26:27-28 NLT

All men need a blood "transfusion" to overcome the genetic sickness called sin. He already gave it, but we must receive it to do us any good. There is a blood bank at the Cross just waiting for people to come and get their transfusion.

In his book "Written in Blood," Robert Coleman tells the story of a little boy whose sister needed a blood transfusion. The doctor explained that she had the same disease the boy had recovered from two years earlier. Her best chance for recovery was a transfusion from someone who had previously conquered the disease. Since the two children had the same rare blood type, the boy was the ideal donor.

> *"Would you give your blood to Mary?" the doctor asked. Johnny hesitated. His lower lip started to tremble. Then he smiled and said, "Sure, for my sister."*
> *Soon the two children were wheeled into the hospital room—Mary, pale and thin; Johnny, robust and healthy. Neither spoke, but when their eyes met, Johnny grinned. As the nurse inserted the needle into his arm, Johnny's smile faded. He watched the blood flow through the tube. With the ordeal almost over, his voice, slightly shaky, broke the silence. "Doctor, when do I die?*
> *Only then did the doctor realize why Johnny had hesitated, why his lip had trembled when he'd agreed to donate his blood. He'd thought giving his blood to his sister meant*

giving up his life. In that brief moment, he'd made his great decision.

(Written in Blood, Robert E. Coleman,
Fleming Revel, 1972)

Johnny, fortunately, didn't have to die to save his sister. Each of us, however, has a health condition much more serious than Mary's, and it required Jesus to give not just his blood but his life.

F. Why Christ had to come to this world

Jesus came to undo the works of the devil. The devil had wreaked havoc in the creation. Since man sinned, the consequences and corruption were passed on to the rest of all that God had made. The only way that the damage could be undone was to redeem the creation by a blood sacrifice of an innocent victim. Then, all things could be made new without the devil's interference.

> *Dear children, don't let anyone deceive you about this: When people do what is right, it shows that they are righteous, even as Christ is righteous. But when people keep on sinning, it shows that they belong to the devil, who has been sinning since the beginning. But the Son of God <u>came to destroy the works of the devil</u>.*
>
> 1 John 3:7-8 NLT

> *This is the message of Good News for the people of Israel—that there is peace with God through Jesus Christ, who is Lord of all. You know what happened throughout Judea, beginning in Galilee, after John began preaching his message of baptism. And you know that God anointed Jesus of Nazareth with the Holy Spirit and with power.*

Then Jesus went around <u>doing good and healing all who</u>
<u>were oppressed by the devil</u>, for God was with Him.
Acts 10:36-38 NLT

Gently instruct those who oppose the truth. Perhaps God
will change those people's hearts, and they will learn the
truth. Then they will come to their senses and escape from
the devil's trap. For they have been held captive by him
to do whatever he wants.   2 Timothy 2:25-26 NLT

Because God's children are human beings—made of flesh
and blood—the Son also became flesh and blood. For only
as a human being could He die, and only by dying could
He <u>break the power of the devil</u>, who had the power of
death. Only in this way could He set free all who have
lived their lives as slaves to the fear of dying.
Hebrews 2:14-15 NLT

The great dragon was hurled down–that ancient serpent
called the devil, or Satan, <u>who leads the whole world astray</u>.
He was hurled to the earth, and his angels with him. Then
I heard a loud voice in heaven say: "Now have come the
salvation and the power and the kingdom of our God, and
the authority of his Christ. For the accuser of our brothers,
who accuses them before our God day and night, has been
hurled down.   Revelation 12:9-11 NIV

The Son of God came to earth on a rescue mission. For thirty
years, he learned the culture and reconnoitered the terrain. For
three years he did "show and tell" so that people would know
the Father. Finally, he poured out his blood for the taking away
of sin, the worst disease of all time that is fatal one hundred
percent of the time unless one gets a blood transfusion from Jesus.

G. God and humanity: a growing relationship between parent and child

Not all human beings are God's children. They are all God's creation and they were made in his image. In spite of that, through the disobedience of Adam and Eve, all of their offspring received their sin nature. When we were born, we inherited a spiritual and physical defect in our makeup, and we are all therefore sons of disobedience and sons of the devil.

> *Jesus said to them, "If God were really your Father, you would love me. I came from God, and now I am here. I did not come by my own authority. God sent me. You don't understand the things I say, because you cannot accept my teaching. Your father is the devil. You belong to him. You want to do what he wants. He was a murderer from the beginning. He was always against the truth. There is no truth in him. He is like the lies he tells. Yes, the devil is a liar. He is the father of lies.*   John 8:42-44

> *Those who are God's children do not continue to sin, because the new life God gave them stays in them. They cannot keep sinning, because they have become children of God. So we can see who God's children are and who the devil's children are. These are the ones who are not God's children: those who don't do what is right and those who do not love their brothers and sisters in God's family.*   1 John 3:9-10

God's purpose remained the same after sin entered the world—he wants to have children like himself and a bride for his Son. He desires to have a personal relationship with every human being who accepts entry into that relationship.

"The great God of the universe who heaped up the mountains, scooped out the oceans, and flung out the stars wants to have a relationship with you."

Adrian Rogers

But the plans of the LORD stand firm forever, the purposes of his heart through all generations.

Psalm 33:11 NIV

He is the God who made the whole world and everything in it. He is the Lord of the land and the sky. He does not live in temples built by human hands. He is the one who gives people life, breath, and everything else they need. He does not need any help from them. He has everything he needs. God began by making one man, and from him he made all the different people who live everywhere in the world. He decided exactly when and where they would live. "God wanted people to look for him, and perhaps in searching all around for him, they would find him. But he is not far from any of us. It is through him that we are able to live, to do what we do, and to be who we are. As your own poets have said, 'We all come from him.'

Acts 17:24-28

God is creating children in his image. He is making a huge family that will one day live with him in his grand mansion called the New Jerusalem. Only those who are spiritually healthy will enter that city. Only those who have received the blood of Christ into their beings will be eligible.

4. Can God answer prayer?

You might ask, "Why a chapter on the effectiveness of prayer? Every Christian knows that God answers prayer." Yes, most Christians say they believe in prayer while at the same time many say that God already knows all the future. If he does, then your prayers cannot change anything at all or God would have been wrong about the future. Which will you believe: 1) that your prayers change what is going to happen in the future, or 2) that the future is already known and therefore set in concrete? They can't both be true. Many Christians don't pray with great expectation. We often just go through the motions because we believe that in the end, *"God's sovereignty will control everything anyway." "Que Será, Será"* — Whatever will be, will be: Or *"It is the will of Allah."* But the truth is that our prayers move the heart and the hand of God, and this ultimately changes things in the present and the future.

> *When He had taken the book, the four living creatures and the twenty–four elders fell down before the Lamb, each one holding a harp and golden bowls full of incense, which are the prayers of the saints.*   Revelation 5:8 (NASB)

*Another angel came and stood at the altar. This angel
had a golden holder for incense. The angel was given
much incense to offer <u>with the prayers of all God's holy
people</u>. The angel put this offering on the golden altar
before the throne. The smoke from the incense went up
from the angel's hand to God. The smoke went up <u>with
the prayers of God's people</u>.*   Revelation 8:3-4

Many times I have seen this motto on the walls of Christian
homes and church buildings:

"Prayer Changes Things."

But then I find that many of my Christian brothers don't really
believe it. They believe that God already knows how everything
is going to turn out. If God's knowledge of the future is absolute,
then we need to change the old motto from "Prayer Changes
Things" to "Prayer Can Change Nothing."

**There is not one of God's faithful servants in the Bible who
believed that prayer could not change the outcome of future events.**

Following are many Scripture quotes showing that God's people
throughout the Bible believed that their prayers would move
God to change the future:

*In the dream God responded, "Yes, I know you are innocent.
That's why I kept you from sinning against Me, and why
I did not let you touch her. Now return the woman to her
husband, and <u>he will pray for you</u>, for he is a prophet. Then
you will live. But if you don't return her to him, you can
be sure that you and all your people will die."*
                                    Genesis 20:6-7 NLT

God believes that the details of the future are still to be
determined.

> *Isaac's wife could not have children. So Isaac* <u>*prayed*</u> *to*
> *the LORD for her. The LORD* <u>*heard Isaac's prayer*</u>*, and*
> *he allowed Rebekah to become pregnant.*
> Genesis 25:21

Some would say that God had promised to make a nation out
of the seed of Abraham and his son Isaac and that it was going
to happen regardless of what Isaac did, but God sure had Isaac
and Rebekah "fooled" into believing he answered their prayer.

> *So the LORD sent poisonous snakes among the people,*
> *and many were bitten and died. Then the people came to*
> *Moses and cried out, "We have sinned by speaking against*
> *the LORD and against you.* <u>*Pray*</u> *that the LORD will*
> *take away the snakes." So Moses* <u>*prayed*</u> *for the people.*
> Numbers 21:6-7 NLT

> *So I bowed down before the LORD 40 days and 40 nights,*
> *because the LORD said he would destroy you. I* <u>*prayed*</u> *to*
> *the LORD. I said, "Lord GOD, don't destroy your people.*
> *They belong to you. You freed them and brought them out*
> *of Egypt with your great power and strength. Remember*
> *your promise to your servants Abraham, Isaac, and Jacob.*
> *Forget how stubborn these people are. Don't look at their*
> *evil ways or their sins."*   Deuteronomy 9:25-27

Moses believed that things turned out differently because of
his prayers.

> *"But will God really dwell on earth? The heavens, even the*
> *highest heaven, cannot contain you. How much less this*

*temple I have built! Yet give attention to <u>your servant's</u>
<u>prayer and his plea</u> for mercy, O LORD my God. Hear
<u>the cry and the prayer</u> that your servant is <u>praying</u> in your
presence this day. May your eyes be open toward this
temple night and day, this place of which you said, `My
Name shall be there,' so that you will <u>hear the prayer</u> your
servant <u>prays</u> toward this place. <u>Hear the supplication of</u>
<u>your servant</u> and of your people Israel <u>when they pray</u>
toward this place. Hear from heaven, your dwelling place,
and when you hear, forgive.*   1 Kings 8:27-30 NIV

Solomon, the wisest man who ever lived until his time, believed
that prayer would bring changes to a man's future.

*Then King Jeroboam said to the man of God, "Please
pray to the LORD your God for me. Ask him to heal
my arm." So the man of God prayed to the LORD, and
the king's arm was healed, as it was before.*
                                                1 Kings 13:6

King Jeroboam believed that prayer changed the future condition
of his hand.

*At the time of sacrifice, the prophet Elijah stepped forward
and <u>prayed</u>: "O LORD, God of Abraham, Isaac and
Israel, let it be known today that you are God in Israel
and that I am your servant and <u>have done all these things</u>
<u>at your command. Answer me, O LORD, answer me</u>, so
these people will know that you, O LORD, are God, and
that you are turning their hearts back again."*
                                        1 Kings 18:36-37 NIV

Elijah believed that God's answer to his prayer would change
the spiritual condition and future of Israel.

David built an altar there to the LORD and sacrificed burnt offerings and peace offerings. And when David prayed, the LORD answered him by sending fire from heaven to burn up the offering on the altar.

1 Chronicles 21:26 NLT

That night God appeared to Solomon and said, "What do you want? <u>Ask, and I will give it to you</u>!" Solomon replied to God, "You showed faithful love to David, my father, and now You have made me king in his place. O LORD God, please continue to keep Your promise to David my father, for You have made me king over a people as numerous as the dust of the earth!

2 Chronicles 1:7-9 NLT

At times I might shut up the heavens so that no rain falls, or command grasshoppers to devour your crops, or send plagues among you. Then if My people who are called by My name will humble themselves and <u>pray and seek My face</u> and turn from their wicked ways, I will hear from heaven and will forgive their sins and restore their land. My eyes will be open and My ears attentive <u>to every prayer</u> made in this place.   2 Chronicles 7:13-15 NLT

God decreed that he would respond to the humble prayers of those who called on him, and that he would change their circumstances.

So when the Aramean chariot commanders saw Jehoshaphat in his royal robes, they went after him. "There is the king of Israel!" they shouted. But <u>Jehoshaphat called out, and the LORD saved him</u>. God helped him by turning the attackers away from him.

2 Chronicles 18:31 NLT

Jehoshaphat learned that God answered his prayers when he saved his life.

> *There near the Ahava River, I announced that we all should fast. We should fast to make ourselves humble before our God. We wanted to ask God for a safe trip for ourselves, our <u>children</u>, and for everything we owned. I was embarrassed to ask King Artaxerxes for soldiers and horsemen to protect us as we traveled. There were enemies on the road. The reason I was embarrassed to ask for protection was because of what we had told the king. We had said to King Artaxerxes, "Our God is with everyone who trusts him, but he is very angry with everyone who turns away from him." So we <u>fasted and prayed</u> to our God about our trip. <u>He answered our prayers</u>.*
>
> Ezra 8:21-23

Ezra believed that God had protected them from what could have happened if he had not asked God for help.

> *Listen to my cry for help, my King and my God, for I pray to no one but You. Listen to my voice in the morning, LORD. <u>Each morning I bring my requests to You and wait expectantly</u>.*   Psalm 5:2-3 NLT

> *In my trouble I called to the LORD. Yes, I cried out to my God for help. There in his temple he heard my voice. He heard my cry for help.*   Psalm 18:6

> *For he has not despised or disdained the suffering of the afflicted one; he has not hidden his face from him but has <u>listened to his cry for help</u>.*   Psalm 22:24 NIV

O LORD my God, I called to you for help and you healed me. Psalm 30:2 NIV

In my alarm I said, "I am cut off from your sight!" Yet you heard my cry for mercy when I called to you for help. Psalm 31:22 NIV

Be pleased, O LORD, to save me; O LORD, come quickly to help me. Psalm 40:13 NIV

Then my enemies will turn back when I call for help. By this I will know that God is for me. Psalm 56:9 NIV

I am worn out calling for help; my throat is parched. My eyes fail, looking for my God. Psalm 69:3 NIV

He will rescue the poor when they cry to him; he will help the oppressed, who have no one to defend them. Psalm 72:12 NLT

LORD, I am asking you to help me! Early each morning I pray to you. Psalm 88:13

Unless the LORD had given me help, I would soon have dwelt in the silence of death. Psalm 94:17 NIV

The Psalms are replete with occasions when David and the other Psalm writers placed their petitions before God believing that his response would change the outcome of their future.

O people of Zion, who live in Jerusalem, you will weep no more. How gracious he will be when you cry for help! As soon as he hears, he will answer you. Isaiah 30:19 NIV

This is what the LORD says: "In the time of my favor <u>I will answer you</u>, and in the day of salvation <u>I will help you</u>; I will keep you and will make you to be a covenant for the people, to restore the land and to reassign its desolate inheritances . . .   Isaiah 49:8 NIV

Then <u>when you call</u>, the LORD will answer. 'Yes, I am here,' He will quickly reply. "Remove the heavy yoke of oppression. Stop pointing your finger and spreading vicious rumors!   Isaiah 58:9 NLT

Isaiah knew that much of the future depended on men's prayers and petitions to God for help.

Then the officials went together to Daniel's house and found him <u>praying and asking for God's help</u>.   Daniel 6:11 NLT

I went on praying and confessing my sin and the sin of my people, pleading with the LORD my God for Jerusalem, His holy mountain. As I was praying, Gabriel, whom I had seen in the earlier vision, came swiftly to me at the time of the evening sacrifice. He explained to me, "Daniel, I have come here to give you insight and understanding. <u>The moment you began praying</u>, a command was given. And now I am here to tell you what it was, for you are very precious to God. Listen carefully so that you can understand the meaning of your vision.   Daniel 9:20-23 NLT

Daniel, one of the most faithful prayers in the Bible, believed that what happened tomorrow was in part dependent on his prayers.

He said, "I cried out to the LORD in my great trouble, and He answered me. I called to You from the land of the dead, and LORD, You heard me!
Jonah 2:2 NLT

But when you pray, go away by yourself, shut the door behind you, and pray to your Father in private. Then your Father, who sees everything, will reward you.
Matthew 6:6 NLT

"Ask and it will be given to you; seek and you will find; knock and the door will be opened to you. For everyone who asks receives; he who seeks finds; and to him who knocks, the door will be opened. Matthew 7:7-8 NIV

Then Jesus said to the disciples, "Have faith in God. I tell you the truth, you can say to this mountain, 'May you be lifted up and thrown into the sea,' and it will happen. But you must really believe it will happen and have no doubt in your heart. I tell you, you can pray for anything, and if you believe that you've received it, it will be yours."
Mark 11:22-24 NLT

To throw a mountain into the sea does not seem like the will of God, yet Jesus says that God will even answer some crazy requests if we have faith when we pray. How is it possible to tell his disciples that they can pray for anything if it is not really true? If everything were already known by God, their prayers could not be answered and wouldn't make any difference in the final outcome. What is already eternally known cannot ever be changed.

Jesus answered, "The truth is, if you have faith and no doubts, you will be able to do the same as I did to this

*tree. And you will be able to do more. You will be able to say to this mountain, 'Go, mountain, fall into the sea.' And if you have faith, it will happen. If you believe, <u>you will get **anything** you ask for in prayer.</u>"*

Matthew 21:21-22

Until now you have not asked for anything in my name. <u>Ask and you will receive</u>, and your joy will be complete.

John 16:24 NIV

Jesus kept teaching over and over that God's answer to men's prayers would help determine their future.

<u>*Pray*</u> *in the Spirit at all times. Pray with all kinds of prayers, and ask for everything you need. To do this you must always be ready. Never give up. Always pray for all of God's people. Also <u>pray for me</u>–that when I speak, God will give me words so that I can tell the secret truth about the Good News without fear. I have the work of speaking for that Good News, and that is what I am doing now, here in prison. <u>Pray</u> that when I tell people the Good News, I will speak without fear as I should.*

Ephesians 6:18-20

Paul believed that the prayers of the saints would change the way things turned out.

So we have not stopped praying for you since we first heard about you. We ask God to give you complete knowledge of His will and to give you spiritual wisdom and understanding. Then the way you live will always honor and please the Lord, and your lives will produce every kind of good fruit. All the while, you will grow as you learn to know God better and better. We also pray that you will be strengthened with all His glorious power so you will have all the endurance and patience you need. May you be filled with joy, always thanking the Father. He has enabled you to share in the inheritance that belongs to His people, who live in the light. Colossians 1:9-12

A widow who really needs help is one who has been left all alone. She trusts God to take care of her. She prays all the time, night and day, and asks God for help.
1 Timothy 5:5

Paul obviously believed in prayer. He mentions how often he intercedes for the believers in the churches, and shows great concern about how things will turn out with them. He didn't believe that the future was unchangeable.

For the eyes of the Lord are on the righteous and his ears are <u>attentive to their prayer</u>, but the face of the Lord is against those who do evil." 1 Peter 3:12 NIV

Peter believed that prayer would influence the lives of those who prayed.

Are any of you suffering hardships? <u>You should pray</u>. Are any of you happy? You should sing praises. Are any of you sick? You should call for the elders of the church to come <u>and pray over you</u>, anointing you with oil in the name of the Lord. Such a <u>prayer offered in faith will heal the sick</u>, and the Lord will make you well. And if you have committed any sins, you will be forgiven. Confess your sins to each other and <u>pray for each other</u> so that you may be healed. <u>The earnest prayer</u>

> *of a righteous person has great power and produces*
> *wonderful results.*   James 5:13-16 NLT

> *Elijah was as human as we are, and yet <u>when he prayed</u>*
> *earnestly that no rain would fall, none fell for three and*
> *a half years! Then, when he <u>prayed again</u>, the sky sent*
> *down rain and the earth began to yield its crops.*
>   James 5:17-18 NLT

James believed that Elijah's prayer affected the climate. He believed that prayer could change the health of a sick person and the length of his life. Prayer is powerful and effective to change the outcome of a person's future circumstances.

> *My dear friends, if we don't feel that we are doing wrong,*
> *we can be without fear when we come to God. And God*
> *gives us what we ask for. We receive it because we obey*
> *God's commands and do what pleases him.*
>   1 John 3:21-22

John taught that our prayers changed what we were going to receive. If we don't pray, we get one result, and if we do, we receive a different outcome.

These are only some of the references throughout the Bible that tell us to pray and that God will answer according to our requests and our faith. They are not empty, impossible promises. They are open-ended: The results are yet to be decided and do not rely on what God already knows. Our prayers, coupled with our faith, enable God to act.

Jesus said we should pray *"Your will be done on earth."* Obviously, from Jesus' own words, God does his will in Heaven;

but on earth, his will in each life is contingent on man's response. God desires to bless us much more than he is able to because the degree of his blessing depends on the size of our faith.

The extremely fruitful evangelist of the nineteenth century, D. L. Moody, is a prime example of God blessing a person according to his faith.

> *Perhaps the line most frequently attributed to Dwight L. Moody (and spoken by his character in the only film on Moody's life) is the famous quotation: "The world has yet to see what God can do with a man fully consecrated to him. By God's help, I aim to be that man."*
>
> *In fact, Moody did not originate the line. Henry Varley, a British revivalist who had befriended the young American in Dublin, recalled that in 1873 Moody asked him to recount words they had spoken in private conversation a year earlier, just before Moody's return to the United States. Varley provides this account (as recorded in Paul Gericke's Crucial Experiences in the Life of D.L. Moody):*
> *During the afternoon of the day of conference Mr. Moody asked me to join him in the vestry of the Baptist Church. We were alone, and he recalled the night's meeting at Willow Park and our conversation the following morning. "Do you remember your words?" he said.*
> *I replied, "I well remember our interview, but I do not recall any special utterance."*
> *"Don't you remember saying, 'Moody, the world has yet to see what God will do with a man fully consecrated to him?' "*
> *"Not the actual sentence," I replied.*
> *"Ah," said Mr. Moody, "those were the words sent to my soul, through you, from the Living God. As I crossed the*

> *wide Atlantic, the boards of the deck of the vessel were*
> *engraved with them, and when I reached Chicago, the very*
> *paving stones seemed marked with 'Moody, the world has*
> *yet to see what God will do with a man fully consecrated*
> *to him.' Under the power of those words I have come*
> *back to England, and I felt that I must not let more time*
> *pass until I let you know how God had used your words*
> *to my inmost soul."*   Mark Fackler

When we pray to the Father, he never puts us on hold, or has us punch numbers on the dial pad, or run through twenty menu options. When we pray to God with a right heart attitude, we are talking to a real person, and a person who can do something about our problem. We don't have to ask to talk to a supervisor or to the owner because our Father is Lord over all. When we pray, we are talking to the chief.

A miracle is divine intervention in the affairs of men —either as a response to prayer, or at God's own initiative. We see in the Scriptures that most miracles happen because God's servants ask for them. If you stop believing in miracles, you are out of business as a Christian.

To whom should we address our prayers?

Jesus told us to pray to the Father.

> *"This, then, is how you should pray:"* `Our Father in
> heaven, hallowed be your name . . . .*
>   Matthew 6:9 NIV

All the references to prayer in the Bible except one say that we should address our prayers to the Father:

Do not be like them, for your <u>Father</u> knows what you need before you <u>ask him</u>.   Matthew 6:8 NIV

So if you sinful people know how to give good gifts to your children, how much more will your heavenly Father give good gifts <u>to those who ask Him</u>.

Matthew 7:11 NLT

"Again, I tell you that if two of you on earth agree about anything you ask for, it will be <u>done for you by my Father</u> in heaven.   Matthew 18:19 NIV

Then the <u>Father</u> will give you <u>whatever you ask</u> in my name.   John 15:16 NIV

At that time you won't need to ask Me for anything. I tell you the truth, <u>you will ask the Father directly</u>, and He will grant your request because you use My name. You haven't done this before. Ask, using My name, and you will receive, and you will have abundant joy.

John 16:23-24 NLT

In that day <u>you will ask in my name</u>. I am not saying that I will ask the Father on your behalf.

John 16:26 NIV

The <u>only exception</u> to these clear instructions about praying to the Father is found in John 14, where Jesus is making the very strong point that he and the Father are one, and that his purpose is to bring glory to the Father.

Jesus answered, "Philip, I have been with you for a long time. So you should know me. Anyone who has seen me

> *has seen the Father too. So why do you say, 'Show us the Father'? Don't you believe that I am in the Father and the Father is in me? The things I have told you don't come from me. The Father lives in me, and he is doing his own work. Believe me when I say that I am in the Father and the Father is in me. Or believe because of the miracles I have done. "I can assure you that whoever believes in me will do the same things I have done. And they will do even greater things than I have done, because I am going to the Father. <u>And if you ask for anything in my name, I will do it for you</u>. Then the Father's glory will be shown through the Son. <u>If you ask me for anything in my name, I will do it</u>.*   John 14:9-14

So, the overwhelming evidence tells us that we should direct our prayers to the Father. There is no indication that we should pray to the Holy Spirit who indwells us. And, there is absolutely no instruction anywhere to pray to the "saints" or other human beings, including Mary, or to angels or evil spirits. In fact, praying to anyone other than to the true God was considered adultery and idolatry in the Old Testament.

As I said at the beginning, you cannot show me one servant of the Lord in the Bible who believed that earnest prayer to the true God would not change the course of his life. If you believe that everything is already known by God and therefore unchangeable, you should ask why God had duped these "gullible" servants of his into believing that their prayers would make any difference in future events?

Prayer does change things, and when we ask our Father in faith (assuming that we are born with his Spirit and are his children), he will respond, and that will change our hearts, our lives and our future.

The promise is clear – God, the Father will answer our prayers when we pray in the right way.

> *We can come to God with no doubts. This means that when we ask God for things (and those things agree with what God wants for us), God cares about what we say. He listens to us every time we ask him. So we know that he gives us whatever we ask from him.*
>
> 1 John 5:14-15

5. The process of salvation

Just like in a normal natural birth of a baby, the spiritual birth is not an instantaneous event, but is preceded by an extended process. First, in a physical human reproduction, there is conception where the sperm encounters the egg; then there is the process of the embryo traveling down the fallopian tube to the uterus; then there is the nine month growth period before the baby is ready to come out of the womb and breath with its own lungs; finally, there is the long period of care needed until the child can function and support himself.

Friends and relatives rejoice when they hear that a woman is pregnant, but they rejoice a whole lot more when they hear that the baby has been delivered.

After years of scratching my head trying to understand all of the biblical statements about the new birth, I now understand that the following is the process by which a person is born again in the Spirit and becomes God's child:

1. People hear from the Father through his revelation in creation (Romans 1:20, Psalm 19:1-4)

2. They respond in faith (believing in God), they learn truth (John 6:43-45), and they are marked as belonging to God (John 8:47, John 17:6)

3. They hear the gospel of salvation in Christ proclaimed (John 20:31, Romans 1:16; 3:22), and they respond in faith recognizing Jesus Christ as God's Son (John 1:12-13, 3:16)

4. They are brought into a Father–son relationship with God by receiving the Holy Spirit (John 1:13, John 3:3-6, I John 3:1-2)

5. They are nurtured and cared for throughout their life on earth

6. They are united with their Heavenly Father and their older brother Jesus and spend eternity with them and all their brothers and sisters

After many years of Bible study, practical analysis of Bible statements, and what I believe is inspiration from the Holy Spirit, I now understand the process that a human being goes through as he comes to eternal life in Christ. Most doctrines of soteriology (the study of salvation), do not fully explain a lot of the biblical statements, especially those by Jesus in the Gospel of John. I have tried to take into account all of the puzzle pieces and carefully fit them together.

1. God reveals himself to men through creation and human conscience

The heavens tell about the glory of God. The skies announce what his hands have made. Each new day tells more of the story, and each night reveals more and more about God's power. You cannot hear them say anything. They don't make any sound we can hear. But

their message goes throughout the world. Their teaching reaches the ends of the earth. The sun's tent is set up in the heavens.   Psalm 19:1-4

God shows his anger from heaven against all the evil and wrong things that people do. Their evil lives hide the truth they have. This makes God angry because <u>they have been shown what he is like</u>. Yes, God has made it clear to them. There are things about God that people cannot see—his eternal power and all that makes him God. But since the beginning of the world, <u>those things have been easy for people to understand</u>. <u>They are made clear in what God has made</u>. So people have no excuse for the evil they do. <u>People knew God</u>, but they did not honor him as God, and they did not thank him. Their ideas were all useless. There was not one good thought left in their foolish minds.   Romans 1:18-21

Even Gentiles, who do not have God's written law, show that they know His law when they instinctively obey it, even without having heard it. They demonstrate that <u>God's law is written in their hearts</u>, for their own conscience and thoughts either accuse them or tell them they are doing right. And this is the message I proclaim—that the day is coming when God, through Christ Jesus, will judge everyone's secret life.   Romans 2:14-15 NLT

There is no one in the whole world today or in the history of the human race who has not heard the truth about God. These Scriptures clearly state that all men have the knowledge of God revealed to them. The key words are that his "power and nature" are revealed through the "creation." After seeing this revelation, all men make a choice to either glorify God or reject him. This is prior to ever hearing the gospel message of salvation through Christ's death on the cross.

> *God sent a man, John the Baptist, to tell about the light so that everyone might believe because of his testimony. John himself was not the light; he was simply a witness to tell about the light. The One who is the true light, who gives light to everyone, was coming into the world.*
> John 1:6-9 NLT

Christ is the light of the world. Not only does he give light to those who hear the Gospel, but he gives light to every human being.

> *They are judged by this fact: The light has come into the world. But they did not want light. They wanted darkness, because they were doing evil things. Everyone who does evil hates the light. They will not come to the light, because the light will show all the bad things they have done. But anyone who follows the true way comes to the light. Then the light will show that whatever they have done was done through God.*
> John 3:19-21

> *And, "He is the stone that makes people stumble, the rock that makes them fall." They stumble because they do not obey God's word, and so they meet the fate that was planned for them. But you are not like that, for you are a chosen people. You are royal priests, a holy nation, God's very own possession. As a result, you can show others the goodness of God, for He called you out of the darkness into His wonderful light.*
> 1 Peter 2:9-10 NLT

> *We heard the true teaching from God. Now we tell it to you: God is light, and in him there is no darkness. So if we say that we share in life with God, but we continue*

living in darkness, we are liars, who don't follow the truth. We should live in the light, where God is. If we live in the light, we have fellowship with each other, and the blood sacrifice of Jesus, God's Son, washes away every sin and makes us clean.   1 John 1:5-7

Jesus answered, "What I teach is not my own. My teaching comes from the one who sent me. <u>People who really want to do what God wants</u> will know that my teaching comes from God. They will know that this teaching is not my own.   John 7:16-17

All of the initiative for light comes from God, but how we respond to that light depends on us. We can resist the light and try to hide from it, or we can make a decision to move toward the light. Our salvation depends on this choice. Some people were already doing evil before Christ came into the world, and some people were already living by the truth before he came. The gospel will only appeal to those who have already chosen to live in the light. Those who are doing evil will reject it, and those who are responding to God's grace by faith will accept it.

The heathen really are lost if they have not believed in what God has already revealed to them in his creation. The gospel will not save people who have intentionally turned away from God as he was revealed to them.

2. People respond in faith to God's revelation and because of their faith he reckons them as righteous

There are many instances in Scripture where people were worshipping God long before they were exposed to the gospel of Christ. Note the following:

When Paul was in Corinth and discouraged, Jesus appeared to him and said, "For I am with you, and no one is going to attack and harm you, because I have many people in this city."   Acts 18:9-10 NIV

Anyone who belongs to God listens gladly to the words of God. But you don't listen because you don't belong to God.   John 8:47 NLT

In the Old Testament, God says the same: *"Yet I reserve seven thousand in Israel—all whose knees have not bowed down to Baal and all whose mouths have not kissed him."*   1 Kings 19:18 NIV

In the New Testament, we see numerous cases of people who were worshipping God before they ever heard the Gospel of Christ's substitutionary death:

In the city of Caesarea there was a man named Cornelius, a Roman army officer in what was called the Italian Unit. He was a religious man. He and all the others who lived in his house were worshipers of the true God. He gave much of his money to help the poor people and always prayed to God. One afternoon about three o'clock, Cornelius had a vision. He clearly saw an angel from God coming to him and saying, "Cornelius!" Staring at the angel and feeling afraid, Cornelius said, "What do you want, sir?" The angel said to him, "God has heard your prayers and has seen your gifts to the poor. He remembers you and all you have done.   Acts 10:1-4

Cornelius was a God worshipper but not a Jew. The fact that he was a Gentile and yet received the Holy Spirit caused great conflict within the early church. Here was a man whom

God accepted based on faith alone and not on fulfilling the requirements of the law given to Moses.

> *There was a woman there named Lydia from the city of Thyatira. Her job was selling purple cloth. <u>She was a worshiper of the true God</u>. Lydia was listening to Paul, and the Lord opened her heart to accept what Paul was saying.*   Acts 16:14

Lydia also was a Gentile, not a Jew, but who worshipped God as she knew him. Where had she gotten this knowledge of who God was, if it wasn't through natural revelation?

> *Paul left the synagogue and moved into the home of Titius Justus, <u>a man who was a worshiper of the true God</u>. His house was next to the synagogue. Crispus was the leader of that synagogue. He and all the people living in his house believed in the Lord Jesus. Many other people in Corinth also listened to Paul. They, too, believed and were baptized.*   Acts 18:7-8

> *Some of the Jews there believed Paul and Silas and decided to join them. Also, a large number of Greeks who were worshipers of the true God and many important women joined them.*   Acts 17:1-4

> *Peter began to speak: "I really understand now that God does not consider some people to be better than others. <u>He accepts anyone who worships him and does what is right</u>. It is not important what nation they come from.*   Acts 10:34-35

This clearly shows that some people were already God's property even before believing in Christ, and before Christ's sacrificial death and resurrection. All Old Testament believers already belonged to God even though they had not been redeemed of their sins until later when Christ died for them.

Worshippers of God existed among the Gentiles and the Jews long before the gospel of Christ was ever revealed or proclaimed to them, and long before the Jews even existed as a race. All of the Old Testament believers from Adam to Malachi worshipped God based on what they had seen in his general revelation. The later ones added to that what Moses had written at God's instruction. But, long before Moses, and long before the Law, Abraham believed God, and it was reckoned to him as righteousness. Job, Enoch, Joseph and multitudes of others only had God's revelation on which to base their faith. People worshipped God long before the name of "Jesus of Nazareth" existed.

Jesus' statements are clearer than anyone else's about how God, the Father teaches and calls people.

> *The Father is the one who sent me, and he is the one who brings people to me. I will raise them up on the last day. Anyone the Father does not bring to me cannot come to me. It is written in the prophets: 'God will teach them all.' People listen to the Father and learn from him. They are the ones who come to me.*   John 6:44-45

> *All your sons will be taught by the LORD, and great will be your children's peace.*   Isaiah 54:13 NIV

General revelation to all mankind has always existed since the world was created, and every human being must respond to it in one way or the other and will worship someone or something. There are two categories of people in the world — those who accept the truth from God and worship him as Creator and Lord, and those who turn away in rebellion and disbelief. Those who turn away from God's general revelation also turn away from Christ and his message of salvation through his blood.

> *I have revealed you to <u>those whom you gave me</u> out of the world. <u>They were yours; you gave them to me</u> and they have obeyed your word.*   John 17:6 NIV

> *I pray for them now. I am not praying for the people in the world. But I am praying for <u>these people you gave me, because they are yours</u>.*   John 17:9

> *"Father, I want these <u>people you have given me</u> to be with me in every place I am. I want them to see my glory–the glory you gave me because you loved me before the world was made. Father, you are the one who always does what is right. The world does not know you, but I know you, and these followers of mine know that you sent me. I showed them what you are like, and I will show them again. Then they will have the same love that you have for me, and I will live in them."* John 17:24-26

> *"I am coming to you now. But I pray these things while I am still in the world. I say all this so that these followers can have the true happiness that I have. I want them to be completely happy. I have given them your teaching. And the world has hated them, because <u>they don't belong to the world</u>, just as I don't belong to the world. "I am not asking you to take them out of the world. But I am asking that you keep them safe from the Evil One. <u>They don't belong to the world</u>, just as I don't belong to the world."*   John 17:13-16

These believers belonged to the Father before they ever belonged to Christ. Because of their faith in what had been revealed to them they were considered God's possession even though they were not yet fully saved.

> *If you love me, you will obey what I command. And I will ask the Father, and he will give you another Counselor to be with you forever– the Spirit of truth. The world cannot accept him, because it neither sees him nor knows him. But you know him, for <u>he lives with you</u> and <u>will be in</u> you. I will not leave you as orphans; I will come to you.*
> John 14:15-18 NIV

The Holy Spirit was already living <u>with</u> the eleven apostles (Judas had already left when Jesus said this), and was soon to take up his permanent residence within them on the day of Pentecost.

> *"I am the shepherd who cares for the sheep. <u>I know my sheep just as the Father knows me</u>. And my sheep know me just as I know the Father. I give my life for these sheep. I have other sheep too. They are not in this flock here. I must lead them also. They will listen to my voice. In the future there will be one flock and one shepherd.*
> John 10:14-16

The sheep from the other pen belonged to God, but they did not yet belong to Christ. These people already had a faith relationship with God the Father. When the time came, the Father gave all of these people to the Son for the purpose of redemption. Their faith, along with the sacrificial work of Christ, resulted in their salvation.

God's children

God often calls these people who have believed in him through general revelation his children, though they were not yet children in the sense of having received the new birth in the Holy Spirit. It was like them being in the womb, but not yet having been spiritually re-born.

> *Caiaphas did not think of this himself. As that year's high priest, he was really prophesying that Jesus would die for the Jewish people. Yes, he would die for the Jewish people. But he would also die for <u>God's other children scattered all over the world</u>. He would die to bring them all together and make them one people.*
> John 11:51-52

This passage says that they were God's children <u>before</u> Christ ever died for them.

> *And again, "I will put my trust in him." And again he says, "Here am I, and <u>the children</u> God has given me."*
> Hebrews 2:13 NIV

They are not Christ's children, but children of the Father, and they were already his "children" when the Father gave them to Christ so that he could give them eternal life.

While some believed God, many others rejected him

> <u>*They traded the truth of God for a lie*</u>. *They bowed down and worshiped the things God made instead of worshiping the God who made those things. He is the one who should be praised forever. Amen.*   Romans 1:25

That is because they hated knowledge. They refused to fear and respect the LORD.   Proverbs 1:29

The Man of Evil will use every kind of evil to fool those who are lost. They are lost <u>because they refused to love the truth and be saved</u>. So God will send them something powerful that leads them away from the truth and causes them to believe a lie. They will all be condemned because <u>they did not believe the truth</u> and because they enjoyed doing evil.   2 Thessalonians 2:10-12

He will give eternal life to those who keep on doing good, seeking after the glory and honor and immortality that God offers. But He will pour out His anger and wrath on those who live for themselves, who refuse to obey the truth and instead live lives of wickedness.
There will be trouble and calamity for everyone who keeps on doing what is evil—for the Jew first and also for the Gentile. But there will be glory and honor and peace from God for all who do good—for the Jew first and also for the Gentile.   Romans 2:5-10 NLT

And the Father who sent Me has testified about Me Himself. You have never heard His voice or seen Him face to face, and you do not have His message in your hearts, because you do not believe Me—the One He sent to you. "You search the Scriptures because you think they give you eternal life. But the Scriptures point to Me! Yet <u>you refuse to come to Me to receive this life</u>. "Your approval means nothing to Me, because I know <u>you don't have God's love within you</u>. For I have come to you in My Father's name, and <u>you have rejected Me</u>. Yet if others come in their own name, you gladly welcome them. No *wonder you can't believe! For you gladly honor each other, but you don't care about the honor that comes from the One who alone is God.* John 5:37-44 NLT

Jesus said to them, "<u>If God were really your Father</u>, you would love me. I came from God, and now I am here. I did not come by my own authority. God sent me. You don't understand the things I say, because you cannot accept my teaching. <u>Your father is the devil.</u> You belong to him. You want to do what he wants. He was a murderer from the beginning. He was always against the truth. There is no truth in him. He is like the lies he tells. Yes, the devil is a liar. He is the father of lies. John 8:42-44

I do not accept praise from men, but I know you. I know that you do not have the love of God in your hearts. John 5:41 NIV

The world would love you as one of its own if you belonged to it, but you are no longer part of the world. I chose you to come out of the world, so it hates you. Do you remember what I told you? 'A slave is not greater than the master.' Since they persecuted Me, naturally they will persecute you. And if they had listened to Me, they would listen to you. They will do all this to you because of Me, for they have rejected the one who sent Me. John 15:19-21 NLT

Yes, <u>the minds of these people are now closed</u>. They have ears, but they don't listen. They have eyes, but they refuse to see. If their minds were not closed, they might see with their eyes; they might hear with their ears; they might understand with their minds. Then they might turn back to me and be healed. Matthew 13:15

God did not close their eyes: it was <u>their decision</u>. They are not innocent victims. Like Curly of the three stooges, who cried out, "I can't see, I can't see". And Moe says "Why not?" Curly responds, "I got my eyes closed." If a man intentionally closes his eyes to God's teaching, he will never understand truth. In order to understand, there must be a response of faith to the revelation of God, or the person's eyes become blind and his heart becomes harder and harder with each revelation.

> *The Good News that we tell people may be hidden, but it is hidden only to those who are lost. The ruler of this world has blinded the minds of those who don't believe. They cannot see the light of the Good News–the message about the divine greatness of Christ. Christ is the one who is exactly like God.*   2 Corinthians 4:3-4

Those who are rebels against God have become blinded so that they cannot see the light in Christ. The gospel will only be received by those who have already believed in God through his general revelation. Salvation comes when we love the truth. We must believe the truth and not delight in wickedness. The people in Romans 1 were given the opportunity to worship God and they refused. Because of their refusal, God sent them a delusion and they began to descend down the stairs into greater and greater wickedness.

> *But some of you do not believe Me." (For Jesus knew from the beginning which ones didn't believe, and He knew who would betray Him.) Then He said, "That is why I said that people can't come to Me <u>unless the Father gives them to Me</u>."*   John 6:64-65 NLT

Why did Jesus choose the 12 disciples? What were his criteria? We know that he chose Judas Iscariot knowing that he was an infidel. We believe he chose the rest because they were persons of faith in God, and they had qualities that would be useful in the proclamation of the gospel. The heart attitude of each of the disciples was probably revealed to him by the Father the night he prayed while choosing them. Jesus knew from the beginning that Judas did not have faith in God and that he would therefore betray him, and he was chosen for that purpose. He also knew from the beginning that some of the many other followers in the crowds did not believe in God's revelation to them. The faithful disciples were not converted to faith through his ministry. They were already faith people before he ever met them, and that is why they were chosen.

> *You brood of snakes! How could evil men like you speak what is good and right? For whatever is in your heart determines what you say. A good person produces good things from the treasury of a good heart, and an evil person produces evil things from the treasury of an evil heart. And I tell you this, you must give an account on judgment day for every idle word you speak.*
>
> Matthew 12:33-35 NLT

> *O Jerusalem, Jerusalem, you who kill the prophets and stone those sent to you, how often I have longed to gather your children together, as a hen gathers her chicks under her wings, but you were not willing!*
>
> Luke 13:34 NIV

Once a person begins to reject God's authority/ownership over him, he goes downhill from there. When we reject God's truth, we get farther and farther away from him, and get more and more evil with every step. On the other hand, if we come toward the light, he illumines us more and more and transforms our nature.

God is patiently pleading and working for the salvation of all men

But the time is coming—indeed it's here now—when true worshipers will worship the Father in spirit and in truth. <u>The Father is looking for those who will worship Him that way</u>. John 4:23 NLT

But don't forget this one thing, dear friends: To the Lord a day is like a thousand years, and a thousand years is like a day. The Lord is not being slow in doing what he promised–the way some people understand slowness. But <u>God is being patient</u> with you. <u>He doesn't want anyone to be lost</u>. <u>He wants everyone to change their ways and stop sinning</u>. 2 Peter 3:8-9

And remember, <u>our Lord's patience gives people time to be saved</u>. This is what our beloved brother Paul also wrote to you with the wisdom God gave him. 2 Peter 3:15 NLT

And since you do the same things as those people you judge, surely you understand that God will punish you too. How could you think you would be able to escape his judgment? God has been kind to you. <u>He has been very patient, waiting for you to change</u>. But you think nothing of his kindness. Maybe you don't understand that <u>God is kind to you so that you will decide to change your lives</u>. Romans 2:3-4

God is patiently and actively looking for faith in the hearts of men everywhere. There is absolutely no reason to say he is patient if he already knows the end of a thing. Patience implies a hopeful waiting for a desired outcome. The passage mentioning the "thousand years" is often quoted to support the belief that God is timeless, but that is not what it is saying. It is telling us that God is fulfilling his promises and his desire <u>no matter how long</u> it seems to take. He is not impatient about waiting for people to respond to him in faith.

> *Now, if evil people change their lives, they will live and not die. They might stop doing all the bad things they did and begin to carefully obey all my laws. They might become fair and good. God will not remember all the bad things they did. He will remember only their goodness, so they will live! The Lord GOD says, "<u>I don't want evil people to die. I want them to change their lives so that they can live!</u>"* Ezekiel 18:21-23

3. Those who are people of faith hear the gospel and respond in a positive way

Forgiveness by God and salvation in Christ are possible for <u>every</u> human being. God offers this salvation to anyone who will receive it, and he has commissioned the church made up of all true believers to publish the Good News to the whole world. God has not predestined who will be saved. To offer something very desirable to a person when the reality is that he cannot receive it is hypocritical and cruel. We try to teach our children not to be evil like that. We don't ask our children if they want a bowl of ice cream if we know there is no ice cream in the house and we don't have money to buy any.

The prospect of everlasting life is presented in God's Word as a possibility for <u>all</u> people. After urging his listeners to '*keep on asking and seeking'* good things from God, Jesus pointed out that a father does not give a stone or a serpent to his child who asks for bread or a fish. Jesus said: *"Therefore, if you, being evil, know how to give good gifts to your children, how much more will your Father who is in heaven give good things to those asking him?"* Matthew 7:11 NIV. God not only offers good things to his children, but he also gives them to them when they do what he says.

> And *everyone who calls on the name of the LORD will be saved;* for on Mount Zion and in Jerusalem there will be deliverance, as the LORD has said, among the survivors whom the LORD calls.   Joel 2:32 NIV

> And *everyone* who calls on the name of the Lord will be saved.   Acts 2:21 NIV

The invitations and opportunities that God offers are bona fide. He, in all sincerity, urges men to *'turn from transgression and live,'* as he did with the people of Israel. His loving nature would not allow him to offer salvation to all if he foreknew that they were individually destined to die in wickedness. If you think that God is capricious and makes offers and promises he has no intention of keeping, you are terribly mistaken about who he is.

In a similar vein, the apostle Peter writes: *The Lord is not being slow in doing what he promised–the way some people understand slowness. But God is being patient with you. He doesn't want anyone to be lost. He wants everyone to change their ways and stop sinning.* (2 Peter 3:9) If God already foreknew and foreordained millenniums in advance precisely which individuals would receive eternal salvation and which individuals would receive eternal destruction, how meaningful could "the patience of God" be and how genuine could be his desire that all come to repentance. The apostle John wrote that *"God is love,"* and the apostle Paul states that love *"hopes all things."* (1 John 4:8; 1 Corinthians 13:4, 7) Even though in some evil people the possibility of repentance is slim, God does not give up hoping that it will happen so that he can forgive them and show them his mercy.

If, by God's foreknowledge, the opportunity to receive the benefits of Christ Jesus' sacrifice were already irrevocably sealed off from some people, even billions of individuals before their birth, it could not truly be said that the ransom was made available to all men. (2 Corinthians 5:14-15); 1 Timothy 2:5-6; Hebrews 2:9) *Peter began to speak: "I really understand now that God does not consider some people to be better than others. He accepts anyone who worships him and does what is right. It is not important what nation they come from.* (Acts 10:34-35; Deuteronomy 10:17; Romans 2:11) The option of forgiveness and salvation is genuinely open to all men, *"God wanted people to look for him, and perhaps in searching all around for him, they would find him. But he is not far from any of us.* (Acts 17:27) It is not an empty hope or hollow promise. Even at the very end of the Scriptures, there is a specific invitation on God's part: *The Spirit and the bride say, "Come!" Everyone who hears this should also say, "Come!" All who are thirsty may come; they can have the water of life as a free gift if they want it.* (Revelation 22:17).

> *Yes, God loved the world so much that he gave his only Son, so that <u>everyone</u> who believes in him would not be lost but have eternal life. God sent his Son into the world. He did not send him to judge the world guilty, but to save the world through him. People who believe in God's Son*

> are not judged guilty. But people who do not believe are
> already judged, because they have not believed in God's
> only Son. They are judged by this fact: The light has come
> into the world. But they did not want light. They wanted
> darkness, because they were doing evil things. Everyone
> who does evil hates the light. They will not come to the
> light, because the light will show all the bad things they
> have done. But _anyone_ who follows the true way comes to
> the light. Then the light will show that whatever they have
> done was done through God.   John 3:16-21

If you don't understand the meanings of the words "everyone"
or "anyone," look them up in any dictionary or ask a six–year
old child.

> He came to that which was his own, but his own did
> not receive him. Yet _to all who received him,_ to _those_
> _who believed_ in his name, he gave the right to become
> children of God–children born not of natural descent,
> nor of human decision or a husband's will, but born
> of God.   John 1:11-13 NIV

> If you openly say, "Jesus is Lord" and believe in your
> heart that God raised him from death, you will be saved.
> _Yes, we believe in Jesus deep in our hearts, and so we are_
> _made right with God. And we openly say that we believe_
> _in him, and so we are saved._ Yes, the Scriptures say,
> "_Anyone who trusts in him_ will never be disappointed."
> It says this because there is no difference between those
> who are Jews and those who are not. The same Lord is
> the Lord of all people. And he richly blesses _everyone_ who
> looks to him for help. Yes, "_everyone_ who trusts in the
> Lord will be saved."If you openly say, "Jesus is Lord"

*and believe in your heart that God raised him from death,
you will be saved.*   Romans 10:9-13

*I am proud of the Good News, because it is the power
God uses to save everyone who believes–to save the Jews
first, and now to save those who are not Jews. The Good
News shows how God makes people right with himself.
God's way of making people right begins and ends with
faith. As the Scriptures say, "The one who is right with
God by faith will live forever."*   Romans 1:16-17

*"I am praying not only for these disciples but also for
<u>all who will ever believe in Me</u> through their message.*
                                    John 17:20 NLT

Anyone who receives by faith the teaching of the Father through
his created works and on-going providence is going to be saved.
Because he becomes a person of faith, he will be led into the
arms of Christ who will give him eternal life and he will never
lose it (*My sheep listen to my voice; I know them, and they
follow me. I give them eternal life, and they shall never perish;
no one can snatch them out of my hand. John* 10:27-28). God
is going to save all true believers no matter their nationality,
their race, their sex, their marital status, their age, their level of
education, or their denomination. Adam and Eve never joined a
church, or attended mass, or had perfect attendance in Sunday
School, but because they put their faith in God and Christ died
for them, they will be with him forever.

*He replied, "You are permitted to understand the secrets
of the Kingdom of Heaven, but others are not. To those
who listen to My teaching, more understanding will be
given, and they will have an abundance of knowledge.*

> *But for <u>those who are not listening</u>, even what little understanding they have will be taken away from them.*
> Matthew 13:11-12 NLT

> *But whenever <u>anyone</u> turns to the Lord, the veil is taken away.*   2 Corinthians 3:16 NIV

When a person responds in faith to what God reveals through his creation, then the blindness is taken away and the person can believe in the gospel.

> *So don't judge anyone now. The time for judging will be when the Lord comes. He will shine light on everything that is now hidden in darkness. He will make known the secret purposes of our hearts. Then the praise each person should get will come from God.*   1 Corinthians 4:5

Hearing and believing the gospel about Christ's incarnation, death and resurrection is the final step in the sealing of salvation. The proclamation of the gospel gives the opportunity to a "God worshipper" to actually be saved. This gospel is proclaimed usually by human beings (2 Corinthians 5:18-20), but was also done by Jesus after his resurrection when he preached the gospel to all of the spirits held in prison (1 Peter 3:18-19), and also by Jesus and angels who appear to people in visions and dreams (example are the multitudes of Muslims who have turned to Christ in the Middle East over the last two decades).

What does the Bible mean by the word "Foreknowledge"?

Foreknew — *"Of whom he was aware and loved beforehand."* He had a personal relationship with them as individuals. This knowing did not take place before these people came into existence. He could not know them as persons until they were conceived.

> *"Not everyone who says to me, `Lord, Lord,' will enter the kingdom of heaven, but only he who does the will of my Father who is in heaven. Many will say to me on that day, `Lord, Lord, did we not prophesy in your name, and in your name drive out demons and perform many miracles?' Then I will tell them plainly, `I never <u>knew you</u>.*
>
> Matthew 7:21-23 NIV

> *God the Father <u>knew</u> you and chose you long ago, and His Spirit has made you holy. As a result, you have obeyed Him and have been cleansed by the blood of Jesus Christ. May God give you more and more grace and peace.*
>
> 1 Peter 1:2 NLT

They were <u>known</u> previously by God because of their faith and therefore chosen to be obedient to Jesus and to be sprinkled with His blood.

> *And we know that God causes everything to work together for the good of those who love God and are called according to His purpose for them. For <u>God knew His people in advance</u>, and He chose them to become like His Son, so that His Son would be the firstborn among many brothers and sisters. And having chosen them, He called them to come to Him. And having called them, He gave them right standing with Himself. And having given them right standing, He gave them His glory.*
>
> Romans 8:28 NLT

> *For he chose <u>**us in him**</u> before the creation of the world to be holy and blameless in his sight. In love he predestined*

> *us to be adopted as his sons through Jesus Christ, in*
> *accordance with his pleasure and will– to the praise of*
> *his glorious grace, which he has freely given us in the One*
> *he loves.* Ephesians 1:4-6 NIV

He chose <u>all those</u> who come into Christ — this is a generic group of people and not name specific.

> *In him <u>we were also chosen</u>, having been predestined*
> *according to the plan of him who works out everything*
> *in conformity with the purpose of his will, in order that*
> *<u>we, who were the first to hope in Christ</u>, might be for*
> *the praise of his glory. And <u>you also **were included** in*
> *Christ when you heard the word of truth</u>, the gospel of*
> *your salvation. <u>Having believed</u>, you were marked in him*
> *with a seal, the promised Holy Spirit, who is a deposit*
> *guaranteeing our inheritance until the redemption of those*
> *who are God's possession–to the praise of his glory.*
> Ephesians 1:11 NIV

No person can be saved without being included "<u>in</u>" Christ. Every person who has a faith relationship with the Father through his revealing himself through creation and life will be included in Christ. People are not saved until they hear the word of truth, believe it, and become part of Christ.

> *"Salvation is found in no one else, for there is no other*
> *name under heaven given to men by which we must be*
> *saved."* Acts 4:12 NIV

No one has ever been saved nor ever will be if he is not "in" Christ. Adam, Enoch, Moses, David, Isaiah, Matthew, Luke and John are all saved because they were put "into" Christ, and Christ paid for their sins on the cross, and he rose as a testimony of payment in full.

God knows the condition of every person's heart

The parable of the four different soils —

> *"This is the meaning of the parable: The seed is the word of God. Those along the path are the ones who hear, and then the devil comes and takes away the word from their hearts, so that they may not believe and be saved. Those on the rock are the ones who receive the word with joy when they hear it, but they have no root. They believe for a while, but in the time of testing they fall away. The seed that fell among thorns stands for those who hear, but as they go on their way they are choked by life's worries, riches and pleasures, and they do not mature. But the seed on good soil stands for those with <u>a noble and good heart</u>, who hear the word, retain it, and by persevering produce a crop.*   Luke 8:11-15 NIV

The soils never get converted from one kind to another. The good soil was already good when the seed fell into it. The bad soils were already bad when the seed fell into them. The seed made no difference in the condition of the soil. The soils are a picture of the condition of the heart of a man before he hears the gospel. A man must believe in God's general revelation in order for his heart to be made right so that he can produce fruit when he receives the gospel. When we preach the gospel we should be looking for people whose heart is ready to receive it. A wise sower will use some intelligence when he distributes the seed. He won't intentionally cast it on the path or on the rocky soil. He will aim to get most of the seed on the good soil.

The parable of the good fish and the bad fish —

> *Also, God's kingdom is like a net that was put into the lake. The net caught many different kinds of fish. It was full, so the fishermen pulled it to the shore. They sat down and put all the good fish in baskets. Then they threw away the bad fish. It will be the same at the end of time. The angels will come and separate the evil people from the godly people. They will throw the evil people into the place of fire. There the people will cry and grind their teeth with pain.*   Matthew 13:47-50

The "good fish" are those people who believe in what God has revealed to them. They are considered righteous because of their faith (like Abraham). The wicked are those who have refused to hear and believe when God revealed his nature to them.

The parable of the tares and the wheat —

> *Jesus told them another parable: "The kingdom of heaven is like a man who sowed good seed in his field. But while everyone was sleeping, his enemy came and sowed weeds (tares) among the wheat, and went away. When the wheat sprouted and formed heads, then the weeds also appeared. The owner's servants came to him and said, `Sir, didn't you sow good seed in your field? Where then did the weeds come from?'*
> *`An enemy did this,' he replied.*
> *The servants asked him, `Do you want us to go and pull them up?'*
> *`No,' he answered, `because while you are pulling the weeds, you may root up the wheat with them. Let both grow together until the harvest. At that time I will tell*

the harvesters: First collect the weeds and tie them in
bundles to be burned; then gather the wheat and bring
it into my barn.'   Matthew 13:24-30 NIV

The tares/weeds never get transformed into wheat. They remain
the same as when they started. They represent evil, unbelieving
people that Satan sows in God's field (the church) and who
appear to be good plants, but in reality are weeds meant to suck
up the nutrition meant for the wheat, and to create confusion.

When we reject God and turn away from the light, we become
more and more evil. Our decision to refuse the right of God to
rule over us starts us down the very slippery slope to increasing
darkness and wickedness. Hell is getting as far from God as is
possible, where his light, his love, his life, and his provision no
longer have any redeeming influence.

My dear friend, don't follow what is bad; follow what
is good. Whoever does what is good is from God. But
whoever does evil has never known God.
                              3 John 1:11

Praise be to the God and Father of our Lord Jesus Christ.
In Christ, God has given us every spiritual blessing in
heaven. In Christ, he chose us before the world was made.
He chose us in love to be his holy people--people who
could stand before him without any fault. And before
the world was made, God decided to make us his own
children through Jesus Christ. This was what God wanted,
and it pleased him to do it.   Ephesians 1:3-5

This is true because he already knew his people and had
already appointed them to have the same form as the

*image of his Son. Therefore, his Son is the firstborn among
many children.*   Romans 8:29
                                      (God's Word)

*"Not everyone who says to me, 'Lord, Lord,' will enter
the kingdom of heaven, but only he who does the will
of my Father who is in heaven. Many will say to me on
that day, `Lord, Lord, did we not prophesy in your name,
and in your name drive out demons and perform many
miracles?' Then I will tell them plainly, 'I never knew you.
Away from me, you evildoers!'*   Matthew 7:21-23

God "knows" the good-doers — He does not "know" the
evil-doers.

*Satan, who is the god of this world, has blinded the minds
of those who don't believe. They are unable to see the
glorious light of the Good News. They don't understand
this message about the glory of Christ, who is the exact
likeness of God. You see, we don't go around preaching
about ourselves. We preach that Jesus Christ is Lord, and
we ourselves are your servants for Jesus' sake. For God,
who said, "Let there be light in the darkness," has made
this light shine in our hearts so we could know the glory
of God that is seen in the face of Jesus Christ.*
                                      2 Corinthians 4:4-6 NLT

*But you aren't in the dark about these things, dear brothers
and sisters, and you won't be surprised when the day of
the Lord comes like a thief.*   1 Thessalonians 5:4 NLT

*After Jesus said these things, he looked toward heaven and
prayed, "Father, the time has come. Give glory to your*

Son so that the Son can give glory to you. You gave the Son power over all people so that he could give eternal life <u>to all those you have given to him</u>. And this is eternal life: that people can know you, the only true God, and that they can know Jesus Christ, the one you sent.
John 17:1-3

I am not talking about all of you. <u>I know the people I have chosen</u>. But what the Scriptures say must happen: 'The man who shared my food has turned against me.'
John 13:18

Jesus did not "know" Judas, but he knew all about him.

God is patiently pleading and working for the salvation of men. This is his greatest desire and most important work.

4. Those who believe in Christ are nurtured and cared for throughout their life on earth

I always thank my God for you because of the grace that he has given you through Christ Jesus. In him you have been blessed in every way. You have been blessed in all your speaking and all your knowledge. This proves that what we told you about Christ is true. Now you have every gift from God while you wait for our Lord Jesus Christ to come again. <u>He will keep you strong until the end</u> so that on the day when our Lord Jesus Christ comes, <u>you will be free from all blame</u>. God is faithful. He is the one who has chosen you to share life with his Son, Jesus Christ our Lord.
1 Corinthians 1:4-9

Jesus has the power of God. And <u>his power has given us</u>
<u>everything we need to live a life devoted to God</u>. We have
these things because we know him. Jesus chose us by his
glory and goodness, through which he also gave us the
very great and rich gifts that he promised us. With these
gifts you can share in being like God. And so you will
escape the ruin that comes to people in the world because
of the evil things they want.   2 Peter 1:3-4

Then Jesus said, "I am the bread that gives life. <u>No one</u>
<u>who comes to me will ever be hungry</u>. No one who
believes in me will ever be thirsty. I told you before that
you have seen me, and still you don't believe. The Father
gives me my people. Every one of them will come to me.
I will always accept them. I came down from heaven to
do what God wants, not what I want. <u>I must not lose</u>
<u>anyone God has given me</u>. But I must raise them up on
the last day. <u>This is what the one who sent me wants me</u>
<u>to do</u>.   John 6:35-39

5. They are all united with their Heavenly Father and Jesus and spend eternity with them.

Father, I want these people you have given me to be with
me in every place I am. I want them to see my glory–the
glory you gave me because you loved me before the world
was made.   John 17:24

Then I saw a new heaven and a new earth. The first heaven
and the first earth had disappeared. Now there was no
sea. And I saw the holy city, the new Jerusalem, coming
down out of heaven from God. It was prepared like a

bride dressed for her husband. I heard a loud voice from the throne. It said, "Now God's home is with people. He will live with them. They will be his people. God himself will be with them and will be their God. He will wipe away every tear from their eyes. There will be no more death, sadness, crying, or pain. All the old ways are gone.

Revelation 21:1-4

Conclusion

Here is the order of salvation: (1) God loves us and sends a remedy for our sin, and then, (2) we must believe. If we do not believe, there is no salvation. God obviously starts the process by making the offer of salvation, but each man must accept the offer. God cannot believe for us, or he would gladly believe for all men.

Salvation is not a question of works or magic words that bring salvation. It is not even a decision we make to go forward at an evangelistic campaign or to pray the sinner's prayer (I am a great supporter of Billy Graham and many others who preach the gospel to multitudes of people, because a public declaration to identify with Christ is an important step in the salvation process). Salvation is about our on-going faith attitude toward God. Though praying the sinner's prayer, or indicating our willingness to receive Christ in a public setting are good things, they are only manifestations of the faith that should already be in our heart. Many have prayed the prayer to no avail because their heart wasn't in it, or faith wasn't in their heart. Salvation is a gift from God that is based on our faith attitude of reverence and worship of the Creator. Any supposed salvation where this faith and worship of God do not exist is a miscarriage and not a live birth.

We should not twist people's arms to make a profession of faith in Christ and then wonder why there is no evidence of a changed life. We should shine the light of the gospel on the lives of everyone we can and in every good way we can, but it is up to them to respond to the light according to what is already in their heart. *"Men did not come to the light, because they loved darkness more than light."* Neither we nor God can do anything about the lack of faith in people's hearts. We can't put it there or make it happen. It is a series of voluntary decisions that each person in the world must make when faced with the truth about God.

6. | Where does faith come from?

Some theologians trying to explain the process of salvation have often tried to eliminate the importance of man's response to God's initiative to save them. In spite of the clarity of the Bible that salvation is based on the faith of the individual, quite a few scholars have argued that Ephesians 2:8-9 says that faith comes from God and not from man. However, "the gift" in this verse does not refer to faith, but rather to salvation.

> *For it is by grace you have been saved, through faith–and this not from yourselves, it is the gift of God–not by works, so that no one can boast.*   NIV

How do we know that this statement is not referring to our faith? Because the Bible says over and over that the faith is "ours" and not God's. The phrase "your faith" is seen forty times throughout the Bible. "Our faith appears four more times, "my faith" once, and we are exhorted to "have faith" twelve times. There is never any mention of "God's faith", or of someone saying "God has given me my faith." We get our love from God as seen in 1 John, but there is no similar mention of getting our faith from God.

The defining statement *"and this not from yourselves"* does not refer to our faith, because our faith comes from our heart. For understanding the meaning more clearly, it could read: *For it is by grace you have been saved —it is the gift of God— not by works, so that no one can boast.* All those who believe in God's word concerning salvation through his Son Jesus, will be saved. The offer is to all men, but only those who have faith will be saved. The Bible clearly states that <u>whoever believes</u> will receive the gift of salvation.

The faith is clearly ours and not something that belongs to God. Even though Jesus exercised faith in his Father throughout his lifetime, there is never any indication that the faith which saves every individual comes from him. Look at just some of the statements in the Bible:

> *But someone might argue, "Some people have faith, and others have good works." My answer would be that you can't show me <u>your faith</u> if you don't do anything. But I will show you <u>my faith</u> by the good I do. You believe there is one God. That's good, but even the demons believe that! And they shake with fear.* James 2:18-19

> *When Jesus heard this, he was amazed. He said to those who were with him, "The truth is, this man <u>has more faith</u> than anyone I have found, even in Israel.* Matthew 8:10

Why would Jesus be so amazed at this man's level of faith if it were only a gift from God? Was he amazed that his Father had given him such a large dose, or was he amazed at the man's depth of belief? The logical conclusion is that he was amazed that there was a man who believed in God so firmly.

> *Then Jesus answered, "Woman, you have great faith! You will get what you asked for." And right then the woman's daughter was healed.*   Matthew 15:28

> *Jesus answered, "You were not able to make the demon go out, because <u>your faith is too small</u>. Believe me when I tell you, if <u>your faith</u> is only as big as a mustard seed you can say to this mountain, 'Move from here to there,' and it will move. You will be able to do anything."*
> Matthew 17:20

> *Jesus answered, "The truth is, <u>if you have faith</u> and no doubts, you will be able to do the same as I did to this tree. And you will be able to do more. You will be able to say to this mountain, 'Go, mountain, fall into the sea.' And <u>if you have faith</u>, it will happen. If you believe, you will get anything you ask for in prayer."*
> Matthew 21:21-22

> *Jesus answered, "<u>Have faith</u> in God. The truth is, you can say to this mountain, 'Go, mountain, fall into the sea.' And if you have no doubts in your mind and believe that what you say will happen, then God will do it for you.*
> Mark 11:22-23

Why would Jesus exhort his followers to have lots of faith if it was something they had only received from God and over which they had no control?

The Lord said, "If your faith is as big as a mustard seed, you can say to this mulberry tree, 'Dig yourself up and plant yourself in the ocean!' And the tree will obey you.
Luke 17:6

Satan has asked to test you men like a farmer tests his wheat. O Simon, Simon, I have prayed that you will not lose your faith! Help your brothers be stronger when you come back to me.   Luke 22:31-32

Jesus answered: "Don't you know me, Philip, even after I have been among you such a long time? Anyone who has seen me has seen the Father. How can you say, `Show us the Father'? Don't you believe that I am in the Father, and that the Father is in me? The words I say to you are not just my own. Rather, it is the Father, living in me, who is doing his work. Believe me when I say that I am in the Father and the Father is in me; or at least believe on the evidence of the miracles themselves. I tell you the truth, anyone who has faith in me will do what I have been doing. He will do even greater things than these, because I am going to the Father.   John 14:9-12 NIV

I never shrank back from telling you what you needed to hear, either publicly or in your homes. I have had one message for Jews and Greeks alike—the necessity of repenting from sin and turning to God, and of having faith in our Lord Jesus.   Acts 20:20-21 NLT

Men must repent, turn to God and have faith. These are all decisions that each man must make. There is nothing here to make us believe that having faith is a gift from God and is in a different category than repenting and turning.

Last night an angel of the God whose I am and whom I serve stood beside me and said, 'Do not be afraid, Paul. You must stand trial before Caesar; and God has graciously given you the lives of all who sail with you.' So keep up your courage, men, for I have faith in God that it will happen just as he told me. Nevertheless, we must run aground on some island." Acts 27:23-26 NIV

What if some did not have faith? Will their lack of faith nullify God's faithfulness? Not at all! Let God be true, and every man a liar. Romans 3:3-4 NIV

God gave Jesus as a way to forgive people's sins through their faith in him. God can forgive them because the blood sacrifice of Jesus pays for their sins. God gave Jesus to show that he always does what is right and fair. He was right in the past when he was patient and did not punish people for their sins. And in our own time he still does what is right. God worked all this out in a way that allows him to judge people fairly and still make right any person who has faith in Jesus. Romans 3:25-26

The emphasis on having faith is clearly placed on men, not on God. God's faithfulness was given primarily to men who had faith.

Is this blessing only for those who are circumcised? Or is it also for those who are not circumcised? We have already said that it was because of Abraham's faith that he was accepted as one who is right with God. Romans 4:9

Therefore, since we have been made right in God's sight by faith, we have peace with God because of what Jesus

*Christ our Lord has done for us. <u>Because of our faith</u>,
Christ has brought us into this place of undeserved
privilege where we now stand, and we confidently and
joyfully look forward to sharing God's glory.*

Romans 5:1-2 NLT

*"You and I are Jews by birth, not 'sinners' like the
Gentiles. Yet we know that a person is made right with
God <u>by faith</u> in Jesus Christ, not by obeying the law. And
<u>we have believed</u> in Christ Jesus, so that we might be
made right with God <u>because of our faith</u> in Christ, not
because we have obeyed the law. For no one will ever be
made right with God by obeying the law."*

Galatians 2:15-16 NLT

*So I am not the one living now–it is Christ living in me.
I still live in my body, but <u>I live by faith</u> in the Son of
God. He is the one who loved me and gave himself to
save me.*

Galatians 2:20

*In the same way, "<u>Abraham believed</u> God, and God
counted him as righteous <u>because of his faith.</u>" The real
children of Abraham, then, are <u>those who put their faith
in God</u>. What's more, the Scriptures looked forward to
this time when God would declare the Gentiles to be
righteous <u>because of their faith</u>. God proclaimed this good
news to Abraham long ago when He said, "All nations
will be blessed through you." So <u>all who put their faith in
Christ</u> share the same blessing Abraham received because
of his faith.*

Galatians 3:6-9

It is obvious that believing and having faith are things which men
do, and because they do it God counts them as righteous. It is

not the other way around: He does not consider them righteous until and unless they first believe in him and his Son Jesus.

> *Once you were alienated from God and were enemies in your minds because of your evil behavior. But now he has reconciled you by Christ's physical body through death to present you holy in his sight, without blemish and free from accusation–if you continue in your faith, established and firm, not moved from the hope held out in the gospel.* Colossians 1:21-23 NIV

> *That is why, when I could bear it no longer, I sent Timothy to find out whether your faith was still strong. I was afraid that the tempter had gotten the best of you and that our work had been useless.* 1 Thessalonians 3:5 NLT

> *Timothy, my son, I give you this instruction in keeping with the prophecies once made about you, so that by following them you may fight the good fight, holding on to faith and a good conscience. Some have rejected these and so have shipwrecked their faith.* 1 Timothy 1:18-19 NIV

> *For I am already being poured out like a drink offering, and the time has come for my departure. I have fought the good fight, I have finished the race, I have kept the faith.* 2 Timothy 4:6-7 NIV

> *I always thank my God as I remember you in my prayers, because I hear about your faith in the Lord Jesus and your love for all the saints. I pray that you may be active in sharing your faith, so that you will have a full understanding of every good thing we have in Christ.* Philemon 1:4-6 NIV

Therefore, since the promise of entering his rest still stands, let us be careful that none of you be found to have fallen short of it. For we also have had the gospel preached to us, just as they did; but the message they heard was of no value to them, because those who heard did not combine it with faith.   Hebrews 4:1-2 NIV

Therefore, since we have a great high priest who has gone through the heavens, Jesus the Son of God, let us hold firmly to the faith we profess.   Hebrews 4:14 NIV

These trials will show that your faith is genuine. It is being tested as fire tests and purifies gold—though your faith is far more precious than mere gold. So when your faith remains strong through many trials, it will bring you much praise and glory and honor on the day when Jesus Christ is revealed to the whole world.
1 Peter 1:7 NLT

He came to His own people, and even they rejected Him. But to all who believed Him and accepted Him, He gave the right to become children of God. They are reborn— not with a physical birth resulting from human passion or plan, but a birth that comes from God.
John 1:11-13 NLT

All those who accepted God's gift by believing in the divinity of his Son Jesus became God's children. If man had no control over his faith, then why does Jesus warn about causing the little ones to lose faith?

But if anyone causes one of these little ones who trusts in me to lose faith, it would be better for that person

WHERE DOES FAITH COME FROM? 131

> *to be thrown into the sea with a large millstone around*
> *his neck.*   Matthew 18:6 NLT

Or why does he recriminate the disciples for having so little faith if it's none of their doing? If faith is a gift from God, shouldn't he blame the Father for being so stingy with his gifts?

> *Jesus said, "You <u>faithless</u> and corrupt people! How long*
> *must I be with you? How long must I put up with you?*
> *Bring the boy here to Me."*   Matthew 17:17 NLT

> *"<u>You don't have enough faith,</u>" Jesus told them. "I*
> *tell you the truth, if you had faith even as small as a*
> *mustard seed, you could say to this mountain, 'Move*
> *from here to there,' and it would move. Nothing would*
> *be impossible."*   Matthew 17:20 NLT

> *Jesus knew what they were saying, so He said, "<u>You have</u>*
> *<u>so little faith</u>! Why are you arguing with each other about*
> *having no bread?*   Matthew 16:8 NLT

The whole Bible is about believing what God says. Those who believe are considered "de facto" righteous, and then made truly righteous through the blood of Christ. This process cannot and will not happen without faith on the part of the one who is to receive the gift of righteousness and salvation.

Is "Total Depravity" taught in the Bible?

Since the time of Augustine in the early fifth century, we have the doctrine usually called the total depravity of man. This says that man is absolutely helpless in regards to his salvation, and plays no part in it whatsoever. It is all a work of God and therefore man is not involved in any way.

I believe that it is true that man cannot initiate the process nor contribute anything to provide the work of salvation. However, the Bible teaches over and over and over again that the gospel message must be combined with faith for salvation to happen. If man had no part in the transaction, then the commandment to preach the gospel to every creature would only be an exercise in futility, and the exhortation to believe would be of no importance whatsoever.

Faith has nothing to do with the preparation of the gift of God; it only has to do with whether we will receive the prepared gift or not. Man is absolutely helpless to make salvation or to even help in wrapping it up and putting a bow on it. When the offer comes from God to man, God has already prepared everything to provide complete salvation for everyone who will accept it.

If man were to play no part whatsoever in obtaining salvation, then faith could only be a gift from God. The reasoning by Augustine and subsequent theologians is that if we were dead, "Then how could we believe?" But the problem is with their understanding of death.

> In the past you were <u>spiritually dead because of your sins and the things you did against God</u>. Yes, in the past your lives were full of those sins. You lived the way the world lives, following the ruler of the evil powers over the earth. That same spirit is now working in those who refuse to obey God. In the past all of us lived like that, trying to please our sinful selves. We did all the things our bodies and minds wanted.

> *Like everyone else in the world, we deserved to suffer God's anger just because of the way we were. But God is rich in mercy, and he loved us very much. <u>We were spiritually dead because of all we had done against him</u>. But he gave us new life together with Christ. (You have been saved by God's grace.)* Ephesians 2:1-5

Death does not mean annihilation. It does not mean that a person ceases to exist. Every human who has died to this world is still alive in the spirit world. Every soul will either end up in the New Jerusalem with God or in the Lake of Fire with Satan. So when the Bible says that someone is dead, it simple means that he has been separated from life of some kind.

When Ephesians says that God *"made us alive with Christ even <u>when we were dead</u> in transgressions–it is by grace you have been saved* (NIV)," it does not mean that humans were unconscious or completely unaware of what God was doing. It means that they were separated from God. We could not escape the bars of death and unite ourselves with the world of spiritual life. But God can cross any gulf because he is fully alive and the Giver of life. God came to all human beings who were cut off from him and made them an offer of pardon through the work of Christ, his eternal Son (2 Corinthians 5:18-20). It is God's initiative but it does not become effective in the life of a person unless it is coupled with faith on the part of the receiver. Faith is not a work, or salvation would no longer be a gift. Faith is a simple trust that God's offer is valid and that we need it. Faith is a humble recognition of our desperate situation, and an acknowledgement of God's abundant mercy. When God says "Would you like this gift of eternal life," we answer "Yes."

> *So do not be ashamed to testify about our Lord, or*
> *ashamed of me his prisoner. But join with me in suffering*
> *for the gospel, by the power of God, who has saved us*
> *and called us to a holy life–<u>not because of anything we</u>*
> *<u>have done but because of his own purpose and grace</u>.*
>
> 2 Timothy 1:9 NIV

The Greek noun translated "done" is *er'gon* which means toil, deed, doing, labor, work. Faith is not an act, a work, or an effort on our part. It needs no toiling, nor requires that we expend anything on our part. We need give nothing, but only receive. Therefore, faith has no merit attributed to our account. Faith is not a work we do to win points with God. It is a response to the work of God around us and in us. Those who believe do not exalt themselves nor take credit for their faith. Instead, they recognize that what has been done has been done by God. All salvation is the work of God: my personal salvation happens when I respond to God's work and his offer. Faith is not a passive belief in which I am not involved. It requires an active decision on my part. Faith is making conscious decisions to trust in God's word and in his character.

We cannot save ourselves by doing good works of any kind. Salvation is not earned. The only thing we can earn by our sin-tainted efforts is separation from God and from life.

> *When people sin, they earn what sin pays–death. But God*
> *gives his people a free gift–eternal life in Christ Jesus our*
> *Lord.* Romans 6:23

The gift was bought and paid for, packaged and delivered by God, but each man chooses whether or not he will receive the gift. God is not like UPS or FEDEX who leave packages on the porch. For this package, you have to *sign for it*, and authorize delivery. Every day God tries to deliver the package and hopes you will take it, but unless you decide to receive it, it will go back on the truck.

> *While they were at Lystra, Paul and Barnabas came upon a man with crippled feet. He had been that way from birth, so he had never walked. He was sitting and listening as Paul preached. Looking straight at him, Paul realized <u>he had faith to be healed</u>. So Paul called to him in a loud voice, "Stand up!" And the man jumped to his feet and started walking.*   Acts 14:8-10 NLT

Faith is something that affects the person who has it and apparently even shows on the countenance.

God wants us to seek him

Man is not totally depraved – man can believe and accept God's help. The Scriptures urge us again and again to seek God. One passage often quoted seems to say that no one seeks him, but multitudes of others tell us to do it.

> *The LORD looks down from heaven on the sons of men to see if there are <u>any who understand, any who seek God</u>. All have turned aside, they have together become corrupt; there is no one who does good, not even one.*   Psalm 14:2-3 NIV

But this does not say that no one <u>ever</u> seeks him. It says that no one does good, and that they are all corrupt. Jesus said there is only one who is good and that is God (Father, Son and Holy Spirit). However, we are exhorted many times in the Scriptures to seek God. No man will seek God on his own initiative, but he can seek God in response to God's revealing his light to him and his prior work in his life. This will result in his doing good.

God says that men should seek him

> The God who made the world and everything in it is the Lord of heaven and earth and does not live in temples built by hands. And he is not served by human hands, as if he needed anything, because he himself gives all men life and breath and everything else. From one man he made every nation of men, that they should inhabit the whole earth; and he determined the times set for them and the exact places where they should live. God did this so that men would seek him and perhaps reach out for him and find him, though he is not far from each one of us.
>
> Acts 17:24-27 NIV

> And it is impossible to please God without faith. Anyone who wants to come to Him must believe that God exists and that He rewards those who sincerely seek Him.
>
> Hebrews 11: 6 NLT

> But if from there you seek the LORD your God, you will find him if you look for him with all your heart and with all your soul.
>
> Deuteronomy 4:29 NIV

> And Solomon, my son, learn to know the God of your ancestors intimately. Worship and serve Him with your whole heart and a willing mind. For the LORD sees every

*heart and knows every plan and thought. <u>If you seek Him,
you will find Him</u>. But if you forsake Him, He will reject
you forever.*   1 Chronicles 28:9 NLT

*He commanded Judah <u>to seek the LORD</u>, the God of
their fathers, and to obey his laws and commands.*
                                                 2 Chronicles 14:4 NIV

*In the eighth year of his reign, while <u>he was still young,
he began to seek the God</u> of his father David.*
                                                 2 Chronicles 34:3 NIV

*The Spirit of God came upon Azariah son of Oded. He
went out to meet Asa and said to him, "Listen to me, Asa
and all Judah and Benjamin. The LORD is with you when
you are with him. <u>If you seek him, he will be found by you</u>,
but if you forsake him, he will forsake you. For a long time
Israel was without the true God, without a priest to teach
and without the law. But in their distress <u>they turned to
the LORD</u>, the God of Israel, and <u>sought him, and he was
found by them</u>.*   2 Chronicles 15:1-4 NIV

*Then they entered into a covenant to seek the LORD, the
God of their ancestors, with all their heart and soul. They
agreed that anyone who refused to seek the LORD, the
God of Israel, would be put to death—whether young or
old, man or woman. They shouted out their oath of loyalty
to the LORD with trumpets blaring and rams' horns
sounding. All in Judah were happy about this covenant,
for they had entered into it with all their heart. They
earnestly sought after God, and they found Him. And the
LORD gave them rest from their enemies on every side.*
                                                 2 Chronicles 15:12-15 NLT

The rest of the events of Asa's reign, from beginning to end, are recorded in The Book of the Kings of Judah and Israel. In the thirty-ninth year of his reign, Asa developed a serious foot disease. Yet even with the severity of his disease, <u>he did not seek</u> the LORD's help but turned only to his physicians.   2 Chronicles 16:11-12 NLT

Those who know your name will trust in you, for you, LORD, have never forsaken <u>those who seek you</u>.
          Psalm 9:10 NIV

The wicked are too proud <u>to seek God</u>. They seem to think that God is dead.   Psalm 10:4 NLT

O God, you are my God, <u>earnestly I seek you</u>; my soul thirsts for you, my body longs for you, in a dry and weary land where there is no water.   Psalm 63:1 NIV

But may <u>all who seek</u> you rejoice and be glad in you; may those who love your salvation always say, "Let God be exalted!"   Psalm 70:4 NIV

For I know the plans I have for you," declares the LORD, "plans to prosper you and not to harm you, plans to give you hope and a future. Then you will call upon me and come and pray to me, and I will listen to you. <u>You will seek me and find me when you seek me with all your heart</u>. I will be found by you," declares the LORD, "and will bring you back from captivity. I will gather you from all the nations and places where I have banished you," declares the LORD, "and will bring you back to the place from which I carried you into exile."
          Jeremiah 29:11-14 NIV

God wants to save all men, but not everyone loves God and accepts his rule over them. When a person rejects God; when a person entirely decides to give up on God, God, in tears, reluctantly gives him up.

The statements in Psalm 14:3 and Isaiah 53:2-3 that say that "no one does good" mean that there are no human beings who take the initiative to seek God. Just because we are imperfect and sinful does not mean that we cannot seek him in response to his initiative. Apparently God doesn't believe that man is so depraved that he cannot desire to know God. When a man repents of his rebellious, self–seeking ways, God is ready and eager to forgive him and receive him because of the blood of Christ. We ourselves cannot remove the sin in our lives, but we can desire to have it taken away. Paul made this very clear in Romans 7 when he said that he had the desire to do what was right, but didn't have the power to do it. When a person truly desires and seeks God's help, God will give him the power to overcome the sin. All he asks is that we be willing to be set free to follow God.

> *I love God's law with all my heart. But there is another power within me that is at war with my mind. This power makes me a slave to the sin that is still within me.*
> Romans 7:22-23 NLT

> *All praise to God, the Father of our Lord Jesus Christ. It is by His great mercy that we have been born again, because God raised Jesus Christ from the dead. Now we live with great expectation, and we have a priceless inheritance—an inheritance that is kept in heaven for you, pure and undefiled, beyond the reach of change and decay. And <u>through your faith</u>, God is protecting you*

> *by His power until you receive this salvation, which is*
> *ready to be revealed on the last day for all to see. So be*
> *truly glad. There is wonderful joy ahead, even though*
> *you have to endure many trials for a little while. These*
> *trials will show that your faith is genuine. It is being*
> *tested as fire tests and purifies gold—though your faith*
> *is far more precious than mere gold. So when your faith*
> *remains strong through many trials, it will bring you*
> *much praise and glory and honor on the day when Jesus*
> *Christ is revealed to the whole world. You love Him even*
> *though you have never seen Him. Though you do not see*
> *Him now, you trust Him; and you rejoice with a glorious,*
> *inexpressible joy. The reward for trusting Him will be*
> *the salvation of your souls.*   1 Peter 1:3-9 NLT

There is a seldom mentioned conversation between Jesus and
some of his would-be followers:

> *Then they asked him, "What must we do to do the works*
> *God requires?" Jesus answered, "The work of God is*
> *this: to believe in the one he has sent."*
>   John 6:28-29 NIV

God only asks men to do one thing to please him, and that is
to believe what he says. He doesn't believe for us.

There are a few problem texts that I should deal with:

1. There are two passages that refer to having received faith

This is a statement that seems to contradict the other statements
listed above. I have no easy explanation for it, but the vast bulk
of evidence says that faith comes from within the individual
and is not a gift from God.

Simon Peter, a servant and apostle of Jesus Christ, To those who through the righteousness of our God and Savior Jesus Christ <u>have received</u> a faith as precious as ours:

2 Peter 1:1 NIV

Bible translators have translated this Greek word: lagchanō in several different ways, for instance:
obtained (the most common interpretation), received, reached, gotten, have a part, shares with us, share in, have been given, etc.

So, the jury is still out on the exact interpretation of the word in this context. It could mean to all who have "reached, "have a share in," or "share with us" a faith as precious as ours.

In His grace, God has given us different gifts for doing certain things well. So if God has given you the ability to prophesy, speak out <u>with as much faith as God has given you</u>.   Romans 12:6 NLT

Here is a statement saying that God has given us faith, but it is in the context of spiritual gifts. It is not talking about faith that brings us salvation, but rather faith to enable us to minister.

2. Another passage mentions the "gift of faith."

Something from the Spirit can be seen in each person. The Spirit gives this to each one to help others. The Spirit gives one person the ability to speak with wisdom. And the same Spirit gives another person the ability to speak with knowledge. The same Spirit gives faith to one person and to another he gives gifts of healing. The Spirit <u>gives to one person</u> the power to do miracles, to another the ability to prophesy, and to another the ability to judge what is from *the Spirit and what is not. The Spirit gives one person the ability to speak in different kinds of languages, and to another the ability to interpret those languages. One Spirit, the same Spirit, does all these things. The Spirit decides what to give each one.*   1 Corinthians 12:7-11

This is also in a list of spiritual gifts, and since we know from first Corinthians 12 that not all gifts are given to all believers, it cannot refer to the general faith that all believers need for salvation. In fact, it is clear from the context that this "gift of faith" is only given to some believers. If this were referring to saving faith (or the faith that saves us), it would have to say that it was given to all who believe.

"Saving" faith is not a spiritual gift which comes from God. Salvation is a gift which God offers to all human beings through his general revelation and through the sacrifice of Christ on the Cross. But, a gift must be believed in and accepted to be of any benefit to the intended receiver.

The gospel of Repentance

Repentance (making a turn-around, or a change in thinking) is a key concept in the process of salvation and it runs through the Bible from cover to cover. A sinner is exhorted to repent and turn from his wicked ways. All of us begin our existence with wicked ways because we are descendants of Adam who had a rebellious and disobedient nature. A person needs to recognize this rebellion in himself and realize that it is no good. He then needs to turn away from his evil, dark, self-centered deeds, and look to God, and God will welcome him. Repentance will only happen after and while the person exercises faith in what God is saying to him through general revelation, through the gospel, through his written word, and through the work of the Holy Spirit.

Conclusion

Faith that saves a person does not come from God. It comes from the heart of the individual as he believes what God says. Grace comes from God; saving faith comes from man. Every man is being wooed by God to turn from his wicked ways and believe in God's Son Jesus. Paul says that God is entreating the world through us to be reconciled with him. God is calling; Jesus is calling; the church is calling; "Oh sinner, come home!" God can't do any more for you than what he has already done. You must respond and say, "Yes, I am a sinner, I believe in God's remedy for my sin, and I want the gift."

7. | Sons of God

The Scriptures are replete with the words "sons of God," and state that anyone who puts his faith in Jesus as God's Son also becomes God's son. No other arrangement could bring forgiveness, righteousness and salvation to a lost human race. As we saw in Chapter 3, God's purpose is to have many children that would be co–heirs with his eternal Son "the Word" (His name only became Jesus when he was born as a human being).

Many have asked the question, "Are we really God's sons?" The clear biblical answer is "Yes." Anyone who is in Christ has received God's nature in his person. We are not just street urchins who have been brought in from the cold and can sit in a corner of God's house, but we are legitimate born sons. It is not physically possible for a person who is born with one father to be born again with a different father. But, it is possible spiritually, and that is exactly what happens when a person believes that Jesus of Bethlehem is God's eternal Son.

So, what does it mean to be a son of God?

Partaking of the Divine Nature

1. A man who is in Christ is reborn spiritually and is a new creature

A saving relationship with God is only finalized when a human being believes that Jesus is God's means for his salvation, and is born a second time with God as his father.

> *Jesus answered, "I assure you, everyone must be born again. Anyone who is not <u>born again</u> cannot be in God's kingdom."*   John 3:3

> *You were cleansed from your sins when you obeyed the truth, so now you must show sincere love to each other as brothers and sisters. Love each other deeply with all your heart. For <u>you have been born again</u>, but not to a life that will quickly end. Your new life will last forever because it comes from the eternal, living word of God.*
> 1 Peter 1:22-23 NLT

> *This means that anyone who belongs to Christ has become <u>a new person</u>. The old life is gone; a new life has begun!*
> 2 Corinthians 5:17 NLT

Once we believe in Christ, we spiritually die to the old nature of Adam, and we receive the new nature of God. This does not make us perfect in our present human body, but it will eventually make us perfect when we leave this body and this world behind. Though we still struggle against the old sinful nature and do not always do what pleases God, as far as he is concerned we are perfect. "There is therefore now no condemnation" (Romans 8:1).

2. A reborn man has a new nature

By His divine power, God has given us everything we need for living a godly life. We have received all of this by coming to know Him, the One who called us to Himself by means of His marvelous glory and excellence. And because of His glory and excellence, He has given us great and precious promises. These are the promises that enable you to <u>share His divine nature</u> and escape the world's corruption caused by human desires. (2 Peter 1:3-4)

2 Peter 1:3-4 NLT

But to all who believed Him and accepted Him, He gave the right to become children of God. They are reborn— not with a physical birth resulting from human passion or plan, but a birth that comes from God.

John 1:12-13 NLT

We know that God's children do not make a practice of sinning, for God's Son holds them securely, and the evil one cannot touch them. We know that we are children of God and that the world around us is under the control of the evil one.   1 John 5:18-19 NLT

"Therefore since we are <u>God's offspring</u>, we should not think that the divine being is like gold or silver or stone–an image made by man's design and skill.

Acts 17:29 NIV

Those who have been <u>born into God's family</u> do not make a practice of sinning, because <u>God's life is in them</u>. So they can't keep on sinning, because <u>they are children of God</u>. So now we can tell who are children of God and

who are children of the devil. Anyone who does not live righteously and does not love other believers does not belong to God.   1 John 3:9-10 NLT

Everyone who believes that Jesus is the Christ has <u>become a child of God</u>. And everyone who loves the Father loves His children, too. We know we love God's children if we love God and obey His commandments. Loving God means keeping His commandments, and His commandments are not burdensome. For every child of God defeats this evil world, and we achieve this victory through our faith.   1 John 5:1-4 NLT

Many years ago as a young missionary pilot in Bolivia, we were also working to plant a church in a poor neighborhood on the outskirts of the city of Cochabamba. The people living there were primarily Quechua speakers from the rural mountain areas. They spoke very poor Spanish, even worse than mine at the time. As I was trying to minister to them and make the gospel clear, I struggled to find illustrations which would help them understand the new birth. Since they were primarily farmers and shepherds, I finally thought of this illustration that made sense for them.

The pig and the cat

A pig is the offspring of two pigs, and acts just like his parents. He loves to wallow in the dirty mud to cool off. He is not concerned about his odor or what people think of him. He often rolls around in what has just come out of his body. Pigs are dirty, smelly, rude, and (until the craze began for pot–bellied pigs some decades back) are not very popular for pets in people's houses.

A cat is the offspring of two cats (this is not rocket science), and acts like its parents. Cats are furry, usually keep clean by washing themselves with their paws and tongues, dig holes before they defecate, like to curl up on people's laps, and are often friendly pets. If they fall in the mud, they get out of it and wash themselves off.

Let's say we have a pig and we want to change his way of living. We want him to be nice like a cat so we can hold him on our lap. We give him a bath, cut his nails (hooves), spray him with perfume, put a nice ribbon around his neck, and bring him in the living room to lie on the carpet or on our lap. What happens? Soon, he will mess the place up. If we leave the door open, he will likely run back to where the other pigs are and roll around in the slop. Even though we cleaned him up on the outside, he was still a pig on the inside and obeyed his porcine nature.

The only way we could possibly make a pig act like a cat would be to have him be born again with two cats as parents. Stop laughing! I know that that can never happen. But do you know that what is impossible for pigs is possible for humans? Yes, a man can be born again and receive a new nature and be a whole different "animal." That's what the gospel is all about. We can be born again and this time God can be our Father. We can receive his nature and we become his offspring. This is the key to living a different lifestyle. We are no longer slaves to the sin nature, but are set free to live like our new Daddy. (By the way, since God is neither male nor female nor dwells in a physical body, we don't need a mother for this to happen.)

When we are born again we receive the nature of our new Father, and become part of his family for the rest of eternity.

We can never get de–born or un-born because we have God's eternal life in us.

3. God calls us his sons many times

> I, God Most High, say, "You are gods, my own sons.
>   Psalm 82:6

> He said to me: "It is done. I am the Alpha and the Omega, the Beginning and the End. To him who is thirsty I will give to drink without cost from the spring of the water of life. He who overcomes will inherit all this, and I will be his God and _he will be my son_.   Revelation 21:6-7 NIV

> Jesus replied, "Marriage is for people here on earth. But in the age to come, those worthy of being raised from the dead will neither marry nor be given in marriage. And they will never die again. In this respect they will be like angels. _They are children of God_ and children of the resurrection.   Luke 20:34 NLT

> The Spirit that we received is not a spirit that makes us slaves again and causes us to fear. The Spirit that we have _makes us God's chosen children_. And with that Spirit we cry out, "Abba, Father." And the Spirit himself speaks to our spirits and _makes us sure that we are God's children_. If we are God's children, we will get the blessings God has for his people. He will give us all that he has given Christ. But we must suffer like Christ suffered. Then we will be able to share his glory.   Romans 8:15-17

> "Yet the time will come when Israel's people will be like the sands of the seashore—too many to count! Then, at

> *the place where they were told, 'You are not My people,'*
> *it will be said, 'You are children of the living God.*
> Hosea 1:10 NLT

4. Many New Testament authors declare us to be God's sons

> *See how very much our Father loves us, for He calls us*
> *His children, and that is what we are! But the people who*
> *belong to this world don't recognize that we are God's*
> *children because they don't know Him. Dear friends, we*
> *are already God's children, but He has not yet shown*
> *us what we will be like when Christ appears. But we do*
> *know that we will be like Him, for we will see Him as*
> *He really is.*   1 John 3:1-2 NLT

John makes sure that we understand that our sonship is not
just a legal title, but that we really have been born of God. He
also says that we are still small children, and that one day we
will pass from this condition to be full–grown sons. The Greek
word sometimes translated "sons" means "children," not fully
grown adult sons.

> *You are all sons of God through faith in Christ Jesus, for*
> *all of you who were baptized into Christ have clothed*
> *yourselves with Christ.*   Galatians 3:26 NIV

> *As you endure this divine discipline, remember that God*
> *is treating you as His own children. Who ever heard of a*
> *child who is never disciplined by its father? If God doesn't*
> *discipline you as He does all of His children, it means that*
> *you are illegitimate and are not really His children at all.*
> *Since we respected our earthly fathers who disciplined*

us, shouldn't we submit even more to the discipline of the Father of our spirits, and live forever?

Hebrews 12:7-9 NLT

Therefore, dear brothers and sisters, you have no obligation to do what your sinful nature urges you to do. For if you live by its dictates, you will die. But if through the power of the Spirit you put to death the deeds of your sinful nature, you will live. For all who are led by the Spirit of God are children of God.   Romans 8:12-14 NLT

Yet what we suffer now is nothing compared to the glory He will reveal to us later. For all creation is waiting eagerly for that future day when God will reveal who His children really are.   Romans 8:18-19 NLT

And we believers also groan, even though we have the Holy Spirit within us as a foretaste of future glory, for we long for our bodies to be released from sin and suffering. We, too, wait with eager hope for the day when God will give us our full rights as His adopted children, including the new bodies He has promised us.

Romans 8:23 NLT

The creation is looking forward to that day when God's children are displayed in a grand ceremony and declared to be fully grown sons (adoption). We, who are the children of God also long to come to full maturity in God's family.

. . . And "It will happen that in the very place where it was said to them, 'You are not my people,' they will be called 'sons of the living God.'   Romans 9:6 NIV

Think of it this way. If a father dies and leaves an inheritance for his young children, those children are not much better off than slaves until they grow up, even though they actually own everything their father had. They have to obey their guardians until they reach whatever age their father set. And that's the way it was with us before Christ came. We were like children; we were slaves to the basic spiritual principles of this world. But when the right time came, God sent His Son, born of a woman, subject to the law. God sent Him to buy freedom for us who were slaves to the law, so that He could adopt us as His very own children. And because <u>we are His children</u>, God has sent the Spirit of His Son into our hearts, prompting us to call out, "<u>Abba, Father.</u>" <u>Now you are no longer a slave but God's own child. And since you are His child</u>, God has made you His heir.

Galatians 4:1-7 NLT

As long as we are in this world, we are God's little children. One day, we will receive our full rights as sons, and then we will receive our inheritance.

Endure hardship as discipline; <u>God is treating you as sons</u>. For what son is not disciplined by his father?

Hebrews 12:7 NIV

He did not say this on his own; as high priest at that time he was led to prophesy that Jesus would die for the entire nation. And not only for that nation, but to bring together and unite all the children of God scattered around the world.   John 11:51-52 NLT

I have been dumbfounded over the last several years at evangelical pastors and theologians who, in spite of this overwhelming evidence, say that we really do not receive God's nature. They find it difficult to believe that God would do something this amazing and make us his very own children.

5. As sons of God, we will participate in the kingdom of God and have important responsibilities

> *Do you not know that the saints will judge the world? And if you are to judge the world, are you not competent to judge trivial cases? Do you not know that we will judge angels? How much more the things of this life!*
>
> 1 Corinthians 6:2-3 NIV

One of our jobs on the new earth will be to help God judge the angels and the peoples of the world.

> *And furthermore, it is not angels who will control the future world we are talking about. For in one place the Scriptures say, "What are mere mortals that You should think about them, or a son of man that You should care for him? Yet You made them only a little lower than the angels and crowned them with glory and honor. [You gave them charge of everything You made.]*
>
> Hebrews 2:5-7 NLT

6. Jesus is our older brother

> *God, for whom and through whom everything was made, chose to bring many children into glory. And it was only right that He should make Jesus, through His suffering, a perfect leader, fit to bring them into their salvation. So now Jesus and the ones He makes holy have the same*

Father. That is why Jesus is not ashamed to call them His brothers and sisters.   Hebrews 2:10-11 NLT

And we know that in all things God works for the good of those who love him, who have been called according to his purpose. For those God foreknew he also predestined to be conformed to the likeness of his Son, that he might be the <u>firstborn among many brothers</u>.
                                        Romans 8:28-29 NIV

If Jesus is divine, so are his brothers and sisters

Are not the children of God also gods? Those born of God have God's nature and God's life. We true believers are all part of God's divine family. The offspring of a cow is a cow. The offspring of a chicken is a chicken. The offspring of a squirrel is a squirrel. Why does it seem so hard for some to believe that the offspring of God is a god?

Being God or a god does not require having absolute authority. The Father has absolute authority, but the Son has authority subject to the Father, and the Holy Spirit has authority subject to the Father and the Son. If a requirement for being God means that the person has to have absolute authority, than neither Christ nor the Holy Spirit would be God.

It does not require having all of God's attributes to be divine. It is not dependent on our powers, our attributes, or our authority. It is only dependent on our nature. First Peter 1:4 says that we have the nature of God, so we are also gods though we do not claim to have his attributes nor his authority.

As we will see in Chapter 9 *(Jesus, a man just like us with one exception)*, Jesus was not omnipresent, omniscient, or omnipotent in his human body. But he was still God every day of his life. The Word, in his human form (Jesus), was like us in that he had no supernatural powers, no supernatural knowledge, no ability to be in two places at the same time, and no immortality. He was joined irrevocably with the human race that he himself had created. Even after his resurrection he has a glorified human body for the rest of eternity. His power came from his intimate relationship with the Father and the Holy Spirit. He submitted 100% to the Father's will and carried out all his instructions without fault.

Jesus was the God-man, a perfect combination of the nature of God and the pre-fallen nature of Adam. He had to be completely human in order to be the advocate and sacrifice for the sins of all mankind. When he came to Bethlehem, he came with no baggage, no divine powers, and no eternal knowledge. He came into the world like all human beings but with one exception – his paternal nature came from God and not from Adam, and that made all the difference.

God is not only not ashamed to call us his children, but he is very proud to do so. We are his pride and joy, the culmination and purpose of his creation. We have seen over thirty times where the Bible refers to us as God's children who have been born of God and who have his nature.

7. The real meaning of adoption

Many Christians mistakenly believe that though we were not God's children, we have now legally become part of his family through adoption. However, that is not what it means to become a son of God. It is true that we were not God's children, but the Bible very clearly and very often says that we were <u>born</u> into God's family and that we have his nature.

When you hear the term "adoption" in the Bible, don't think of it in the same way as human beings adopt. A couple takes a child who does not have their genes, their nature, their lifeblood in them, and then that child is declared legally theirs, although he still has the same old genes as before.

With God, although we were not his children, he causes us to be <u>born again</u>, this time with his nature, and so we are not just smelly, repugnant urchins brought into the house by the grace and goodwill of our new adoptive "Father." He is indeed our Father in every sense of the word. So, biblical adoption means a whole lot more than plain human adoption. God takes those who were not his children, and makes them his children in every way possible. Humanly, we have no way to do that.

Adoption

uihothesia *hwee-oth-es-ee'-ah* —
The placing as a son, that is, adoption (figuratively Christian sonship in respect to God): –adoption (of children, of sons).

What does the Bible mean when it talks about the adoption as God's children? The Greek word appears five times in the New Testament.

<u>Romans 8:15</u> *For you did not receive a spirit that makes you a slave again to fear, but you received the Spirit of sonship (adoption). And by him we cry, "Abba, Father."* NIV

<u>Romans 8:23</u> *Not only so, but we ourselves, who have the firstfruits of the Spirit, groan inwardly as we wait eagerly for our adoption as sons, the redemption of our bodies.* NIV

<u>Romans 9:4</u> . . . *the people of Israel. Theirs is the adoption as sons; theirs the divine glory, the covenants, the receiving of the law, the temple worship and the promises.* NIV

<u>Galatians 4:5</u> *to redeem those under law, that we might receive the full rights (adoption) of sons.* NIV

<u>Ephesians 1:5</u> *He predestined us to be adopted as his sons through Jesus Christ, in accordance with his pleasure and will–to the praise of his glorious grace, which he has freely given us in the One he loves.* NIV

In one of these passages, Paul says that the adoption has not yet happened:

> *We know that the whole creation has been groaning as in the pains of childbirth right up to the present time. Not only so, but we ourselves, who have the firstfruits of the Spirit, groan inwardly as <u>we wait eagerly for our adoption as sons</u>, the redemption of our bodies. For in this hope we were saved. But hope that is seen is no hope at all. Who hopes for what he already has? But if we hope for what we do not yet have, we wait for it patiently.*
>
> Romans 8:22-25 NIV

In some sense, we are still waiting for the adoption, so obviously the full measure of it hasn't happened yet. In Ephesians he gives us a better understanding of the different stages in our progress from being God's little children to being his full grown sons with all rights.

Think of it this way. If a father dies and leaves an inheritance for his young children, those children are not much better off than slaves until they grow up, even though they actually own everything their father had. They have to obey their guardians until they reach whatever age their father set. And that's the way it was with us before Christ came. We were like children; we were slaves to the basic spiritual principles of this world. But when the right time came, God sent His Son, born of a woman, subject to the law. God sent Him to buy freedom for us who were slaves to the law, so that He could adopt us as His very own children. And because we are His children, God has sent the Spirit of His Son into our hearts, prompting us to call out, "Abba, Father." Now you are no longer a slave but God's own child. And since you are His child, God has made you His heir.

Galatians 4:1-7 NLT

The meaning of "adoption" in the Bible means being placed in a distinctive position in the family. It is like the Bar Mitzvah of the Jews, when the child comes of age and is now considered a son.

"Bar Mitzvah" literally means "son of the commandment." "Bar" is "son" in Aramaic, which used to be the vernacular of the Jewish people. "Mitzvah" is "commandment" in both Hebrew and Aramaic. Technically, the term refers to the child who is coming of age, and it is strictly correct to refer to someone as "becoming a bar mitzvah. A Jewish boy automatically becomes a bar mitzvah upon reaching the age of 13 years, and a girl upon reaching the age of 12 years. No ceremony is needed to confer these rights and obligations. Today, it is common practice for the bar mitzvah celebrant to do much more than just say the blessing. It is most common for the celebrant to learn the entire haftarah portion, including its traditional chant, and

*recite that. In some congregations, the celebrant reads the
entire weekly torah portion, or leads part of the service,
or leads the congregation in certain important prayers.
The celebrant is also generally required to make a speech,
which traditionally begins with the phrase "today, I am
a man." (http://www.jewfaq.org/barmitz.htm)*

Our adoption as sons of God means that we are <u>placed in a new
position</u> in the family. We are considered adult sons with new
responsibilities. Based on Romans 8:22-23, our "adoption" will
be finalized on the day of the resurrection when Christ returns.
At that point, we will pass from being called the little children
of God to being called the sons of God, and will assume new
rights and responsibilities.

Conclusion

The only way to get into God's family is to be born into it.
That occurs when a person by faith believes that Jesus is God's
eternal son who became a man and died for us on the cross.
This means that Mormons and Jehovah's Witnesses and many
others who believe like them are not yet saved because they do
not believe in the eternal divinity of Jesus.

> *"For God loved the world so much that He gave His one
> and only Son, so that everyone who believes in Him will
> not perish but have eternal life. God sent His Son into
> the world not to judge the world, but to save the world
> through Him. "There is no judgment against anyone who
> believes in Him. But anyone who does not believe in Him
> has already been judged for not believing in God's one
> and only Son.*   John 3:16-18

Any person who does not believe that Christ is God's son who came from Heaven to save the world is not saved nor can he be as long as he rejects the divinity of the babe in Bethlehem. When Jesus was born, he was already God, and that nature distinguished him from every other human who ever lived.

8. What does it mean to be "in Christ?"

The key to understanding our salvation and having the power to be a spiritual victor in the Christian life is found in the little phrase "in Christ."

As Noah and his family were saved by being <u>in</u> the ark, we are saved by being <u>in</u> Christ. The emphasis is not so much on a personal relationship, but rather on a <u>position</u>. In the NIV New Testament, we find the phrase "In Christ" 234 times. The meaning has to do with our legal position.

en — A primary preposition denoting (fixed) **position** (in place, time or state), and (by implication) *instrumentality* (medially or constructively), that is, a relation of *rest*.

A very good example that shows that our relationship to Christ is positional is in Ephesians 1:1:

> *Paul, an apostle of Christ Jesus by the will of God, To the saints <u>in Ephesus</u>, the faithful <u>in Christ Jesus</u>.* NIV

These believers were physically located in the city of Ephesus. But, they were also located "in" Christ. The first shows the physical location of their body, and the other shows their spiritual location as a person. Another clear example is in verse 3:

> *Praise be to the God and Father of our Lord Jesus Christ, who has blessed us <u>in the heavenly realms</u> with every spiritual blessing <u>in Christ</u>.*   NIV

I will not include the text of the 234 times that the NIV Bible repeats the phrase "in Christ", or the many times it uses the phrase "in him", etc. I will, however, provide a list of many of the references to show you that the concept of our position in Christ is at the heart of the meaning of our salvation.

In Christ – eighty-nine times – AC 24:24, RO 6:11, RO 6:23, RO 8:1, RO 8:39, RO 9:1, RO 12:5, RO 15:17, RO 16:3, RO 16:7, RO 16:9, RO 16:10, 1 CO 1:2, 1 CO 1:4, 1 CO 1:30, 1 CO 3:1, 1 CO 4:10, 1 CO 4:15, 1 CO 4:17, 1 CO 15:18, 1 CO 15:19, 1 CO 15:22, 1 CO 15:31, 1 CO 16:24, 2 CO 1:20, 2 CO 1:21, 2 CO 2:14, 2 CO 2:17, 2 CO 3:14, 2 CO 5:17, 2 CO 5:19, 2 CO 12:2, 2 CO 12:19, GAL 1:22, GAL 2:4, GAL 2:16, GAL 2:17, GAL 3:26, GAL 3:28, GAL 5:6, EPH 1:1, EPH 1:3, EPH 1:9, EPH 1:12, EPH 1:13, EPH 1:20, EPH 2:6, EPH 2:7, EPH 2:10, EPH 2:13, EPH 3:6, EPH 3:11, EPH 3:21, EPH 4:32, PHP 1:1, PHP 1:26, PHP 3:3, PHP 3:9, PHP 3:14, PHP 4:7, PHP 4:19, PHP 4:21, COL 1:2, COL 1:4, COL 1:28, COL 2:5, COL 2:9, COL 2:10, COL 2:17, 1 TH 2:14, 1 TH 4:16, 1 TH 5:18, 1 TI 1:14, 1 TI 3:13, 2 TI 1:1, 2 TI 1:9, 2 TI 1:13, 2 TI 2:1, 2 TI 2:10, 2 TI 3:12, 2 TI 3:15, PHM 1:6, PHM 1:8, PHM 1:20, PHM 1:23, HEB 3:14, 1 PE 3:16, 1 PE 5:10, 1 PE 5:14

In Him – referring to Christ – **seventy-four times** – JN 1:4, JN 2:11, JN 3:15, JN 3:16, JN 3:18, JN 4:14, JN 4:39, JN 6:40,

JN 6:56, JN 7:5, JN 7:31, JN 7:39, JN 7:48, JN 8:30, JN 8:44,
JN 9:36, JN 11:45, JN 11:48, JN 12:11, JN 12:37, JN 12:42,
JN 13:31, JN 13:32, JN 15:5, AC 10:43, AC 17:28, RO 4:24,
RO 9:33, RO 10:11, RO 15:12, RO 15:13, 1CO 1:5, 2 CO
1:19, 2 CO 5:21, 2 CO 13:4, EPH 1:4, EPH 1:7, EPH 1:11,
EPH 1:13, EPH 2:21, EPH 2:22, EPH 3:12, EPH 4:21, PHP
3:9, COL 1:17, COL 1:19, COL 2:6, COL 2:7, COL 2:11, 1
TH 4:14, 2 TH 1:12, HEB 2:13, 1 PE 1:8, 1 PE 2:6, 1 JN 1:5,
1 JN 2:4, 1 JN 2:5, 1 JN 2:6, 1 JN 2:8, 1 JN 2:10, 1 JN 2:15,
1 JN 2:27, 1 JN 2:28, 1 JN 3:3, 1 JN 3:5, 1 JN 3:6, 1 JN 3:9,
1 JN 3:15, 1 JN 3:17, 1 JN 3:24, 1 JN 4:13, 1 JN 4:15, 1 JN
4:16, 1 JN 5:20

Plus the following for an additional forty-nine times:

In the Beloved – referring to Christ – EPH 1:6
In Whom – EPH 1:7, EPH 1:11, EPH 1:13x2, EPH 2:21, Eph
    2:22, EPH 3:12, COL 2:3, COL 2:11
In Himself – EPH 1:9, EPH 2:15
In the Lord Jesus – EPH 1:15
In Christ Jesus – EPH 2:6, EPH 2:10, EPH 2:13, PH 1:1, COL
    1:28, 1 TH 2:14, 1 TI 3:14, 1 TI 3:13, 1 TI 1:1, 2 TI
    1:9, 2 TI 1:13, 2 TI 2:1, 2 TI 2:10, 2 TI 3:12, 2 TI 3:15,
    PHL 1:23
Through Christ Jesus – EPH 2:7
In One body – EPH 2:16
Through Him – EPH 2:18
By Christ Jesus – EPH 3:21
In Jesus – EPH 4:21
In the Lord – EPH 5:8, EPH 6:1, EPH 6:10, EPH 6:21, PH 1:14,
    PH 4:1, PH 4:2, PH 4:4, COL 4:7, COL 4:17, 1 TH 3:8,
    1 TH 5:12, PHL 1:16, PHL 1:20
Through Christ Jesus – PH 4:7

Support for the concept of our position in Christ is overwhelming. Jesus is the container in which we are placed, and our being there gives us every right and every privilege as God's beloved children.

> *This is what God told us: God has given us eternal life, and this life is <u>in his Son</u>. Whoever has the Son has life, but whoever does not have the Son of God does not have life.*
> 1 John 5:11-12

> *Everything was made through him, and nothing was made without him. <u>In him</u> there was life, and that life was a light for the people of the world.*   John 1:3-4

Ephesians is a book that has been one of the principle ones used to defend what is called "predestination," and the absolute foreknowledge of God. However, the first two chapters are very often misinterpreted. Let's examine those chapters and make some observations. As we start, let me say that these chapters are not about who will be saved, but about the vessel of salvation. We think they are about the contents of the vessel, but they are really all about the container. Notice all of the words I have underlined.

¹   Paul, an apostle of Christ Jesus by the will of God, To the saints in Ephesus, the faithful <u>in Christ Jesus</u>:
²   Grace and peace to you from God our Father and the Lord Jesus Christ.
³   Praise be to the God and Father of our Lord Jesus Christ, who has blessed us in the heavenly realms with every spiritual blessing <u>in Christ</u>.
⁴   For he chose us <u>in him</u> before the creation of the world to be holy and blameless in his sight. In love

⁵ he predestined us to be adopted as his sons <u>through Jesus Christ</u>, in accordance with his pleasure and will—

⁶ to the praise of his glorious grace, which he has freely given us <u>in the One he loves</u>.

⁷ <u>In him</u> we have redemption through his blood, the forgiveness of sins, in accordance with the riches of God's grace

⁸ that he lavished on us with all wisdom and understanding.

⁹ And he made known to us the mystery of his will according to his good pleasure, which he purposed in <u>Christ,</u>

¹⁰ to be put into effect when the times will have reached their fulfillment–to bring all things in Heaven and on earth together <u>under one head, even Christ</u>.

¹¹ <u>In him</u> we were also chosen, having been predestined according to the plan of him who works out everything in conformity with the purpose of his will,

¹² in order that we, who were the <u>first to hope in Christ</u>, might be for the praise of his glory.

¹³ And you also were <u>included in Christ</u> when you heard the word of truth, the gospel of your salvation. Having believed, you were <u>marked in him</u> with a seal, the promised Holy Spirit,

¹⁴ who is a deposit guaranteeing our inheritance until the redemption of those who are God's possession–to the praise of his glory.

¹⁵ For this reason, ever since I heard about <u>your faith in the Lord Jesus</u> and your love for all the saints, ¹⁶ I have not stopped giving thanks for you, remembering you in my prayers.

¹⁷ I keep asking that the God of our Lord Jesus Christ, the glorious Father, may give you the Spirit of wisdom and revelation, so that you may know him better.

¹⁸ I pray also that the eyes of your heart may be enlightened in order that you may know the hope to which he has called you, the riches of his glorious inheritance in the saints,

[19] and his incomparably great power for us who believe. That power is like the working of his mighty strength,

[20] which he exerted in Christ when he raised him from the dead and seated him at his right hand in the heavenly realms,

[21] far above all rule and authority, power and dominion, and every title that can be given, not only in the present age but also in the one to come.

[22] And God placed all things under his feet and appointed him to be head over everything for the church,

[23] which is his body, the fullness of him who fills everything in every way.

2 [1] As for you, you were dead in your transgressions and sins,

[2] in which you used to live when you followed the ways of this world and of the ruler of the kingdom of the air, the spirit who is now at work in those who are disobedient.

[3] All of us also lived among them at one time, gratifying the cravings of our sinful nature and following its desires and thoughts. Like the rest, we were by nature objects of wrath.

[4] But because of his great love for us, God, who is rich in mercy,

[5] made us alive with Christ even when we were dead in transgressions–it is by grace you have been saved.

[6] And God raised us up with Christ and seated us with him in the heavenly realms in Christ Jesus,

[7] in order that in the coming ages he might show the incomparable riches of his grace, expressed in his kindness to us in Christ Jesus.

[8] For it is by grace you have been saved, through faith–and this not from yourselves, it is the gift of God—

[9] not by works, so that no one can boast.

[10] For we are God's workmanship, created in Christ Jesus to do good works, which God prepared in advance for us to do.

[11] Therefore, remember that formerly you who are Gentiles by birth and called "uncircumcised" by those who call themselves "the circumcision" (that done in the body by the hands of men)—

[12] remember that at that time you were <u>separate from Christ</u>, excluded from citizenship in Israel and foreigners to the covenants of the promise, without hope and without God in the world.

[13] But <u>now in Christ Jesus</u> you who once were far away have been brought near through the blood of Christ.

[14] For <u>he himself</u> is our peace, who has made the two one and has destroyed the barrier, the dividing wall of hostility,

[15] by abolishing in his flesh the law with its commandments and regulations. His purpose was to create <u>in himself</u> one new man out of the two, thus making peace,

[16] and <u>in this one body</u> to reconcile both of them to God through the cross, by which he put to death their hostility.

[17] He came and preached peace to you who were far away and peace to those who were near.

[18] For <u>through him</u> we both have access to the Father by one Spirit.

[19] Consequently, you are no longer foreigners and aliens, but fellow citizens with God's people and members of God's household,

[20] built on the foundation of the apostles and prophets, with Christ Jesus himself as the chief cornerstone.

[21] <u>In him</u> the whole building is joined together and rises to become a holy temple in the Lord.

[22] And <u>in him</u> you too are being built together to become a dwelling in which God lives by his Spirit.

NIV

In Chapter 1, there are **sixteen times** in which Paul refers in some way to our position in Christ in only twenty-three verses.

In Chapter 2, he refers to our position in Christ **fourteen times** in twenty-two verses. I cannot claim to be very observant about many things, but it is hard to miss the meaning of what God is telling us here. **Thirty** times in forty-five verses, God is telling us that what is important is the vessel or vehicle of salvation and our position in him. The foreknowledge and predetermination all have to do with Christ. These chapters are not about us. They are about the Christ and our relationship to him.

In verse 12, Paul mentions those who were the *"first to hope in him."* Later, he says that *"you also were <u>included in Christ</u> when you heard the word of truth, the gospel of your salvation. Having believed, you were <u>marked in him</u> with a seal, the promised Holy Spirit.*

Until a person believes in Christ, he is not included in him. Faith in God's word regarding his Son is what places us into Christ and gives us salvation and all the many other benefits of being God's child.

Illustration – Take a container of some kind with a lid, and write Jesus Christ on it (the word "Christ" is not his last name; it is his title – "Christ Jesus", or "Messiah Jesus"). Then write your name on a small slip of paper and place it into the container and put the lid on. Now, the paper with your name on it is hidden inside the container with Christ's name on it. Whatever happens to the container will happen to the slip of paper. This is an illustration that once you are put into Christ through faith, you are hidden in him. Everything that happens to him happens to you. Everything that he has is yours also.

The next time you read Ephesians think of this illustration and it will all make sense. Everything that we are and have depends on our relationship with Jesus. We are not exalted here: Jesus is exalted. The letter is about him, not about us.

We cannot correctly apply verse 4 of chapter 1 to individuals, but only to the vessel of salvation which is Christ. Only the group of those who come into Christ through faith have been chosen before the creation of the world. This choosing also is not about who will be saved, but about what will happen to those who believe – *"to be holy and blameless in his sight."* He predestined all who are in this group to be adopted as sons.

Everything in this passage centers on Christ. Because of him there is redemption. Because of him there is glorification of all who are placed in his body. This whole letter and particularly the early chapters are immersed with praise for Christ, the chosen vehicle of salvation.

> *So do not be ashamed to testify about our Lord, or ashamed of me his prisoner. But join with me in suffering for the gospel, by the power of God, who has saved us and called us to a holy life–not because of anything we have done but because of his own purpose and grace. This grace was given us in Christ Jesus before the beginning of time, but it has now been revealed through the appearing of our Savior, Christ Jesus, who has destroyed death and has brought life and immortality to light through the gospel.*
> 2 Timothy 1:8-10 NIV

The vessel of salvation was determined before the beginning of time, and as Ephesians 1:13 says: *And you also were included in Christ when you heard the word of truth, the gospel of your salvation. Having believed, you were marked in him with a seal, the promised Holy Spirit, . . .*

> *Since, then, you have been raised with Christ, set your hearts on things above, where Christ is seated at the right hand of God. Set your minds on things above, not on earthly things. For you died, and your life is now hidden with Christ in God.* Colossians 3:1-3 NIV

For the true Christian, our identity before God is irreversibly linked to Christ. When the Father looks toward us, he sees the life and perfection of Jesus. He sees his righteousness, his obedience, his loyalty and his love. He sees the container, not the contents. Because we are in him, we are free from condemnation. Because of our faith in believing the Word of God, we were placed into Christ. This is the meaning of spiritual baptism.

> *His intent was that now, through the church, the manifold wisdom of God should be made known to the rulers and authorities in the heavenly realms, according to his eternal purpose which he accomplished in Christ Jesus our Lord. In him and through faith in him we may approach God with freedom and confidence.* Ephesians 3:10-12 NIV

Paul's writings are like a broken record, saying over and over and over again "in Christ," "in Christ," "in Christ." All of our benefits and blessings come because we are "in Christ," and we came into Christ as a result of our faith. Faith is not a work. It is nothing that we can take any credit for, but when the simple–minded believe what God says, it is reckoned to them as righteousness.

> *When anyone is in Christ, it is a whole new world. The old things are gone; suddenly, everything is new!*
> 2 Corinthians 5:17

So now anyone who is in Christ Jesus is not judged guilty.
Romans 8:1

This is a point worth re-emphasizing over and over. Christ is all in all. God has never given nor ever will give a spiritual blessing apart from Christ. It all flows through him and because of him.

My old self has been <u>crucified with Christ</u>. It is no longer I who live, but <u>Christ lives in me</u>. So I live in this earthly body by trusting in the Son of God, who loved me and gave Himself for me. Galatians 2:20 NLT

For <u>in Christ</u> all the fullness of the Deity lives in bodily form, and you have been given <u>fullness in Christ</u>, who is the head over every power and authority.
Colossians 2:9-10 NIV

He is the One all the prophets testified about, saying that <u>everyone who believes in Him</u> will have their sins forgiven through His name. Acts 10:43 NLT

Christ had no sin, but God made him become sin so that <u>in Christ</u> we could be right with God.
2 Corinthians 5:21

No one can see God, but the Son is exactly like God. He rules over everything that has been made. Through his power all things were made: things in heaven and on earth, seen and not seen— all spiritual rulers, lords, powers, and authorities. Everything was made <u>through him</u> and <u>for him</u>. The Son was there before anything was made. And all things continue because of him. He is the head of the body, which is the church. He is the beginning of *everything else. And he is the first among all who will be raised from death. So in everything he is most important. God was pleased for all of himself to live in the Son. And through him, God was happy to bring all things back to himself again– things on earth and things in heaven. God made peace by using the blood sacrifice of his Son on the cross.* Colossians 1:15-20

Notebook illustration

Take a loose leaf or spiral ring notebook and at the top of a clean page write your name with a line under it. Then start to write all of the sins you have ever committed. Write small so that you won't fill up the page too quickly. Everything you have ever said and done that was not in submission to the will of God, your creator and source of life, is a sin. Sin is missing the mark from an absolute and perfect love and obedience toward God. You will probably need a 300 gigabyte hard drive to get it all on.

Next, turn to a new page, and write the name "Jesus" followed by the title "Christ" at the top with a line under it. Now write all of the things that Jesus has done in disobedience to his Father. Guess what, there isn't one thing. He was perfectly righteous and the Father finds no fault whatsoever in his life.

Now, take a ruler and tear both pages just below the lines that you have drawn. Now, open your Bible to 2 Corinthians 5:21 and read it. As you do, start on Jesus' page *(and God made him who had no sin)*, and turn the bottom part of your page to fit under Jesus name *(to be sin for us)*. Now turn back to the page with your name, and place the bottom part of Jesus page under your name *(so that in him we might become the righteousness of God* – NIV).

Our righteousness before the Father is perfect righteousness because it is Christ's righteousness. We can neither add to it nor subtract from it. We are either 100% righteous because we are <u>in</u> Christ, or we are completely unrighteous because we are not <u>in</u> him. It is not a question of balancing the scales by my good works, or piety, or anything else. My only hope is to be in Christ, and if I am, than I am completely acceptable to God <u>forever</u>. I cannot lose my salvation or fall out of God's family.

Our only claim to fame before God is that we are "in" Christ. We are not our own, and we don't have our own identity apart from him. Because we are in him, God the Father treats us as if we were Jesus, the perfect obedient Son. Everything Christ deserves, we are going to get. We have his righteousness, his purity, his future destiny. We are already seated with him in the heavenly places. Wherever Christ is, there we will be because we are a part of him.

The little word "in" is one of the most important words in the whole Bible, and the phrase "in Christ" transforms the destiny of millions of human beings who by faith have been placed in Jesus.

PS: If you are not yet "in Christ," what are you waiting for?

9. Jesus, a man just like us with one exception

Based on many biblical statements, we see that there are different levels of authority in the Trinity. This does not mean that either person in the Triune God is of lesser value, or is any less God.

The Father is the source of all things and all persons. Everything that has life proceeds from the Father. Everything in existence issues out from him. Even the Son and the Holy Spirit have their eternal source in the Father. They were not created, but exist in him from and for all eternity.

The Council of Nicaea in AD 325 overwhelmingly concluded that *the Father was always a Father, and both Father and Son existed always together, eternally, coequally and con–substantially* (being of the same substance). They reacted against, and condemned, the view of Arius who said that the Son had a beginning. This belief is one of the most common errors of groups like the Mormons and the Jehovah's Witnesses who believe that Jesus <u>became</u> a God.

Nevertheless, the terms "Father" and "Son" clearly indicate a dependent relationship. A son is a product of his father and derives his life from him. It is hard for us to fathom that a father would not exist before a son, but that is what happens with God. Since both Father and Son are eternal and have no beginning, there is no order of origin in time.

The Father, Son and Holy Spirit are equal in nature, in attributes, in purpose, and in moral values. However, they are not equal in authority or role. Each has a distinct function and a different responsibility in the Godhead. The Trinity is not a triumvirate in which all three rule equally. For instance, Paul says that Christ is subject to the Father.

> *As the Scriptures say, "God put everything under his control." When it says that "everything" is put under him, it is clear that this does not include God himself. God is the one putting everything under Christ's control. After everything has been put under Christ, then the Son himself will be put under God. God is the one who put everything under Christ. And Christ will be put under God so that God will be the complete ruler over everything.*
>
> 1 Corinthians 15:27-28

The Son is subject to the Father. The Holy Spirit is subject to both the Father and the Son. An example is the relationship that God gave us is in marriage (even though most women don't like this any more than sinners like God to rule over them) – God said that the man is the head of the family, and the woman should be submissive to him. *(To the woman he said, "I will greatly increase your pains in childbearing; with pain you will give birth to children. Your desire will be for your husband, and <u>he will rule over you.</u>"*   Genesis 3:16 NIV)

This does not mean that she is of lesser value, or a lesser person. It only means that she is under authority just like Christ and the Holy Spirit are under the authority of the Father. To the degree that Christ is devalued and debased for being under the authority of the Father, to that same degree the woman is devalued and debased for being under the authority of her husband; or in other words "not debased at all." It has nothing to do with merit or value as an individual. The same is true in healthy military forces – as a person, a private is just as worthy of respect as a general, although as soldiers they have different ranks and each must submit to the authorities above them.

The Son is under authority

In marriage, God says that the husband and wife are one, but he also makes it clear that they do not have the same authority. So it is with the Father and the Son and the Holy Spirit.

> *I give them eternal life, and they will never perish. No one can snatch them away from Me, for My Father has given them to Me, and <u>He is more powerful than anyone else</u>. No one can snatch them from the Father's hand. The Father and I are one.*   John 10:28-30 NLT

> *Jesus told them, "You will indeed drink from My bitter cup. But <u>I have no right</u> to say who will sit on My right or My left. My Father has prepared those places for the ones He has chosen."*   Matthew 20:23 NLT

> *But Jesus answered, "I assure you that the Son <u>can do nothing alone</u>. He does only what he sees his Father doing. The Son does the same things that the Father does. The Father loves the Son and shows him everything*

he does. This man was healed. But <u>the Father will show</u>
<u>the Son</u> greater things than this to do. Then you will
all be amazed.   John 5:19-20

And you know that the Scriptures cannot be altered. So
if those people who received God's message were called
'gods,' why do you call it blasphemy when I say, 'I am
the Son of God'? After all, <u>the Father</u> set Me apart and
<u>sent Me</u> into the world.   John 10:35-36 NLT

This is how God showed his love to us: <u>He sent</u> his only
Son into the world to give us life through him. True love
is God's love for us, not our love for God. <u>He sent</u> his Son
as the way to take away our sins.   1 John 4:9-10

We have seen that the <u>Father sent his Son</u> to be the Savior
of the world, and this is what we tell people now.
                                                    1 John 4:14

I don't speak on My own authority. The Father who sent
Me has commanded Me what to say and how to say it. And
I know His commands lead to eternal life; so I say <u>whatever</u>
<u>the Father tells Me to say.</u>"   John 12:49-50 NLT

Christ makes it very clear that he is under the authority of the
Father and does whatever he orders him to do even though he
says that he and the Father are One.

The Holy Spirit is under authority

But when the right time came, <u>God sent His Son</u>, born
of a woman, subject to the law. God sent Him to buy

freedom for us who were slaves to the law, so that He could adopt us as His very own children. And because we are His children, <u>God has sent the Spirit</u> of His Son into our hearts, prompting us to call out, "Abba, Father."
Galatians 4:4-6 NLT

But the Helper will teach you everything and cause you to remember all that I told you. This Helper is the Holy Spirit that the <u>Father will send</u> in my name.
John 14:26

<u>I will send you</u> the Helper from the Father. The Helper is the Spirit of truth who comes from the Father. When he comes, he will tell about me.   John 15:26

The person who has authority to send another is the greater of the two. This does not mean that their natures or value are any different.

Believe me, servants are not greater than their master. Those who are sent to do something are <u>not greater than the one who sent them</u>.   John 13:16

The human Jesus was very much like any other human baby

When Jesus was born in Bethlehem the only difference between him and other human beings was that his father was God. Our original father was Adam (or in Jesus' words – the devil). Baby Jesus had no supernatural powers, no supernatural knowledge, and no sense of purpose that was different from other human babies.

After the Fall, Jesus was the only human being to be born without" Adam's sin nature. He was God and man at the same time. He almost always referred to himself as the "Son of Man." From the eternal perspective, he had always been the Son of God, and now he was also the Son of Man. This combination of natures made it possible for him to be our representative on the cross, and also to resist the temptation to sin against his Father. He was a sinless man, although he became associated with sin and was condemned because of it. As mentioned earlier, second Corinthians 5: 21 tells us that: *God made him who had no sin to be sin for us, so that in him we might become the righteousness of God* NIV). He was condemned for sin, but it was our sin and not his own.

Many well–intentioned Christians try to give baby Jesus all kinds of powers, knowledge and attributes that he never had. They allow no possibility that he learned his identity and his purpose after he was born. They believe that to deny that Jesus had all the divine attributes is to deny that he was God. In Chapter 7 we saw that the requirement for being god/a god is to have the nature of God, not to have his authority. If we are born of God, than we are gods as the Bible clearly states over and over.

When Jesus left Heaven and was born as a human in Bethlehem, he didn't come in his royal "attire." He clothed himself with weakness, frailty, dependence, and need, just like other human beings. He left behind his super powers because they would have made it impossible for him to fulfill his mission on earth. He was to be one of us, and be tempted in all things just like we are. It is worth saying again, that the only thing that made Jesus different from other men was that his Father was God and that he had an on–going personal relationship with him. The only time that that eternal relationship was ever broken was for the three days that Jesus was separated from his Father as he bore the sins of this world on the cross and in the tomb.

When Jesus returned to the Father, he reclaimed all the attributes that he had given up in his incarnation. He is again omnipresent, omniscient, omnipotent, etc., and is living in every believer, knows every human heart, has power to help and deliver, and is pleading for us before the heavenly throne. He is <u>here</u> on earth and <u>there</u> in Heaven and <u>everywhere</u> at the same time, but he could not do that while he was limited in his mortal human body.

Debunking the myth of Jesus' omnipresence in his human body

Some Christians believe that Christ was omnipresent (able to be everywhere at all times) in his human body. That is an absurd belief since a physical body cannot be in two places at one time, not even in Star Trek. When Philippians 2:7 says, *"but made himself nothing (literally "emptied himself" or "stripped himself"), taking the very nature of a servant, being made in human likeness* NIV)," it means that he left something behind when he became a man. Those theologians who believe in his human omnipresence don't believe he left anything behind. They find it hard to accept that Christ became a human being in a human body with physical limitations. To them, the incarnation never really happened. The Jews were looking for a Messiah who would confine his influence to the physical world. Classical theologians want a Messiah who never really experienced human life at all, but floated far above it.

The reason they defend his omnipresence is because if they admit that he left <u>any</u> of his attributes behind, then he could have left others behind, like omnipotence (having all power) and omniscience (knowing all things). Yet, the Scriptures clearly reveal that Jesus, as incarnated man, did not have unlimited powers nor unlimited knowledge. He also did not have unlimited authority because he himself said after his resurrection, *"All authority has been given to me."* It was given to him after his life of obedience, his suffering, his death and resurrection. The statement *"has been given"* indicates that it wasn't always so. Since his authority in the heavenly realms was from eternity, this new "giving" can only refer to the new authority that was given to him as the victorious God–man.

Christ in his earthly body was not omnipotent

Some theologians and pastors have said that Jesus had all the divine attributes/abilities that he had before his incarnation, but that he simple did not use them. This is twisting logic to agree with pre–conceived beliefs. Let's look at some Scriptures which show that Jesus did not have absolute power, and that the supernatural power he had came from his Father and from the Holy Spirit.

It is worth noting that Jesus did not do any miracles for thirty years. He only began to do miracles after the Holy Spirit descended upon him at his baptism.

> *About that time Jesus came from the town of Nazareth in Galilee to the place where John was. John baptized Jesus in the Jordan River. As Jesus was coming up out of the water, he saw the sky torn open.* <u>*The Spirit came down on him like a dove.*</u> *A voice came from heaven and said, "You are my Son, the one I love. I am very pleased with you."* Mark 1:9-11(MT 3:16-17)

> *So Jesus explained, "I tell you the truth, <u>the Son can do nothing by Himself</u>. He does only what He sees the Father doing. Whatever the Father does, the Son also does.*
>
> John 5:19 NLT

His power was limited

> *Then Jesus told them, "A prophet is honored everywhere except in his own hometown and among his relatives and his own family." And because of their unbelief, <u>He couldn't do any miracles</u> among them except to place His hands on a few sick people and heal them.*
>
> Mark 6:4-5 NLT

He didn't always have the power to heal

> *One day as he was teaching, Pharisees and teachers of the law, who had come from every village of Galilee and from Judea and Jerusalem, were sitting there. And the <u>power of the Lord was present</u> for him to heal the sick.*
>
> Luke 5:17 NIV

Unfortunately, this statement is very seldom, if ever, a topic for a sermon because if doesn't fit our ethereal image of Christ. The fact that Luke says it indicates that the power to heal was not always present with Jesus during his three years of ministry.

Christ in his earthly body was not omniscient

One of the main attributes or abilities that well–intentioned Christians try to assure that Jesus had is omniscience. Omniscience means absolute knowledge of everything and therefore there is no need to learn anything new. From the dictionary – *"having complete or unlimited knowledge, awareness, or understanding: perceiving all things; having total knowledge; knowing everything."*

To prove the omniscience of Jesus, we would need to prove that he knew <u>all things</u>, or at least many things that only an omniscient person could know. To disprove it, I only need to prove that there is <u>one thing</u> he did not know. The following Scriptures show that there were at least twenty things he did not know.

A. We see Jesus learning

> *Then He returned to Nazareth with them and was obedient to them. And His mother stored all these things in her heart. Jesus <u>grew in wisdom</u> and in stature and in favor with God and all the people.*   Luke 2:51-52 NLT

If he had been omniscient, he could not have grown in wisdom since he would have already known all of the answers to all of the questions.

> *Jesus <u>learned</u> that the Pharisees had heard the report that he was making and baptizing more followers than John.*
> John 4:1

You cannot learn something you already know.

> *Some time later, Jesus went up to Jerusalem for a feast of the Jews. Now there is in Jerusalem near the Sheep Gate a pool, which in Aramaic is called Bethesda and which is surrounded by five covered colonnades. Here*

a great number of disabled people used to lie–the blind,
the lame, the paralyzed. One who was there had been an
invalid for thirty-eight years. When Jesus saw him lying
there and <u>learned</u> that he had been in this condition for
a long time, he asked him, "Do you want to get well?"
John 5:1-6 NIV

Jesus found out in some way that the man had been lying there
for most of his life. If he had been omniscient, he would have
already known the man's condition and all his history. Some
would say that his asking the invalid if he wanted to get well
was a rhetorical question, but that is only a poor attempt at
trying to support his omniscience.

We presume that everyone wants to get well, but that may not
be true. We might ask the question to someone, "Do you want
to get off of welfare?' and perhaps the answer would be "No, I
am comfortable just the way I am." After thirty-eight years of
lying by the pool and living off of the gifts of others, the man
might not have wanted to make such a radical change.

For years in Uruguay, we worked with a large group of people
living in a shanty town. Most had been born and spent all their
lives there. To us, it was a terrible situation: to them it was
home, and they were afraid to have to change their culture and
way of living, even though in our eyes it was horrible.

But Jesus answered, "I assure you that the Son can do
nothing alone. He does <u>only what he sees his Father doing</u>.
The Son does the same things that the Father does. The
Father loves the Son and shows him everything he does.
This man was healed. But the Father <u>will show the Son</u>
greater things than this to do. Then you will all be amazed.
John 5:19-20

Why would the Father need to show Jesus anything if he already knew all things? Jesus said that in the future the Father would show him more things that he didn't already know. Jesus did not know everything that was happening but he had a direct line of communication with someone who did.

> *I no longer call you servants, because servants don't know what their master is doing. But now I call you friends, because I have told you <u>everything that my Father told me</u>.*   John 15:15

How could Jesus keep learning things from his Father if he already knew everything?

> *Although he was a son, he learned obedience from what he suffered and, <u>once made perfect</u>, he became the source of eternal salvation for all who obey him and was designated by God to be high priest in the order of Melchizedek.*
> Hebrews 5:8-10 NIV

The Greek word often translated "perfect" is teleos and really means "complete." Jesus' qualifications as our redeemer were not complete until he had lived a life of perfect obedience, having suffered temptation. Then, and only then, could he be the source of eternal salvation. He was not complete until he had passed the test of temptation to disobey.

B. We see Jesus asking for information

> *Jesus immediately felt power go out from him, so he stopped and turned around. "<u>Who touched my clothes?</u>" he asked. The followers said to Jesus, "There are so*

many people pushing against you. But you ask, 'Who touched me?'"   Mark 5:30-31

Then Jesus said, "<u>Who touched me?</u>" They all said they had not touched him. And Peter said, "Master, people are all around you, pushing against you." Jesus said, "<u>Someone touched me</u>. I felt power go out from me."
                                                                Luke 8:45-46

Jesus knew that someone had touched him because he felt the power go out of him, but he **did not know** who did it.

Jesus took the blind man by the hand and led him out of the village. Then, spitting on the man's eyes, He laid His hands on him and asked, "<u>Can you see anything now?</u>" The man looked around. "Yes," he said, "I see people, but I can't see them very clearly. They look like trees walking around." Then Jesus placed His hands on the man's eyes again, and his eyes were opened. His sight was completely restored, and he could see everything clearly.
                                                            Mark 8:23-25 NLT

Apparently, Jesus did not know what the man was seeing and had to ask.

Jesus asked the man, "<u>What do you want me to do for you?</u>" He answered, "Teacher, I want to see again."
                                                                Mark 10:51

Jesus stopped there and said, "Bring that man to me!" When he came close, Jesus asked him, "<u>What do you want me to do for you?</u>" He said, "Lord, I want to see again."
                                                                Luke 18:40-41

After Jesus told them this, he showed them his hands and his feet. The followers were amazed and very, very happy to see that Jesus was alive. They still could not believe what they saw. He said to them, "<u>Do you have any food here?</u>" They gave him a piece of cooked fish.

Luke 24:40-42

Why ask about food if he already knew everything that was in the room? He could have just gone to the fish and picked it up.

Jesus asked him, "What is your name?" The man answered, "Legion." (He said his name was "Legion" because many demons had gone into him.)   Luke 8:30

Jesus did not know what the name of this demon was and he had to ask. Why would Jesus ask, "Who touched me?" or "What is your name?" or "Do you see anything?" or "How long has he been like this?" if he already knew the answers? These clearly are not rhetorical questions, but authentic requests for information.

Early the next morning, Jesus was going back to the city. He was very hungry. He saw a fig tree beside the road and went to get a fig from it. But there were no figs on the tree. There were only leaves. So Jesus said to the tree, "You will never again produce fruit!" The tree immediately dried up and died.   Matthew 21:18-19

The next day as they were leaving Bethany, Jesus was hungry. Seeing in the distance a fig tree in leaf, <u>he went to find out if it had any fruit</u>. When he reached it, he found nothing but leaves, because <u>it was not the season for figs</u>.   Mark 11:12-13 NIV

Jesus didn't know that there were no figs on the tree.

C. We see Jesus not knowing ahead of time what he was going to do

> *Two days later there was a wedding in the town of Cana in Galilee, and Jesus' mother was there. Jesus and his followers were also invited. At the wedding there was not enough wine, so Jesus' mother said to him, "They have no more wine." Jesus answered, "Dear woman, why are you telling me this? <u>It is not yet time for me to begin my work.</u>" His mother said to the servants, "Do what he tells you."* John 2:1-5

It was clearly not his intention to do a miracle at this wedding. Jesus learned <u>after</u> he made this statement that his time had indeed come. Because of his respect for and perhaps obedience to his mother, and due to new instructions from his Father, he began his miraculous ministry.

> *A Canaanite woman from that area came out and began shouting, "Lord, Son of David, please help me! My daughter has a demon inside her, and she is suffering very much." But Jesus did not answer her. So the followers came to him and said, "Tell her to go away. She keeps crying out and will not leave us alone." Jesus answered, "<u>God sent me only to the lost people of Israel.</u>" Then the woman came over to Jesus and bowed before him. She said, "Lord, help me!" He answered her with this saying: "<u>It is not right to take the children's bread and give it to the dogs.</u>" The woman said, "Yes, Lord, but even the dogs eat the pieces of food that fall from their master's table." Then Jesus answered, "<u>Woman, you have great</u>*

> *faith! You will get what you asked for.*" *And right then the woman's daughter was healed.*   Matthew 15:22-28

Jesus, because of his great compassion, acceded to the request of this Gentile woman who demonstrated more faith than most people in Israel. The text clearly shows that he had no original intention of helping her but changed his mind and did.

> *Then Jesus said to them, "People everywhere give honor to a prophet, except in his own town, with his own people, or in his home." Jesus was not able to do any miracles there except the healing of some sick people by laying his hands on them. He was surprised that the people there had no faith. Then he went to other villages in that area and taught.*   Mark 6:4-6

Apparently, Jesus wanted to do much more for these people, but their lack of faith put a limit on his plans. It is strongly implied in the text that he would have done many more miracles if he could have. If so, he did not have absolute foreknowledge of what he was going to do.

D. We see Jesus praying

> *Then Jesus went on a little farther away from them. He fell to the ground and prayed, "My Father, if it is possible, don't make me drink from this cup. But do what you want, not what I want."*   Matthew 26:39 NIV

This fervent prayer would have been a futile exercise if he knew that nothing could change.

> *While Jesus was here on earth, He offered prayers and pleadings, with a loud cry and tears, to the One who*

could rescue Him from death. And God heard His prayers
because of His deep reverence for God.
Hebrews 5:7

Don't you realize that I could ask My Father for thousands
of angels to protect us, and He would send them instantly?
But if I did, how would the Scriptures be fulfilled that
describe what must happen now? Matthew 26:53-54 NLT

Jesus is saying that he could escape if he wanted to. This possibility
of escape was perhaps his greatest temptation ever (much greater
than turning stones into bread because he was hungry), but he
submitted to his Father's will and fulfilled the Scriptural prophecies.

E. We see lots of people who believed that Jesus was not omniscient

No one knows when that day or time will be. The Son
and the angels in heaven don't know when it will be.
Only the Father knows.   Matthew 24:36

Jesus is making it very clear that he was not omniscient.

Then the followers came to Jesus and asked, "Do you know
that the Pharisees are upset about what you said?"
Matthew 15:12

The disciples, who by this time knew Jesus very well, did not believe
in Christ's omniscience or they would not have asked the question.

But some of you don't believe." (Jesus knew the people
who did not believe. He knew this from the beginning.
And he knew the one who would hand him over to his
enemies.)   John 6:64

This statement would be unnecessary/superfluous if Jesus already knew everything. It would be easier to make a blanket statement saying that Jesus knew everything than it was to state that he knew a particular detail. No such statement of general omniscience was ever made by the gospel writers. Apparently John, the writer of this Gospel did not believe that Jesus was omniscient.

How did Jesus learn all the things he knew if he wasn't omniscient?

Jesus learned from the Father after he was born who he was and what his mission was. Jesus says very clearly that he had gone up to Heaven after his incarnation (very probably on multiple occasions and certainly at least once before he was twelve years old – Luke 2:41-47).

> *I have told you about things here on earth, but you do not believe me. So I'm sure you will not believe me if I tell you about heavenly things! The only one who has ever gone up to heaven is the one who came down from heaven–the Son of Man.*   John 3:12-13

(note: In most Greek texts, the words, *"who is in Heaven"* are also included at the end of the statement. This does not change in any way Christ's statement that he had gone into Heaven **after** he came down from Heaven.)

> *I don't mean that there is anyone who has seen the Father. The only one who has ever seen the Father is the one who came from God. He has seen the Father.*
> John 6:46

This could be interpreted in two ways: 1) that Jesus saw the Father before his incarnation; or 2) that he saw him after his incarnation. If it had been before, then the statement could not be true because many beings had seen the Father, including The Holy Spirit, all the angels, the 24 elders, the four living creatures and all those around the throne of God. When he says that only he has seen the Father, it has to mean that he is the only human being to ever see him. The "seeing" by Jesus occurs after his being sent.

Jesus is telling his audience what he learned while in the presence of his Father in Heaven. The apostle Paul made a similar claim in his letter to the Corinthians.

> *I know a man in Christ who was taken up to the third heaven. This happened 14 years ago. I don't know if the man was in his body or out of his body, but God knows. And I know that this man was taken up to paradise. I don't know if he was in his body or away from his body, but he heard things that he is not able to explain. He heard things that no one is allowed to tell.*
>
> 2 Corinthians 12:2-4

It should not be strange to believe that Jesus, like Paul, could be taken up into Heaven to learn from his Father. Christ's tutor was God the Father. This obviously had to be after his incarnation since before it he shared all the divine attributes with the Father and the Holy Spirit and already knew all things that had happened and were happening. Since he was omniscient before his incarnation, he could not have <u>learned</u> anything. The learning had to take place after the incarnation.

> *I no longer call you servants, because a servant does not know his master's business. Instead, I have called you*

friends, for <u>everything that I learned from my Father</u> I have made known to you.   John 15:15 NIV

They asked, "Then who are you?" Jesus answered, "I am what I have told you from the beginning. I have much more I could say to judge you. But I tell people <u>only what I have heard from the one who sent me</u>, and he speaks the truth."   John 8:25-26

They did not understand that he was telling them about his Father. So Jesus said, "When you have lifted up the Son of Man, then you will know that I am the one I claim to be and that I do nothing on my own but <u>speak just what the Father has taught me</u>.   John 8:27-28 NIV

I am telling you what I saw <u>when I was with My Father</u>. But you are following the advice of your father."   John 8:38 NLT

For the Father loves the Son and <u>shows</u> Him everything He is doing. In fact, the Father <u>will show</u> Him how to do even greater works than healing this man. Then you will truly be astonished.   John 5:20 NLT

In addition to Jesus' special transportation into the presence of the Father (whether in body or not we do not know), he also had an on–going, intimate, timeless relationship with the Father that was never broken until he was on the cross. The Father was continually showing Jesus what he was doing and what needed to be done on earth. These are things that Jesus did not already know or the Father would not have needed to show them to him. Jesus was the Father's messenger, Deliverer and Rescuer for the people of the world. In order to accomplish all that was necessary, Jesus had to be a man just like us through whom the Father and the Holy Spirit could work.

Also, we know that Jesus had numerous contacts with angels in his lifetime —

> *So the devil left him. Then some angels came to Jesus and helped him.*   Matthew 4:11

> *Then an angel from heaven came to help him.*
>   Luke 22:43

> *Then the Spirit sent Jesus into the desert alone. He was there for 40 days, being tempted by Satan. During this time he was out among the wild animals. Then angels came and helped him.*   Mark 1:12-13

> *Jesus said to him, "Do you believe this just because I said I saw you under the fig tree? You will see much greater things than that!" Then he said, "Believe me when I say that you will all see heaven open. You will see 'angels of God going up and coming down' on the Son of Man."*
>   John 1:50-51

He also had access to Old Testament prophets —

> *Six days later, Jesus took Peter, James, and John the brother of James and went up on a high mountain. They were all alone there. While these followers watched him, Jesus was changed. His face became bright like the sun, and his clothes became white as light. Then two men were there, talking with him. They were <u>Moses and Elijah</u>.*
>   Matthew 17:1-3

Jesus did not need to be omniscient to be our Savior

For classified information in the military we used a term "need to know" to help determine who could have access to classified documents. If a person didn't need to know, he was denied access even though his security clearance would have permitted it. Jesus didn't need to be omnipresent, omnipotent, nor omniscient to accomplish his mission. His mission was to be an obedient son to every instruction of his Father and to take that obedience to the hardest test of all – the cross of Calvary where he died helpless, at the mercy of his human persecutors. Even his Father had to turn his back on him in order for the redemption to be complete. He died alone and in so doing suffered the penalty which we all deserve.

Conclusion

You have to be more agile than a circus contortionist to distort these Scriptures in order to try to prove that the human Jesus was omnipresent, omnipotent and omniscient. To believe that Jesus was omniscient in his human body is errant theology. It defies all the evidence to the contrary. Many people believe that we have to make God's power and abilities as big as possible to protect him, but they do so at the cost of violating Scripture and reason. God is who he is, and we need to accept him as he is and to know him as he is, not as we imagine he ought to be. We should not make the mistake of applying all of the eternal divine attributes to Christ in his incarnate human form. Divinity is not determined by what attributes a being has, but by the nature of his person.

Jesus was born just like us, except his Father was God. Because he had a divine nature, he did not rebel against his Father's authority as all other human beings did. He was the one and only sinless man, and in obedience to his Father offered himself up as a sacrifice for the sins of all other men, including his very own earthly mother.

> *For this reason, Jesus had to be made like us, his brothers and sisters, in every way. He became like people so that he could be their merciful and faithful high priest in service to God. Then he could bring forgiveness for the people's sins.*   Hebrews 2:17

If Jesus had not been weak and dependent like we are, he could not have been our Savior.

> *"You know what has happened all over Judea. It began in Galilee after John told the people they needed to be baptized. You know about Jesus from Nazareth. God made him the Messiah by <u>giving him the Holy Spirit and power</u>. Jesus went everywhere doing good for people. He healed those who were ruled by the devil, showing that God was with him.*   Acts 10:37-38

Jesus did not do the miracles he did with his own power. He did it with the power of the Holy Spirit and that same power is available to us to also do what is God's will.

10. | Does God change his mind?

Many people have asked the question, "Can God change his mind about something? If he can change his mind about something he was going to do, then obviously, the future was not already determined. Some pretzel theologians have said that he does change his mind, but that he already knew he would. That reminds me of the sign behind the commander's desk in ROTC basic training, "I thought I made a mistake once in 1955, but I was wrong." You can't have it both ways. If God can change his mind, then he could not know every detail of the future. I can't understand why this is so hard for some people to grasp. I can't understand why this is so hard for some people to grasp. I can't understand why this is so hard for some people to grasp. They hold onto their theological view of God regardless of all the evidence to the contrary. If God already infallibly knew every detail of the future, then he could never change his mind about anything or it would prove that he had been wrong.

In this chapter, we will see very clearly that God can and does change his mind. We will see that the Scriptures say that he did it at least twenty-seven times in the Old Testament.

To understand this, we must look at the meaning of the word repent – literally to re-think.

Repent

nacham *naw-kham'*
A primitive root; properly to *sigh*, that is, *breathe* strongly; by implication to *be sorry*, that is, (in a favorable sense) to *pity*, console or (reflexively) *rue*; or (unfavorably) to *avenge* (oneself): - comfort (self), ease [one's self], **Repent** (-er, -ing, self).

Half the times in the Old Testament, this word is translated "repent" and the other half it is translated "comfort." I think that this means that it is referring to something that comes from deep within the heart, especially when referring to God. In the New Testament, the somewhat equivalent word is "metanoia," to change one's thinking.

There are four places in the Bible where it is stated that God does not "repent." Two of these verses refer to a specific case, and two say that he doesn't repent "like a man does." Twenty-seven other verses say that God repented/changed his mind.

> *God is not a man; he will not lie. God is not a human being; his decisions will not change. If he says he will do something, then he will do it. If he makes a promise, then he will do what he promised.*   Numbers 23:19

This verse is the one most often cited by people who want to show that God never changes his mind about anything. It was spoken by Balaam, a pseudo-prophet, and not by God, nor any of his approved prophets. It cannot be taken as absolute truth and should fit into the category of the advice of Job's comforters, or even of Job himself before he was enlightened by God. It is a true statement of what Balaam said, but not everything people said in the Bible is true. Many men made threats or promises or declarations of things that did not come true. The Bible is an accurate record of history, but not all statements in the Bible were made by God or his spokesman. Take Satan's word for example as stated in Job: It never came true.

> *Satan answered the LORD, "But Job has a good reason to respect you. You always protect him, his family, and everything he has. You have blessed him and made him successful in everything he does. He is so wealthy that his herds and flocks are all over the country. But if you were to destroy everything he has, I promise you that he would curse you to your face."* Job 1:9-11

Or other statements like that of Pharaoh:

> *Pharaoh called for Moses and Aaron and said, "Ask the LORD to remove the frogs from me and my people. I will let the people go to offer sacrifices to the LORD."*
> Exodus 8:8

This is what he said, but it was not a true statement, only an accurate description of what he said.

The Bible always accurately records what was said and what happened, but the statements made by some people are not true. There are very many instances of this throughout the Bible. With Balaam's claim – it may or may not be true. Certainly, he was not always speaking at the behest of God.

> *When Samuel turned to leave, Saul caught Samuel's robe. The robe tore. Samuel said to Saul, "In this same way*

> the LORD has torn the kingdom of Israel from you
> today. He has given the kingdom to one of your friends,
> a man who is a better person than you. The one who
> lives forever, the God of Israel, <u>does not lie and will not
> change his mind. He is not like a man who is always
> changing his mind.</u>"   1 Samuel 15:27-29

Samuel was obviously an approved and inspired prophet and we
have no reason whatsoever to doubt what he is saying. However,
he does add the part comparing God to man and saying in essence
that God doesn't change his mind in the same way that men
do. Also, Samuel's statement might not be a blanket statement
about God, but rather refer to the specific case where God was
going to tear the kingdom away from Saul and give it to David.

The other two instances where it is stated that God won't change
his mind are of a specific case in which he is referring to Jesus'
priesthood and not to a general description of God.

> The LORD has made a promise with an oath and <u>will
> not change his mind</u>: "You are a priest forever– the kind
> of priest Melchizedek was."   Psalm 110:4

If there were no possibility of God changing his mind about
anything, then this statement saying that he will not change his
mind about this declaration of the priesthood would be superfluous.

There is no airtight statement in the whole Bible that says that God
will <u>never, ever</u> change his mind. But there are many cases in the Bible
that show that he did change his mind. Scripture is interpreted by
Scripture. That means to say that all of Scripture must be harmonized
and that we understand one part by what we see in other parts.
Sometimes statements seem to contradict each other, but we believe
that the whole truth is revealed by the whole Scripture.

Many translations avoid using the word "repent" in referring to God. They substitute the word "relent." Is "relenting" the same as "repenting"?

> Then the LORD _relented_ and did not bring on his people the disaster he had threatened.   Exodus 32:14 NIV

> . . . for their sake he remembered his covenant and out of his great love he _relented_.   Psalm 106:45 NIV

> So the LORD _relented_. "This will not happen," the LORD said.   Amos 7:3 NIV

> So the LORD _relented_. "This will not happen either," the Sovereign LORD said.   Amos 7:6 NIV

All four of these times where the NIV translators used the word "_relented_," it is the same Hebrew word as "_repented._" Translators are also human and sometimes allow their pre-conceived theology to influence their translation. There is no valid reason in the context to translate this word in a different way than in other contexts. In translation, when the context dictates, different words can be used to express the intent of the passage, but we should not change the words when it is not warranted.

Here are two other cases where the translators used a different English word to express the same Hebrew word when it referred to God's course of action.

> When God saw what they did and how they turned from their evil ways, he had compassion and _did not bring upon them_ (repented of) the destruction he had threatened.
> Jonah 3:10 NIV

> *Nevertheless, the LORD <u>did not turn away</u> (repent) from the heat of his fierce anger, which burned against Judah because of all that Manasseh had done to provoke him to anger.*   2 Kings 23:26 NIV

Following are twenty-five additional references (all from the KJV because that translation does not change the word usage) that clearly state that God does or can "repent:"

> *And it <u>Repented</u> the LORD that he had made man on the earth, and it grieved him at his heart. And the LORD said, I will destroy man whom I have created from the face of the earth; both man, and beast, and the creeping thing, and the fowls of the air; for it <u>repenteth</u> me that I have made them.*   Genesis 6:6-7 KJV

> *Wherefore should the Egyptians speak, and say, For mischief did he bring them out, to slay them in the mountains, and to consume them from the face of the earth? Turn from thy fierce wrath, and <u>repent</u> of this evil against thy people...And the LORD repented of the evil which he thought to do unto his people.*   Exodus 32:12, 14 KJV

> *And when the LORD raised them up judges, then the LORD was with the judge, and delivered them out of the hand of their enemies all the days of the judge: for it <u>repented</u> the LORD because of their groaning by reason of them that oppressed them and vexed them.*   Judges 2:18 KJV

> *It <u>repenteth</u> me that I have set up Saul to be king: for he is turned back from following me, and hath not performed*

my commandments. And it grieved Samuel; and he cried unto the LORD all night. 1 Samuel 15:11 KJV

And Samuel came no more to see Saul until the day of his death: nevertheless Samuel mourned for Saul: and the LORD <u>repented</u> that he had made Saul king over Israel.
1 Samuel 15:35 KJV

And when the angel stretched out his hand upon Jerusalem to de-stroy it, the LORD <u>repented</u> him of the evil, and said to the angel that destroyed the people, It is enough: stay now thine hand. And the angel of the LORD was by the threshing place of Araunah the Jebusite.
2 Samuel 24:16 KJV

And God sent an angel unto Jerusalem to destroy it: and as he was destroying, the LORD beheld, and he <u>repented</u> him of the evil, and said to the angel that destroyed, It is enough, stay now thine hand. And the angel of the LORD stood by the threshing floor of Ornan the Jebusite.
1 Chronicles 21:15 KJV

And he remembered for them his covenant, and <u>repented</u> according to the multitude of his mercies.
Psalm 106:45 KJV

For the LORD will judge his people, and he will <u>repent</u> himself concerning his servants Psalm 135:14 KJV

For this shall the earth mourn, and the heavens above be black: because I have spoken it, I have purposed it, and will not <u>repent</u>, neither will I turn back from it.
Jeremiah 4:28 KJV

God is speaking of this special case – not a generality. If he never changed his mind, then he would not have needed to make this statement.

> *Thou hast forsaken me, saith the LORD, thou art gone backward: therefore will I stretch out my hand against thee, and destroy thee; I am weary with <u>repenting</u>.*
>
> Jeremiah 15:6 KJV

God is saying that he is tired of changing his mind so often to show mercy to this stiff-necked people.

> *If that nation, against whom I have pronounced, turn from their evil, I will <u>repent</u> of the evil that I thought to do unto them.*   Jeremiah 18:8 KJV

> *If it do evil in my sight, that it obey not my voice, then I will <u>repent</u> of the good, wherewith I said I would benefit them.*   Jeremiah 18:10 KJV

> *If so be they will hearken, and turn every man from his evil way, that I may <u>repent</u> me of the evil, which purpose to do unto them because of the evil of their doings.*
>
> Jeremiah 26:3 KJV

> *Therefore now amend your ways and your doings, and obey the voice of the LORD your God; and the LORD will <u>repent</u> him of the evil that he hath pronounced against you.*   Jeremiah 26:13 KJV

> *Did Hezekiah king of Judah and all Judah put him at all to death? Did he not fear the LORD, and besought the LORD, and the LORD <u>repented</u> him of the evil which*

he had pronounced against them? Thus might we procure
great evil against our souls.   Jeremiah 26:19 KJV

If ye will still abide in this land, then will I build you, and
not pull you down, and I will plant you, and not pluck you
up: for I <u>repent</u> me of the evil that I have done unto you.
                                        Jeremiah 42:10 KJV

I the LORD have spoken it: it shall come to pass, and I
will do it; I will not go back, neither will I spare, neither
will I <u>repent</u>; according to thy ways, and according to
thy doings, shall they judge thee, saith the Lord GOD.
                                        Ezekiel 24:14 KJV

And rend your heart, and not your garments, and turn
unto the LORD your God: for he is gracious and merciful,
slow to anger, and of great kindness, and <u>repenteth</u> him
of the evil.   Joel 2:13 KJV

The LORD <u>repented</u> for this: It shall not be, saith the
LORD.   Amos 7:3 KJV

The LORD <u>repented</u> for this: This also shall not be, saith
the Lord GOD.   Amos 7:6 KJV

Who can tell if God will turn and <u>repent</u>, and turn away
from his fierce anger, that we perish not?
                                        Jonah 3:9 KJV

And God saw their works, that they turned from their
evil way; and God <u>repented</u> of the evil, that he had said
that he would do unto them; and he did it not.
                                        Jonah 3:10 KJV

*And he prayed unto the LORD, and said, I pray thee,
O LORD, was not this my saying, when I was yet in my
country? Therefore I fled before unto Tarshish: for I knew
that thou art a gracious God, and merciful, slow to anger,
and of great kindness, and <u>repentest</u> thee of the evil.*
Jonah 4:2 KJV

*For thus saith the LORD of hosts; As I thought to punish
you, when your fathers provoked me to wrath, saith the
LORD of hosts, and I <u>repented</u> not:*
Zechariah 8:14 KJV

He didn't change his mind in this case, but by the very statement
of saying that he didn't proves that he could have.

Twenty-seven verses use the word "repent" referring to God
changing his mind about his plans. Two verses (the source of
one of these is questionable as to his divine inspiration) say
that he does not change his mind like a man does (which could
mean that he is not wishy-washy or does not do it on a whim).
The <u>overwhelming bulk of the evidence</u> of Scripture states that
God does change his mind when he wants to because of his
mercy and also because of his justice.

Let's say you are on a jury and twenty-seven witnesses were
presented who said that they saw a man commit murder, and
the defense presents two witnesses who say that he didn't. You
know that one of the witnesses is of questionable character
(Balaam), and the other is reliable but says he is only 90% sure,
how would you vote?

God has the prerogative and the freedom to change his mind.
"I will show mercy on whom I will show mercy." This means

that his decisions and their future consequences are not already determined.

The word we have looked at is the same Hebrew word that is translated as "repent" when it refers to men

> *And it came to pass, when Pharaoh had let the people go, that God led them not through the way of the land of the Philistines, although that was near; for God said, Lest peradventure the people <u>repent</u> when they see war, and they return to Egypt:* Exodus 13:17 KJV

> *Wherefore I abhor myself, and <u>repent</u> in dust and ashes.* Job 42:6 KJV

> *And let that man be as the cities which the LORD overthrew, and <u>repented</u> not: and let him hear the cry in the morning, and the shouting at noontide;* Jeremiah 20:16 KJV

The immutability of God means that his character, his virtue, his justice, his morals, his sovereignty, his power, etc. are forever the same. Just because he chooses to not control every detail of a man's life doesn't change his being. He remains immutable, but his omniscience of the future is limited by his very own design. He made the decision to delegate freedom to make choices to other living beings. This in no way threatens his sovereignty since it is his choice.

The future is in the hands of God, but what God does in the future depends to a significant degree on what you and I do in

212 GOD IS WITH US

the present. God initiates according to his plan, but then also acts in response to our decisions. This is seen over and over and over again in the Scriptures. The future is subject to God. God is not subject to the future. God is truly sovereign over all.

Conclusion

The biblical evidence is overwhelming that God does change his mind. Because of his mercy, he changes his plans to destroy people who do evil but who then repent, and because of his justice he changes his original plans and punishes people who turn to doing evil. No matter in which translation of the Bible, or in which language you look, you cannot legitimately say that the details of God's plans are all set in concrete and cannot be changed. God is not subject to our theology, and he changes his mind whenever he desires.

11. Foreknowledge, fore-ordination, omniscience and the sovereignty of God

To understand God and his plan for us, we should know his character and something of his attributes. What is he like? What is he trying to do? What are his plans and desires for human beings? If we are gravely mistaken about how God works and what he is doing, then we will have great difficulty fulfilling his will for us.

To believe that God already knows everything that will happen in the future is a serious error in the church because it cannot be supported by the Scriptures. As Evangelical Christians we pride ourselves on adhering strictly to the Bible, but in practice we are sometimes as bad or worse than the sects and cults we criticize for forcing their own interpretations on the Bible text. We approach the Bible with our pre–existing belief system and try to make the Bible agree with us. (This is called eisogesis – reading meaning into the text). We skip over passages that contradict our system; we even unwittingly alter words and meanings in new Bible translations because they conflict with our prior beliefs. This does great damage to the church and the work of God.

214 GOD IS WITH US

> *There is a great danger, when once we have adhered to one particular school of thought or adopted one particular system of theology, of reading the Bible in the light of that school or system and finding its distinctive features in what we read. One reader may tend to do less than justice to those texts which stress man's responsibility; another will be inclined to modify the force of those which emphasize God's eternal election. The remedy for this is to bear resolutely in mind that our systems of doctrine must be based on biblical exegesis, not imposed upon it.*

From the foreword of the book by Paul Marston and Roger Forster, *God's Strategy in Human History,* Millennium Edition 2000, by Wipf and Stock Publishers, Eugene, OR 97401

In this chapter and in Section Two, I will show that God does not have absolute foreknowledge of the future, and in some cases does not know in the present everything that is in the heart of men. I also am going to show that there is not one person in the Bible who believed in God's absolute foreknowledge. I will show you an overwhelming number of Bible texts that are all contrary to the theory of God's absolute foreknowledge of all things future.

> *Paul, in his letters, continually makes logical arguments, he assumes that his gospel makes sense and is consistent with the Old Testament which he knows to be inspired by God. Allowing blatant inconsistency in theology is not only wrong but dangerous, it can lead to all kinds of immoral or wrong behavior in the name of God.*
>
> Marston and Forster,
> Page 28

God has given us a sound mind and there is never any indication that he expected men to throw aside all reason in order to follow him. In philosophy, the first lesson they try to teach you is how to apply reason and logic. The most common example is:

Socrates is a man
All men are mortal
Socrates is mortal

If the first two statements are true, then logically we must conclude that the third is also true. Here are some more logical conclusions if God's foreknowledge of the future were absolute:

The future is perfectly known
What is perfectly known cannot be changed
The future cannot be changed

No one can change that which is perfectly known
One who can change nothing is powerless
God is powerless (impotent)

Obviously, most Christians or even believers in god from other religions would not agree with this conclusion, yet it is the logical conclusion if the future is already determined in every detail.

> *Without faith no one can please God. Whoever comes to God must believe that he is real and that <u>he rewards those who sincerely try to find him</u>.* Hebrews 11:6

If God could not change the future, how could he reward someone who seeks him? Our decisions and actions would have no consequence whatsoever in how the future turns out, or in what reward each of us would receive. If God already knows the future, then our rewards are already determined before the race begins.

The belief that the future is already fully known and therefore unchangeable is absurd both by biblical and rational standards. Though it is the most common belief of western evangelicals does not make it true due to its popularity. Other beliefs in the past have been popular but just as wrong. For example, the belief that the world was flat was almost universally accepted until the time of Columbus and even by many people for years after that. The Reformers like Luther, Calvin, and Zwingli were all born before the discovery of America and most likely were skeptics of the round earth "theory".

Also, before Galileo and Copernicus, nearly everyone, including the reformers believed that the sun and the stars revolved around the earth.

> "The geocentric model held sway into the early modern age, but from the late 16th century onward was gradually superseded by the heliocentric model of Copernicus (1473-1543), Galileo (1564-1642) and Kepler (1571-1630). However, the transition between these two theories met much resistance, not only from Christian theologians, who were reluctant to reject a theory that was in agreement with Bible passages (e.g. "Sun, stand you still upon Gibeon", Joshua 10:12 - KJV), but also from those who saw geocentrism as an accepted consensus that could not be subverted by a new, unknown theory."
>
> Wikipedia

Another very commonly practiced medical/scientific belief helped to kill George Washington. When he was very sick at the end of his life, three times the doctors removed some of his blood to "relieve" the pressure, and very soon thereafter, he died. Blood-letting was the most common medical practice performed by physicians from antiquity until the late nineteenth century, a span of almost 2,000 years. The practice has now been abandoned for all except a few very specific conditions. History shows that the popularity of a belief does not prove something to be true.

Therefore, common acceptance of a theological belief is not a guarantee of truth, and though the belief that God already knows all the future is very popular among evangelicals today, that is no good reason to blindly believe that it is true in a blatant disregard of the biblical evidence to the contrary.

The role of the prophet in the plan of God

Many people believe that the prophets were only foretellers of the future, but that was only a small part of their ministry. Most of the time they told the people what God was thinking, seeing and planning. God revealed his plans and intentions to his servants the prophets, and they told them to the people. Sometimes this involved revelations of things that only God could know about the present as well as what God said he would do in the future. Even the apostle John in the book of Revelation is not seeing into the future, but is seeing the revelation of the plans of God. John was not transported to the future to see what he saw. God revealed to him in the present what he is going to make happen in the future.

God doesn't say he knows the future and is declaring it to us: he says that he is making things happen according to his plan.

He is not a passive God who watches things unfold according to a script, but he is an active God who guides and shapes what happens in the future. As mentioned earlier, the deists believe that God made the universe and then went away, and is no longer in control of things. The "closed theist" who believes that the future is already known and therefore unchangeable is in the same category. In both cases, God would be unable to do anything to help us.

Jonah knew God very well. He knew that after announcing the destruction of Nineveh that it was probable that if they repented God would forgive them and not destroy them as he threatened. He hated the Assyrians, and didn't want God to forgive them, so he ran away to Joppa. He knew that his pronouncements were not telling the future. They were only revealing God's plans and that those plans could change.

Aaron was called Moses' prophet/spokesman, and is an example of what prophets do.

> The LORD said to Moses, "See how important I have made you? In speaking to Pharaoh, you will be like God, and your brother <u>Aaron will be your prophet. You will tell Aaron everything that I command you. Then he will tell the king what I say</u>. And Pharaoh will let the Israelites leave this country.　　　　Exodus 7:1-2

The meaning of "knowing" and "foreknowing"

Here is the definition of one Greek word to "know:
　　eido　　　　i'-do

A primary verb; used only in certain past tenses, the others being borrowed from other verbs; properly <u>to see</u> (literally or

figuratively); by implication (in the perfect only) _to know:_ –
be aware, behold, consider, (have) known (–ledge), look (on),
perceive, see, be sure, tell, understand. To gaze at, see, etc.

> *The people asked, "Where is your father?" Jesus answered,
> "You don't <u>know</u> me or my Father. But if you <u>knew</u> me, you
> would know my Father too."*   John 8:19

> *Your father Abraham was very happy that he would see
> the day when I came. He <u>saw</u> that day and was happy."*
>   John 8:56

The same Greek word translated "know" in the first reference is
translated "saw" in the second. Abraham did not "foresee" the
Lord's Day in the future, but he "knew" it when it happened.
Abraham was spiritually alive to see the birth of the Messiah.
To the Saducees, who did not believe in the resurrection, Jesus
said, *"I am the God of Abraham, Isaac, and Jacob. God is not
the God of the dead, but of the living"* (Matthew 22:31 - NIV).

> *His parents answered, "We <u>know</u> that this man is our
> son. And we <u>know</u> that he was born blind. But we <u>don't
> know</u> why he can see now. We <u>don't know</u> who healed his
> eyes. Ask him. He is old enough to answer for himself."*
>   John 9:20-21

The same Greek word is used to say that they knew he was their
son, as well as to say that they knew he was born blind. When
this word refers to a person, it means to "know personally with
certainty," as in having a personal relationship. In English, we
have the same rule with the word "know." When we refer to
a person, we mean a personal relationship. When we refer to a
thing, it means knowledge of some fact. "I know John Baker,"

versus "I know that he got home late last night." When you see the word "know" in the Bible, if it refers to a person, it means having a personal relationship with that person.

Sometimes, we might say "I know the mayor of our city," when we haven't really met him. What we are saying is that we know something about him, but do not have a personal relationship with him. The context of the statement tells us whether we are talking about a personal relationship or just some information.

The word "foreknew" is a word found in the Bible text in only two places (Romans 8:29, and Romans 11:2). The word "foreknowledge" also appears only twice, once in Acts 2:23 and in 1 Peter 1:2. These two words literally mean knowing <u>someone</u> beforehand. The text never says how long in the past this person was known, but only that it is previous to salvation. Supporters of God's absolute foreknowledge of all things say it means that <u>all things</u> (information) were known to God from eternity past. However, the Bible texts do not say such a thing, and three of the four references to "foreknew" or "foreknowledge" clearly refer to <u>knowing people</u> and not to knowing things. Foreknowledge means a prior relationship with another person. This is problematic for the doctrine of God's absolute foreknowledge of everything future because persons did not exist before their conception. If they did not exist as persons, God could not have had a personal, knowing relationship with them.

The meaning of the word "Foreknew" —
Greek: proginōskō   *prog-in-oce'-ko*
to *know beforehand,* that is, foresee: - foreknow (ordain), know (before), acquainted (before).

proegnō	acquainted-before
prognōsin	to-an-acquainting-before
prognōsei	unto-an-acquainting-before

> *For those whom He foreknew, He also predestined to become conformed to the image of His Son, so that He would be the firstborn among many brethren;*
>
> Romans 8:29 NASB

> *God has not rejected His people whom He foreknew. Or do you not know what the Scripture says in the passage about Elijah, how he pleads with God against Israel?*
>
> *Romans 11:2 NASB*

Both of these verses refer to knowing people and having a personal relationship with them. They are not about having knowledge of the future.

> *Peter, an apostle of Jesus Christ, To God's elect, strangers in the world, scattered throughout Pontus, Galatia, Cappadocia, Asia and Bithynia, who have been chosen according to the foreknowledge of God the Father, through the sanctifying work of the Spirit, for obedience to Jesus Christ and sprinkling by his blood:*
>
> 1 Peter 1:1-2 NIV

This reference also refers to knowing people and not to knowing something.

> *This man was handed over to you by God's set purpose and foreknowledge; and you, with the help of wicked men, put him to death by nailing him to the cross.*
>
> *Acts 2:23 NIV*

This second use of the word "foreknowledge" seems to say that it refers to knowing some "thing" instead of knowing people. However, the "foreknowledge" could refer to the people to whom Christ was handed over. He knew what was in the hearts of the people God handed him over to and that they would put Christ to death because of it. Also, to use the terms "purpose" and "foreknowledge" in the same sentence to describe the same event seems superfluous. A <u>purpose</u> defines what someone intends to do whereas a <u>foreknowledge</u> implies that it is already known. Purpose indicates a work in progress. Foreknowledge of a thing would indicate a work already done.

As used in the Bible, foreknowledge means having a personal relationship prior to some secondary event. God knew us personally before making us his sons, declaring us righteous, predestining us to become like Jesus, giving us an inheritance, and preparing a place for us in Heaven.

Open Theology

In recent years, a school of theology that is often referred to as "Open Theism" has become better known. It basically says that God does not know all of the future, and that some of it will be decided by what choices a man makes in his life. This is not a new theology, but somewhat of a revival of the old theology of the early church. The spokesmen for this branch of theology have been bitterly attacked by the proponents of absolute foreknowledge. "Open theists" have been branded heretics, false teachers and other derogatory terms, and have been shunned by many in the Evangelical community. But heresy is not defined by whether or not I agree with you: it is defined by whether or not I agree with God and the Bible. Those branded as heretics and rebels are in good company because that's the way the Israelites treated the prophets of old, the Pharisees treated Jesus and his disciples, and the way the Catholic Church treated the Reformers and their predecessors. God's servants have not often enjoyed the favor of the religious leaders or of the masses.

I confess that the more I study the Scriptures, the more I am happy to be called an "open theist." I'm open to learning the truth. I'm open to God's acting in my life. I'm open to receiving guidance from the Almighty. I would much rather be an "open theist" than a "closed theist" who believes that the future is already set in concrete and can't be changed, even by God.

While there may be some differences in the details, supporters of "open theism" can roughly be divided into two groups.

The first one claims that while the future is knowable by God, he <u>voluntarily limits</u> his knowledge of the future so that free will choices can remain truly free.

The second group believes that since the future hasn't happened yet, it is not knowable . . . even by God. They hold that if God were to know what we are going to choose whenever we make a choice, we could not choose to do something other than what is 'known' by God, thus we would not be truly free, but bound to fulfill the future that God already knows.

I am happy to fall in the latter group. I believe that the future is still a work in progress and although the skeleton for the future is already decided by God, the flesh is still growing on the bones.

Foreordination

Foreordination means to "fix the horizons", or to "set the limits" (from the Greek *pro·o·rizo* - from pro, before, and *ho·rizo*, mark out or set the bounds). The pages of Scripture are heavy with examples of God telling people what his future purpose and intentions are and what he plans to make happen. The most outstanding example being, of course, the birth, life and death of Jesus about which there were over 300 prophecies.

The primary emphasis in the Scriptures is on God "doing," not on his "knowing."

> *Remember what happened long ago. Remember, I am God and there is no other God. There is no other like me. "In the beginning, I told you what would happen in the end. A long time ago, I told you things that have not happened yet. When I plan something, it happens. I do whatever I want to do.*   Isaiah 46:9-10

> *"Long ago I told you what would happen. I told you about these things. And suddenly I made them happen.*   Isaiah 48:3

> *Listen to what the LORD has planned to do to Babylon. Listen to what he has decided to do to the Babylonians. "I promise that an enemy will drag away the young kids of Babylon's flock, and Babylon will become an empty pasture.*   Jeremiah 50:45

There is no hint here in any of these statements that God is revealing what he sees is going to happen in the future. They clearly state that he is going to do what he has decided.

> *These people who came together against Jesus made*
> *your plan happen. It was done because of your power*
> *and your will.* Acts 4:28

We see in this passage both God's plan and determination (foreordination). Many people equate foreordination with foreknowledge, thinking that when God says something will happen it is because he already knows it. However, the words are by no means the same, and there is a vast distinction between knowing something will happen and being able to make it happen. A prophet might be able to tell you what is going to happen, but only someone who has power and authority can make it happen. Only someone with the power to change what will happen can be considered sovereign. If the future is already known by God, it is as if it has already happened and even God could not make it any different.

Omniscience

Omniscience is a word that theologians (those who study God) came up with to describe God, but it is not found in the Bible. The Bible reveals God as knowing everything in the past and most things in the present. It does not say that he knows everything in the future or every decision that man is going to make. Contrary to common belief, there are a number of biblical cases in which God did not know in the present everything about the heart of a person. He had to test them to find it out. Therefore, according to the Bible, God does not know everything in the present time. God is not shown to be 100% omniscient when it concerns what is in the heart of a man. Here are two of many examples:

> *It was Hezekiah who stopped up the upper source of the waters of the Gihon Spring in Jerusalem and made the waters flow straight down on the west side of the City of David. And he was successful in everything he did. One time the leaders of Babylon sent messengers to Hezekiah. The messengers asked about a strange sign that had happened in the nations. When they came, <u>God left Hezekiah alone to test him and to know everything that was in Hezekiah's heart</u>.*   2 Chronicles 32:30-31

> (God speaking to Abraham)*"Do not lay a hand on the boy," he said. "Do not do anything to him. <u>Now I know that you fear God, because you have not withheld from me your son, your only son</u>."*   Genesis 22:12 NIV

God found out by testing Abraham what he did not know for sure before. The idea that God doesn't know every detail of everything, past, present and future is unimaginable to some people. But it is what the Scriptures say even if we try to explain these passages by saying that God already knew it, but he wanted Hezekiah and Abraham to know. If we asked a sixth grader to read these statements and tell us what they meant, he would come to the same conclusions that I do. It often helps to read the Bible as though we only had a sixth grade education.

As I said earlier, to prove the omniscience of God, we must prove that he knows all things, or at least a great multitude of things. To disprove it, I only need to prove that there is one thing he does not know. If I look at a house and say "That house is red," that is no proof that I know the color of all the other houses in the neighborhood. It only proves that I know the color of the particular house to which I am referring. Just because God reveals that he knows something that will happen in the future is no proof that he knows everything that will happen.

God is absolutely sovereign. He does what he desires and is only limited by his own nature. For instance, he cannot sin, he cannot be impure, he cannot stop loving, he cannot stop being good, he cannot change from being who and what he is. God has no power to change his own nature, nor would he ever have a desire to do so. There is no conflict in his intentions or in his morality. God cannot make a rock so big he cannot lift it because he is not stupid.

People fear that if God does not know all the future, that it would diminish God, but that is not true. If God, in his freewill and sovereignty chooses to leave some of the future open to men's choices, it shows his greatness, and is not a weakness. God is very secure: he is not afraid to allow his creation to have some freedom to make choices. Closed theists would dictate to God what he can and cannot do.

What is Sovereignty?

The dictionary says: *jurisdiction, rule, supremacy, dominion, power. Synonyms are: ascendency, hegemony, domination, authority, control, influence.*

This means that someone or some state that is sovereign has authority and responsibility for whatever it is sovereign over. Unfortunately, religion has redefined the word to mean that God <u>controls</u> every little detail of everything that ever happens. According to religion's definition, nothing can happen but what he causes. That is a very errant idea of what biblical sovereignty

228 GOD IS WITH US

is supposed to mean. God doesn't have to control what I have for lunch in order to be sovereign over his creation.

If a sovereign government decides to grant certain freedoms to departments in its territory, it doesn't lose its sovereignty by doing so. It loses some control, but control and sovereignty are not the same thing. God is not a control freak. He doesn't want or need to insert his influence into every little decision or event within his creation. He does not become less sovereign by allowing his creatures to make some of their own decisions. He is sovereign even though Satan rebelled and has caused terrible destruction within God's handiwork. God is not the author of evil, but he is still responsible over the world in which evil works, and that is why there is going to be a judgment day and appropriate measures taken to destroy the evil and the evil ones. The judge will have the final say and will exert his sovereign will over his creatures.

God made man in his image and gave him a free will just like he himself has

The fishing tackle box — Let's suppose I have a ten-year old son, and I decide to buy him a fishing tackle box and a whole assortment of hooks and lures and fishing tackle to put into it. I give him all of the stuff, but I don't tell him how to put it in the box. I know that he can't put the rolls of line or the bobbers in the very little compartments on the top drawers, so I have some idea of how he might arrange his tackle. But, I don't know, nor do I have a desire to control, how he will arrange his tackle. He can put his selection of hooks, sinkers, lures, swivels, etc. in whatever compartment he wishes. (Women – perhaps the example of a large sewing basket and all the spools of thread, pins, needles, buttons, etc. will serve you better).

God knows all of the compartments and layers and he knows what we have to put into the compartments, but he doesn't know how we are going to do it. He has, <u>by his own volition and sovereignty</u>, left that for us to determine.

We have all known of autocratic dads and moms who want to control everything their child does (I pity you if that's the way your parents were or are). The child grows up never being able to make decisions on his own. For a child to mature and learn to function in our world, he must be given graduated freedom to make his own choices. God is not an autocratic father who believes that it is necessary for him to control every decision we will ever make. He is a loving, trusting Father who will help us every time we need help, but won't impose his will upon our lives. Giving man the power to make a genuine, independent choice does not diminish God's control over his universe.

God respects man's freedom to make choices

There are two other matters of vital importance in relation to man's salvation which God cannot do: he cannot force anyone to love him; and he cannot force anyone to accept a gift. By the very nature of love and giving, man must have the power to choose. The reception of God's love and of the gift of salvation through Jesus Christ can only be by an act of man's free will.

Giving man the power to make a genuine, independent choice does not diminish God's control over his universe. Being omnipotent and omniscient, God certainly could so arrange circumstances as to keep man's rebellion from frustrating his purposes. In fact, God could even use man's free will to help fulfill his own plans and thereby be even more glorified.

God's grand design from the foundation of the world to bestow upon man the gift of his love precludes any ability to force that gift upon any of his creatures. Both love and gifts of any kind must be received. Force perverts the transaction.

It is the power of genuine choice from man's own heart and will which God has sovereignly given him that enables God to love man and for man to receive that love and to love God in return "because he first loved us" (1 John 4:19). It is impossible that the power of choice could challenge God's sovereignty since it is God's sovereignty which has bestowed this gift upon man and set the conditions for both loving and giving.

Dave Hunt, The Berean Call, Feb 1, 2001

Some believe that in order to be God he must control everything, or else he would be in danger of losing his place. Part of the essence of sin is that we want to control everything, and we think that God must be like that also. The argument that God's not foreknowing all future events and circumstances in full detail would evidence imperfection and weakness on his part is a view of perfection from man's viewpoint. Perfection, correctly defined, does not demand such an absolute, all-embracing conclusion. Perfection in the ultimate analysis is equal to what and who God is.

If indeed God knows every choice I am going to make, I would rather find out about it at the end of my earthly life than to live believing that my life is purposeless and without any meaning whatsoever. I am a much happier person believing that my prayers make a difference in the future and that God really is at my side working with me and helping me to live a life pleasing to him. If he already knows what I will do, than no matter what I try to do, it won't make any difference. So, let me enjoy the moment of believing that I am important to God and that I really am made in his image. Man could not truly have been created in "God's image" if he did not have some moral freedom.

> And there is <u>no creature hidden from His sight</u>, but all things are open and laid <u>bare to the eyes of Him</u> with whom we have to do. Hebrews 4:13 NASB

Our feelings and thoughts were not created by God. That is why he often needs to search a man's heart to find out what is in it. God would have no need to <u>see</u> anything if he already knew everything.

Since it does not fit into human reasoning to believe that 1) man has a free choice, and yet 2) God already knows what it is, we invent unreasonable explanations like "it is like two parallel railroad tracks that never seem to meet, but will eventually meet in eternity:" or that there is a sign on the gate of Heaven that says, "Whosoever will may come," but once we enter and look back, the sign reads "You have not chosen me, but I have chosen you." God has the power and freedom to do whatever he likes because he is God and is in the driver's seat. But, when he has clearly revealed a truth about himself over and over and over again throughout the Scriptures, we should not twist our logic into banana pudding to deny it.

The reason the two theological rails of "predestination" and "free-will" don't meet is because they are logically incompatible. We were taught over and over in science classes that if you have two theories that defy reconciliation, look for the one that is false. Don't pretend that they are both correct.

With the example of the two sides of the sign at Heaven's gate, the Bible says a multitude of times that salvation is open to "whosoever will." The supposed statement on the other side is something that Jesus said to the disciples, not to the church in general; "I have chosen you." He never said this to the crowds or to believers other than the twelve chosen disciples. And even one of these "chosen" ones was a devil who never made it to Heaven to see the other side of the sign.

Besides, God has not told us what is on the other side of the sign: he has only revealed what is written on this side. Which side of the sign is uncertain? - the one in which we guess what is written there, or the one where he has told us again and again that "Whosoever will may come?" He doesn't need us to be "guessing" about what is written on the other side. We must trust that the Divine Revealer knows what he is doing and that he really is as he reveals himself to be.

In the Lord's Prayer, Jesus teaches his disciples to pray, "Your will be done." Why should we bother to ask for this? In the first place, if the future is already known, then God can't do anything that is not already limited by his knowledge. Second, is God's will not always done? Apparently, it is not; he doesn't always get his preferred way with people. What he desires for people is not what they always do.

God has a desire for people that is often not fulfilled. If that is so, it means that he is disappointed when we make wrong choices, and delighted when we make right ones. He is not an unfeeling, distant, unconcerned person, but one of compassion, love, patience, and pity. He is a feeling Father, and identifies with our struggles, but doesn't control everything we do.

Jesus is a feeling Savior who understands what we are going through because he went through it himself. *For this reason he had to be made like his brothers in every way, in order that he might become a merciful and faithful high priest in service to God, and that he might make atonement for the sins of the people. Because he himself suffered when he was tempted, he is able to help those who are being tempted* (Hebrews 2:17-18 NIV). *For we do not have a high priest who is unable to sympathize with our weaknesses, but we have one who has been tempted in every way, just as we are—yet was without sin* (Hebrews 4:15 NIV).

Jesus is not like the person who comes to visit us in the hospital and repeatedly says, "Oh, I know how you feel," even though they have never had an operation nor even been in the hospital. Jesus and the Father share our feelings and emotions. They know what it is like to love, be angry, rejoice, be sad, and walk in our moccasins. They live our lives with us like a tender, loving Father who knows the needs of his little child.

God is not a cruel teaser, who offers something without there being any possibility of it ever happening. That would be a God made in the image of evil man. But Jesus said that even man was morally better than doing something like that. If sincere people ask God for things which are good for them, he will delight in giving them. If God offers us a fish we can be sure that having the fish is possible, and is not some kind of scam.

It became very common in recent years for scammers to send out emails to unsuspecting people telling them that they could get millions of dollars if they would help move some money from one place to another. I had a friend in Uruguay who got sucked in and borrowed money (in one case from the church offerings and without permission) so that he could travel to Europe and get a share of all these millions. He never got his money back (or the church's either). I used to receive these kinds of scams almost every day through my email address (usually from Nigeria or some other questionable country). They made great promises, but had no intention of delivering the goods.

God is not like that. If he makes a promise, or gives us a choice, it is because it is legitimate. Our choice is not already known or decided, but the outcome depends on what we choose, and our choice will help determine the future. God is neither a cruel tyrant nor a scam artist who offers things which we can never have.

12. What is predestination?

I believe in predestination, but not the way most people understand it. The word as used in the Bible has nothing whatsoever to do with the identity of who will be saved. It has to do with what happens to those who do get saved. The words <u>predestination</u> or <u>predestinate</u> appear six times in Greek in the Bible.

proorizo   *pro-or-id'-zo*
to *limit in advance,* that is, (figuratively) *predetermine:* - determine before, ordain, predestinate.

> 1. Uses 1-2. *And we know that in all things God works for the good of those who love him, who have been called according to his purpose. For those God foreknew he also <u>predestined</u> to be conformed to the likeness of his Son, that he might be the firstborn among many brothers. And those he <u>predestined</u>, he also called; those he called, he also justified; those he justified, he also glorified.*
>
> Romans 8:28-30 NIV

All those whom God "foreknew" were then predestined to become like Jesus. Everything in this verse depends on the statement that God <u>knew</u> certain persons beforehand. This text does not reveal how long beforehand he knew them. It could be a few days, a few years, or an eternity, but no one can legitimately use this text to build a case for some people being saved and others not from before time began.

> 3. *Praise be to the God and Father of our Lord Jesus Christ, who has blessed us in the heavenly realms with every spiritual blessing <u>in Christ</u>. For he chose us <u>in him</u> before the creation of the world to be holy and blameless in his sight. In love he <u>predestined</u> us to be adopted as his sons <u>through</u> Jesus Christ, in accordance with his pleasure and will–to the praise of his glorious grace, which he has freely given us <u>in the One</u> he loves.*
>
> Ephesians 1:3-6 NIV

Again, predestination is subsequent to being "in Christ." If someone is not in Christ, he is predestined for the wrath of God. Adoption does not mean being made his child, but rather coming of age as his child, and receiving the rights and responsibilities as sons. All those who come into Christ through faith will receive all these benefits of being associated with him. Salvation is a group experience — it has to do with being in Christ, the salvation vessel.

> 4. *<u>In him</u> we were also chosen, having been <u>predestined</u> according to the plan of him who works out everything in conformity with the purpose of his will, in order that we, who were the first to <u>hope in Christ</u>, might be for the praise of his glory. And you also were <u>included in Christ</u> when you heard the word of truth, the gospel of*

> *your salvation. Having believed, you were <u>marked in him</u> with a seal, the promised Holy Spirit, who is a deposit guaranteeing our inheritance until the redemption of those who are God's possession—to the praise of his glory.*
>
> Ephesians 1:11-14 NIV

This passage is about what happens to those who have come to believe in Christ. It says nothing whatsoever about individuals having been chosen beforehand. The emphasis is on Christ and all those who come to believe in him. Being in Christ depends on believing that he is God's eternal Son and man's Savior. We are predestined to be *for the praise of his glory.*

> 5. *In fact, this has happened here in this very city! For Herod Antipas, Pontius Pilate the governor, the Gentiles, and the people of Israel were all united against Jesus, Your holy servant, whom You anointed. But everything they did <u>was determined beforehand</u> according to Your will.*
>
> Acts 4:27-28 NLT

This is speaking about the plan of God and how he would sacrifice his Son Jesus to be the payment for all sinners who believe in him. Again, it says nothing whatsoever about which individuals will be saved.

> 6. *We teach wisdom to people who are mature, but the wisdom we teach is not from this world. It is not the wisdom of the rulers of this world, who are losing their power. But we speak God's secret wisdom that has been hidden from everyone until now. God planned this wisdom for our glory. <u>He planned it before the world began</u>.*
>
> 1 Corinthians 2:6-7

This is saying that God had a plan to save sinful human beings even before time began and even before creation. This says nothing whatsoever about the personal identity of those people.

Like salvation in the flood, spiritual salvation is a group experience. All those who belong to Christ and have been placed in him will be saved, will become like Jesus, and will receive his glory. Getting into this group depends on believing in Christ as God's anointed Messiah. We must enter by the door which is Jesus. The biblical use of the word "predestination" says nothing whatsoever about <u>who</u> will be saved. It shows only what is in store for those who are saved.

13. Does time affect God?

Some theologians say that time only exists on earth and within God's creation, and that therefore there is no time in Heaven and God is not affected by time. They often quote the verse:

> *But don't forget this one thing, dear friends: <u>To the Lord a day is like a thousand years, and a thousand years is like a day</u>. The Lord is not being slow in doing what he promised–the way some people understand slowness. But God is being patient with you. He doesn't want anyone to be lost. He wants everyone to change their ways and stop sinning.* 2 Peter 3:8-9

However, this refers to the relativity of time, and not whether God is affected by it or not. Also, as mentioned in Chapter 5, it refers to God's patience for the salvation of men. The Scriptures do make it clear that time *as we know it* did not exist before creation:

> *No, we speak of God's secret wisdom, a wisdom that has been hidden and that God destined for our glory <u>before time began</u>.* 1 Corinthians 2:7 NIV

So never be ashamed to tell others about our Lord. And don't be ashamed of me, either, even though I'm in prison for Him. With the strength God gives you, be ready to suffer with me for the sake of the Good News. For God saved us and called us to live a holy life. He did this, not because we deserved it, but because that was His plan <u>from before the beginning of time</u>—to show us His grace through Christ Jesus. And now He has made all of this plain to us by the appearing of Christ Jesus, our Savior. He broke the power of death and illuminated the way to life and immortality through the Good News.

2 Timothy 1:8-10 NLT

Greetings from Paul, a servant of God and an apostle of Jesus Christ. I was sent to help God's chosen people have faith and understand the truth that produces a life of devotion to God. This faith and knowledge make us sure that we have eternal life. God promised that life to us <u>before time began</u>—and God does not lie. At the right time, God let the world know about that life. He did this through the telling of the Good News message, and he trusted me with that work. I told people that message because God our Savior commanded me to.

Titus 1:1-3

Our "time" began at creation when God created the heavens and the earth, and the lights to rule the day and the night. At that point, days of twenty-four hours and years of approximately 365 days were instituted.

Since time *as we know it* is a creation of God, that does not mean that some form of time does not exist in Heaven. Throughout the Bible, we see a progression of events that God is superintending.

In the book of Revelation we see a chronology of events that occur in order (though the book itself is not always chronological). God is working toward a final product in the forming of his family and the revealing of his sons. The new earth will be made after the old earth is burned up. God's Son became a man in "the fullness of time," and not necessarily referring to time in this world. The New Jerusalem does not appear before the Old Jerusalem has gone by the wayside. The New Covenant is not given before the Old. The saints under the altar of God in Heaven cry out "How long, how long o Lord?" The rewards and punishment of men and angels are dealt out after the deeds of the people are done.

God has an order and a time-table that we cannot fully comprehend. But to say that there is not "some form of time" in Heaven, and therefore the past, present and future are all the same to God has no scriptural support. The whole Bible reveals a progression toward fulfillment of God's plans and to say otherwise is not good scholarship.

> I make known the end from the beginning, from ancient times, what is still to come. I say: My purpose will stand, and I will do all that I please.   Isaiah 46:10 NIV

Ancient times is not only referring to time when God worked with his creation, but even before creation. God states that there is an end and a beginning and that they are not the same.

God doesn't say that he sees the end of a thing from the beginning, but that he declares it. The emphasis is not on his knowledge, but on his power to do what he desires.

> The first century philosopher Philo, as far as we know, first expounded the idea that, since time is only known

through movement in space, God created time along with the physical universe. Though Philo was a devout Jew, this really arose in development of his Platonic ideas. The idea, adopted by Augustine, Boethius, and fairly standard western theology, involved a sophisticated philosophical notion of time, and also became associated with the idea that God was "timeless".

Marston and Forster Page 249

The Bible reveals a time table, not of twenty-four hours, but of the ordering of events. There is some kind of time with God. Every day is not the same, and there is a progression toward a final end. So, with God the past, present and future are not all the same as some would argue. God is not timeless, but has a plan and a purpose that he is fulfilling. God is looking forward to the exaltation of Christ, the revealing of the sons of God, the Royal Wedding, the Marriage Supper of the Lamb, the creation of the new heavens and the new earth, and living with his family forever in the New Jerusalem.

Also, if there were not a progression in the plans and the work of God, all creation would have already existed and he would not have needed to create anything. He rested on the seventh day because his creative work was a finished act. The past, present, and future all exist apart from each other and God does not move willy–nilly back and forth between them.

14. The problem of the origin of evil

No matter what school of theology you adhere to, you should, of necessity, be able to give a reasonable explanation for the origin of evil that exists in our world.

If you believe in God's absolute foreknowledge of all things future, and believe that he has absolute control over every minute element within his creation, then logically he must be the Creator of evil since it could not have come from any other source.

If on the other hand you believe that God, in his sovereignty gives freedom for angels and for men to choose to obey him or not, then he is not the author of evil. By making angels and men in his own image (though the Bible does not state this about angels – we only conclude this from the fact that some rebelled and some didn't which reveals that they have wills like God does), he of necessity gives them the freedom to make choices. God never made these evil choices, but for his creatures to be free like he is, they had to have the freedom to be like him or be something different. This freedom resulted in the devil's rebellion, the mutiny of one–third of the angels, and the fall of Adam and Eve who then passed their perverted nature on to all their descendents. God did not desire this and was deeply saddened that it happened, but it was a possible consequence of creating these creatures with intellect, emotion and will.

Post–Augustinian theology

In "theological fatalism" or "closed theology," there can be no variants to what is already known about the future. That means that according to this theology, when God began to create (he created the angels before creating earth and humans), he could only create according to what he knew would happen. This means that when he created the world, he of necessity created evil. He created Satan knowing that he would rebel and cause tremendous destruction to God's creation. If he already knew the future, he was powerless to do anything other than create evil. In this theological view, God's sovereignty means absolute control of every detail. The proponents believe that if God surrenders control of even one element, he is no longer sovereign. But as seen earlier this interpretation of sovereignty is not based on biblical revelation, but on man's own imagination of what God should be like.

Pre–Augustinian theology

In what is usually called "open theology" (and I prefer to call literal theology), God took some chances in creation. In order to achieve his desire and purpose of making children in his own image, he had to create beings, both angelic and human, that could make choices that he did not control. He knew this was an "experiment" where he could not assure every outcome, but one that he would not let get out of control. He knew that individual elements could go towards rebellion and destruction or towards obedience and wholeness. But, there was no other way to achieve his purposes than to permit this to happen. He did not cause any of the elements to turn evil: he just gave them the freedom to do so, as well as the freedom to make right choices. In this theological view, he is not the author of evil as he must be in "closed theology."

By giving freedom to these created beings he did not surrender his sovereignty: he still held the process in his hand. It takes a greater, more secure God to invest certain freedom in his creatures, than a god who needs to control every little detail within his creation.

Examples of God's control versus man's freedom

God's control over his creatures can be illustrated by a dog on a leash

The dog walker permits the dog certain freedom to walk where he wants, to do his business on somebody else's lawn, etc., but he never lets go of the leash. The dog has limited freedom, but the dog walker has ultimate control.

It can also be illustrated by a horse in a large fenced-in pasture

A horse inside the fence has a lot of freedom. He can sleep under the trees, drink water from the stream, run and romp across the pasture, get close to the fence, or eat grass in any place within the limits. The one thing he cannot do is get outside the fence. He is restricted by a stronger power that limits his freedom.

Another example is fish in an aquarium

Some time back, we went with our son and his step-son to the Baltimore aquarium and were very impressed with the multitudes of fish and other creatures they have there. The building is huge and there are many separate tanks and cages in many different shapes. All of the fish, turtles, sharks, crustaceans, birds, etc. have limited freedom, but they are all trapped inside their tank or their cage. They can act mean and treat other creatures in an evil way, or be docile and kind; they can swim or fly to the top or the bottom, or to the right or the left, or hide under the coral or the brush. They can go about their business most anyway they want, but they are in a controlled and limited environment.

In the "closed theology" view, these creatures are not only trapped in the tank, but they are trapped in a video presentation where they have no choices whatsoever of where they will swim or how they will act. Their actions are predetermined because the video has already been filmed. For absolute control, the aquarium keepers could superglue the fish to the inside of the aquarium glass, but they wouldn't be much fun to watch. God hasn't super–glued us to his absolute foreknowledge of the future, but allows us to interact with him to determine how our future is going to turn out.

God's control/sovereignty is a lot more complicated than these simple examples, but this helps us understand how both free will and sovereign control can exist at the same time and not be mutually exclusive.

Man is trapped in time and in a contained environment, but that does not mean that he does not have freedom to make choices. Based on those choices, God will reward or punish every action at the proper time. A whole thread runs through the Bible from cover to cover telling us that God will reward each man according to his works (Psalm 62:12, Proverbs 19:17, Matthew 6:4, 6:6, 6:18, 16:27, 25:21, Revelation 22:12). What purpose could these Scriptures have if man had no choices to make?

God did not create evil people or evil deeds. God is everything good and there is no evil in him whatsoever. When he finished his creation he said over and over again, "It is good." There was no evil in it when he made it, but the possibility of rebellion existed because there was no other way to make free agents. Living with robots and computers is not very emotionally rewarding, and God wanted children and other beings who could relate to him as a person, and not as a thing.

We have some nice furniture in our house, and I spend lots of time in bed or on the couch or at the table, but I don't ask advice of, or give opinions to, or talk to the furniture. They are inanimate objects with no soul, no life of their own. We do have a cat, and we do talk to her and have a limited relationship with her. However, I cannot relate to her like I do with my wife, or like I did with my kids when they were still at home. There is no comparison between relating to inanimate objects like my computer, and to a live, breathing human being.

God wanted children like himself, whom he could "know" as people and interact with. You can't laugh or cry or have a great time with a desk lamp, or a tree, or a grain of sand. You can appreciate their beauty and functionality, but you can't have a give and take on a personal level. There are tree–huggers, but if that's all they hug they are very lonely people.

Conclusion

God wanted people whom he could hug, and lavish his gifts on. He wanted one big happy family to inhabit the mansion he was planning to build, where there would be laughter and rejoicing in abundance. He didn't create evil, but it was a by–product of creating creatures with so much freedom that they could make wrong choices as well as right ones.

15. Examining the "proof texts" used to support belief in the absolute foreknowledge of God

Following are most of the biblical texts that supporters of absolute foreknowledge use to support their belief. Let's look at them one by one and see if they prove this doctrine:

The most often cited passage to support God's foreknowledge is Psalm 139. Let's analyze the significant references and see what they teach:

> O LORD, you have <u>searched</u> me and you know me.
> Psalm 139:1 NIV

Some interpret this to mean that he knows all about me, including my future. However, the reason God knows us is that he has searched our hearts. There is no evidence here that he knew us before the search began. So, his knowing us is not foreknowledge, but knowledge discovered as he examined us.

> You know when I sit and when I rise; you <u>perceive</u> my thoughts from afar.
> Psalm 139:2 NIV

This doesn't say that he knows when we would sit or rise ahead of time, but learns it in the present by his observation. He <u>sees</u> my thoughts as I think them, not a millennium ago. He is attentive to our actions and our thoughts as they occur.

> *You <u>discern</u> my going out and my lying down; you are familiar with all my ways.*   Psalm 139:3 NIV

There is nothing here about foreknowledge, but rather it emphasizes his constant observation and examination of our lives.

> *Before a word is on my tongue you know it completely, O LORD.*   Psalm 139:4 NIV

This verse is one of the most commonly quoted ones used to prove his omniscience of the future. However, it proves nothing of the kind. The meaning here is that God knows us so intimately that he knows the thoughts in our minds before they can ever get to our lips. It is no sure evidence for saying that he knew our words yesterday or from eternity.

> *For you created my inmost being; you knit me together in my mother's womb.*   Psalm 139:13 NIV

The emphasis is on what God did for me while in the womb, not from any time previous to that.

> *My frame was not hidden from you when I was made in the secret place. When I was woven together in the depths of the earth, your eyes saw my unformed body. <u>All the days</u> ordained for me were written in your book before one of them came to be.*   Psalm 139:15-16 NIV

Experts say that a study of this text in Hebrew shows that this translation is problematic at best. It refers to "future <u>things</u>," but not to <u>days</u> of our life. The text is talking about the creation of the body in the womb, not about the length of life of the person. A much better translation says "all the <u>members</u> ordained for me were written in your book before my body was made." This is the interpretation in several significant translations:

> *Thine eyes did see my substance, yet being unperfect; and in thy book all my members were written, which in continuance were fashioned, when as yet there was none of them.* KJV

> *Thine eyes did see my substance yet being imperfect; and in thy book all my members were written, which were then formed, without lacking one of them.* Jubilee Bible

From the time the sperm and the egg united, God knew how the body would turn out *(your eyes saw my unformed body)*. In the day this was written, it was hard to fathom, but in our day of genes and DNA, it is not difficult at all. To switch subjects in mid–stream from "body parts" to "days" is incoherent either in Hebrew or English. To say that this passage unequivocally states that all the <u>days</u> of our lives were already determined is a very slender, fragile thread on which to hang such a significant doctrine.

> *The LORD clearly sees everything you do. He <u>watches</u> where you go.* Proverbs 5:21

Closed theists understand this to mean that God knows ahead of time all the steps in a man's path. But, if he already knew everything there is to know, why would he need to watch a man? This does not prove foreknowledge, but goes against it.

252 GOD IS WITH US

> *In the beginning, I told you what would happen in the*
> *end. A long time ago, I told you things that have not*
> *happened yet. When I plan something, it happens. I do*
> *whatever I want to do.*   Isaiah 46:10

The emphasis here is on God accomplishing his plans. He is stating that he will not be thwarted in fulfilling all that he intends to do and what he has said he will do. This statement is not a passive declaration about God's knowledge of the future, but one that says that God is the main mover behind all that happens in the future. If God already knew the future, he would say, "Everything will turn out as it has been destined to happen."

This very clearly refers, not to what God knows, but to what he does. He can declare what is going to happen because he is going to make it happen. If he were only declaring his knowledge of the future, then he could not do all that he pleases to do. His own will and freedom to work would be limited by his own predetermined knowledge. He does not say, "I have done all that I please", but rather "I do whatever I want to do." So, the future is not already done but God still has the power to determine the future.

> *"I knew you before I formed you in your mother's womb.*
> *Before you were born I set you apart and appointed you*
> *as My prophet to the nations."*   Jeremiah 1:5 NLT

"Before being formed in the womb" does not unequivocally mean known from eternity. It only means "former to growing" in the womb. Today, we understand a lot more about how a baby is formed. An egg and a sperm interact and a person is conceived. That fertilized egg begins to make its way down the Fallopian tube towards the womb. There is plenty of time for God to know the heart and per-sonality of this miniscule human being before it gets to the womb and starts to grow into the body it will be at birth. "Before getting to the womb, I already knew you"

This is also a statement about Jeremiah, not about the whole world. A likely meaning of this is that God knew Jeremiah and his personality from the moment of conception, and he liked what he saw so he chose him as a prophet. God had his own reasons for choosing Jeremiah, but there is nothing said here to show that this choosing was before Jeremiah's conception.

> *"No one knows when that day or time will be. The Son and the angels in heaven don't know when it will be. Only the Father knows.*   Matthew 24:36

This certainly proves that Christ was not omniscient in his human body. But also, just because the Father knows the day and hour of the Lord's return, does not prove that he knows or wants to know every detail of our future lives.

> *Jesus was handed over to you, and you killed him. With the help of evil men, you nailed him to a cross. But God knew all this would happen. It was his plan—a plan he made long ago.*   Acts 2:23

It was God's plan since before the foundation of the world to make a savior for the human race. Just because God had foreknowledge of this plan and event does not prove that he has or wants to have foreknowledge of every detail of the future.

> *As it is written: "I have made you a father of many nations." He is our father in the sight of God, in whom*

> *he believed–the God who <u>gives</u> life to the dead and <u>calls</u>*
> *things that are not as though they were.*
>
> Romans 4:17 NIV

This verse shows that it is God who makes these things happen.
He doesn't <u>reveal what has already existed</u>, but makes them
come into being. He is not a passive observer of things, but an
active creator.

> <u>*In Christ*</u>*, he chose us before the world was made. He*
> *chose us in love to be his holy people–people who could*
> *stand before him without any fault. And before the world*
> *was made, God decided to make us his own children*
> <u>*through*</u> *Jesus Christ. This was what God wanted, and*
> *it pleased him to do it.*   Ephesians 1:4-5

This verse tells of the wonderful plan of God for all of those who
trust him and come into Christ. It does not refer to salvation
or what is mistakenly called "predestination," but to what is
going to happen to those who believe.

> *Nothing in all the world can be hidden from God. He can*
> *clearly see all things. Everything is open before him. And*
> *to him we must explain the way we have lived.*
>
> Hebrews 4:13

This is a verse that really conflicts with absolute foreknowledge
because it says that God is presently watching us and based on
what he finds will hold us to account.

> *Peter, an apostle of Jesus Christ, To God's elect, strangers*
> *in the world, scattered throughout Pontus, Galatia,*
> *Cappadocia, Asia and Bithynia, who have been chosen*

> *according to <u>the foreknowledge of God the Father</u>,*
> *through the sanctifying work of the Spirit, for obedience*
> *to Jesus Christ and sprinkling by his blood:*
>
> 1 Peter 1:1-2 NIV

The foreknowledge here refers to God's elect being destined to "obey the Lord Jesus and to be sprinkled by his blood" *(chosen . . . for obedience to Jesus Christ)*. All who are placed in Christ are destined for this end. According to Jesus, this foreknowledge is based on the requirement that a person <u>learns</u> from God *(It is written in the Prophets: `They will all be taught by God. Everyone who listens to the Father and learns from him comes to me* – John 6:45 NIV)*. This learning from God could not have happened in eternal ages, but after the person was alive. So the term "foreknowledge" is referring to a short time prior to being born-again in Christ, and not to some eternal predetermination.

> *God <u>chose Him</u> as your ransom long before the world*
> *began, but He has now revealed Him to you in these last*
> *days. Through Christ you have come to trust in God. And*
> *you have placed your faith and hope in God because He*
> *raised Christ from the dead and gave Him great glory.*
>
> 1 Peter 1:20-21 NLT

This choosing before the world began refers to Christ the Savior. It does not refer to us.

> *We will know by this that we are of the truth, and will*
> *assure our heart before Him in whatever our heart*
> *condemns us; for God is greater than our heart and <u>knows</u>*
> *<u>all things</u>.* 1 John 3:19-20 NASB

This is referring to what is in our hearts right now. It makes no statement about knowing them in the future.

All the "proof texts" for the doctrine of the absolute foreknowledge of God are no proof at all. Everyone of them has holes, and some even contradict the doctrine. The few references that seem to support God's absolute foreknowledge of all things future do so in a weak way, and when compared to the thousands of biblical references that refute the doctrine are not even equal to a snowball in a hail storm.

16. The questionable legacy of Augustine and the sixteenth century reformers

In seminary, I had a Church History professor who was an excellent instructor. He also was sometimes referred to as "the resident Arminian on campus." I once asked him about that, and he replied that he wasn't an Arminian, but rather a "pre–Augustinian." I never understood that very well until I started writing this book. Now, I am happy to agree wholeheartedly with him. Arminians (not to be confused with the people of Armenia, the first declared Christian nation in the world around AD 300), are accused of teaching the free–will of man and that a saved person can lose his salvation. Often, they are set up as theology's strawmen and things are attributed to Arminius that he never believed.

They say it is not good to speak ill of the dead, but something must be said about the legacy that came down to the present–day church from Augustine (fifth century) and the reformers of the sixteenth century (namely Calvin, Zwingli, and Luther). First, let me say that I have a great respect for the reformers and their wives who in the face of overwhelming odds and at the peril of their lives stood up for the gospel and for adherence to the Holy Scriptures. These brave Christians are to be commended for trying to purify the corrupt church of their time and reinstate biblical Christianity. I only hope that I will be considered worthy to stand in their shadows when the eternal rewards are given out in Heaven.

However, anyone with a little experience in the Christian life has learned that no Christian, other than Christ himself, is without fault. Each Christian forms his theology partly out of rebellion against God, partly out of biblical revelation, partly out of his surrounding circumstances, partly out of personal experience, and partly out of convenience. The reformers were no different. For example, neither Luther, nor Zwingli, had a missionary vision for reaching a lost world (Calvin was instrumental in sending two missionaries to Brazil). This was mostly due to the fact that they were fighting for survival against the Roman Church which had rotted morally and spiritually, but still had a strong military influence. The reformers formed state–related churches as a means of defense against the might of Rome. They baptized infants and anyone else they could find within their territorial domain to make sure that no one would join Rome against them. Partly because of their circumstances, they ended up with some errors in their theology. We don't want to throw rocks at them, because under the same circumstances we probably would have done the same thing or worse. However, we also do not want to imitate their errors.

In AD 312, the Roman Emperor Constantine had a profound spiritual experience, and he ceased persecution of the Christian church in the Roman Empire in 313. Persecution had been rampant off and on for 270 years, but now the Empire, over a transition period of twenty or more years, adopted

Christianity as its major religion. This brought the purity of the church to a low level. Now, there was no risk involved in declaring oneself a Christian. In fact, to be a Christian was even an advantage. Where there is no cost to be a Christian, the quantity of the church goes up and the quality takes a nosedive. The pre–Constantinian church was small but pure: the post–Constantinian church mushroomed, but opened itself to all kinds of heresy and immorality.

Into this new tolerant environment was born a man who would have a profound influence on the development of Christian theology. Many Protestants, especially Calvinists, consider Saint Augustine to be one of the theological fathers of the sixteenth century Protestant Reformation due to his teachings on salvation, infant baptism, and divine grace. Let's look at the history of Augustine's life:

> **Augustine of Hippo** *Latin: Aurelius Augustinus Hipponensis; 13 November 354 – 28 August 430), also known as Saint Augustine was an early Christian theologian and philosopher whose writings were very influential in the development of Western Christianity and Western philosophy. He was bishop of Hippo Regius (present–day Annaba, Algeria) located in the Roman province of Africa. Writing during the Patristic Era, he is viewed as one of the most important Church Fathers in the West. Among his most important works are City of God and Confessions, which continue to be read widely today.*
>
> *According to his contemporary, Jerome, Augustine "established anew the ancient Faith."*
>
> *After his conversion to Christianity and his baptism in 387, Augustine developed his own approach to philosophy and theology, accommodating a variety of methods and*

different perspectives. Believing that the grace of Christ was indispensable to human freedom, he helped to formulate the doctrine of original sin and made seminal contributions to the development of the "just war" theory. When the Western Roman Empire began to disintegrate, Augustine developed the concept of the Catholic Church as a spiritual City of God (in a book of the same name), distinct from the material earthly City. His thoughts profoundly influenced the medieval worldview.

This famous son of St. Monica was born in Africa and spent many years of his life in wicked living and in false beliefs. Though he was reputed to be one of the most intelligent men who ever lived and though he had been brought up a Christian, his sins of impurity and his pride darkened his mind so much, that he could not see or understand the divine truth anymore. Through the prayers of his holy mother and the marvelous preaching of St. Ambrose, Augustine finally became convinced that Christianity was the one true religion. Yet he did not become a Christian then, because he thought he could never live a pure life. One day, however, he heard about two men who had suddenly been converted on reading the life of St. Antony, and he felt terribly ashamed of himself. "What are we doing?" he cried to his friend Alipius. "Unlearned people are taking Heaven by force, while we, with all our knowledge, are so cowardly that we keep rolling around in the mud of our sins!"

Full of bitter sorrow, Augustine flung himself out into the garden and cried out to God, "How long more, O Lord? Why does not this hour put an end to my sins?" Just then he heard a child singing, "Take up and read!" Believing that God had intended him to hear those words, he picked up the book of the Letters of St. Paul, and read

THE QUESTIONABLE LEGACY OF AUGUSTINE AND THE...

the first passage his gaze fell on. It was just what Augustine needed, for in it, St. Paul says to put away all impurity and to live in imitation of Jesus. That did it! From then on, Augustine began a new life.

He was baptized, became a priest, a bishop, a famous Catholic writer, founder of a sect of priests, and one of the greatest saints that ever lived. He became very devout and charitable, too.

http://en.wikipedia.org/wiki/Augustine_
of_Hippo- cite_note-6

After his conversion, Augustine was an ardent follower of the Lord. He rose to a very high position of influence within the Christian church of his day. Unfortunately, he was not a tolerant man of what he perceived to be errors in other men. In spite of the commonly accepted view of Augustine, some things should be noted:

Augustine did not know Greek or Hebrew, and did all of his research and writings in Latin. He could not read the Scriptures or the writings of the early church Fathers in their original languages. Up until this time, most of the earlier church fathers were fluent and wrote in Greek. With Augustine's generation, the text of the Bible for the church changed from Greek to Latin. This was lamentable because the church moved away from the original manuscripts and the tradition of the early church.

The Latin Vulgate is a late fourth–century translation of the Bible that became the Catholic Church's officially promulgated Latin version of the Bible. The translation was largely the work of St. Jerome, who, in 382, was commissioned by Pope Damasus I to revise the *Vetus Latina* ("Old Latin") collection of biblical texts in Latin then in use by the Church.

Augustine had a profound influence on the theology of his time and the beginning of new practices in the church. We can trace the erroneous doctrines of "irresistible grace," the teaching that the Holy Spirit proceeds from the Son as well as from the Father, the practice of infant baptism and baptism of other persons who were not true believers, the concept of a state church, the roots of the Roman Catholic Church, the celibacy of the priesthood, a–millennial theology, the compelling of people to believe by force, the persecution of other Christians, and the roots of the medieval world view all to the time of Augustine, and much of it directly to his door. He believed that the Virgin Mary was sinless, which probably contributed to the Roman church's acceptance of this doctrine at a later date.

The statement that *"Augustine developed his own approach to philosophy and theology, accommodating a variety of methods and different perspectives"* sounds similar to what Joseph Smith did in the nineteenth century. He reinvented basic doctrine in disregard of what had gone before, and by distancing himself from the original Scriptures.

> *One of the decisive developments in the western philosophical tradition was the eventually widespread merging of the <u>Greek philosophical tradition</u> and the Judeo–Christian religious and scriptural traditions. <u>Augustine is one of the main figures through and by whom this merging was accomplished</u>. He is, as well, one of the towering figures of medieval philosophy whose authority and thought came to exert a pervasive and enduring influence well into the modern period, and even up to the present day, especially among those sympathetic to the religious tradition which he helped to shape.*
> (Fri Mar 24, 2000; substantive revision Fri Nov 12, 2010 http://plato.stanford.edu/entries/augustine/)

Augustine's philosophy and theology became a model for the Catholic Church, and later for the Reformers like Luther, Calvin and Zwingli who not only adopted his theology, but also his practice of the persecution of fellow believers.

Partly because of Augustine, we have the state churches like the Roman Catholic, the Eastern Orthodox, the Lutheran, the Reformed, and the Anglican. Some of the Reformers of the sixteenth century were nearly as barbaric as the Catholics in their torture, imprisonment, and execution of nonconformist Christians. Both the Catholics and Protestants used torture, imprisonment, threat and execution to control or exterminate those who wanted to follow a more radical Biblical Christianity like the Anabaptists (Mennonites, Baptists, Amish, Quakers, Church of the Brethren, Brethren Church, Grace Brethren, Dunkard Brethren, and the German Baptists), the Waldensians, and the Moravians (originally United Brethren).

Augustine was born 300 years after the time of Paul and twenty years after Constantine's transformation of the Empire, and therefore he should not be referred to as an "early" church father. For over eighty-five years, there was almost no persecution of Christians in the Roman world; Augustine was the person most responsible for reinstating it. This time, it wasn't the persecution of Christians by unbelievers, but the persecution of Christians by other Christians because they didn't agree on some doctrines of the faith.

If you want a thorough analysis of the many fallacies in Augustine's theology and his departure from sound biblical practice, please refer to Paul Marston and Roger Forster's *"God's strategy in Human History"* pages 305-342. I will rest my case for being suspect of Augustine's theology and "sainthood" with this quote from F. W. Farrar, *"Lives of the Fathers"* (1889), page 536:

> *Augustine must bear the fatal charge of being the first as well as one of the ablest defenders of the frightful cause of persecution and intolerance. He was the first to misuse the words, "Compel them to come in" – a fragmentary phrase wholly unsuited to bear the weight of horror for which it was made responsible. He was the first and ablest asserter of the principle that led to the Albigensian crusades, Spanish armadas, Netherlands butcheries, St Bartholomew massacres, the accursed infamies of the inquisition, the vile espionage, the hideous balefires of Seville and Smithfield, the racks, the gibbets, the thumbscrews, the subterranean torture-chambers used by churchly torturers who assumed the "garb and language of priests with the trade and temper of executioners, to sicken, crush, and horrify the revolted conscience of mankind. It is mainly because of his intolerance that the influence of Augustine falls like a dark shadow across the centuries. It is thus that an Arnold of Citeaux, a Torquemada, a Sprenger, an Alva, a Philip the Second. a Mary Tudor, a Charles IX and a Louis XIV can look up to him as an authorizer of their enormities and quote his sentences to defend some of the vilest crimes which ever caused men to look with horror on the religion of Christ and the church of God.*

The birth of the doctrine of irresistible grace

The Augustinian sympathizer Alister E. McGrath admits: *"The pre-Augustinian theological tradition is practically of one voice in asserting the freedom of the human will."* (Page 296 Marston – Forster)

Prior to Augustine, no church father wrote about irresistible grace, but instead emphasized the free will of man. Here are some excerpts from the writings of several early–church fathers on this topic:

Justin Martyr (c100-165) – "God, wishing men and angels to follow his will, resolved to create them free to do righteousness."

Iraneus of Gaul (c130-200) – ". . . in man as well as in angels, he has placed the power of choice. Man is possessed of freewill from the beginning, and God is possessed of freewill in whose likeness man was created . . ."

Athenagoras of Athens (second century) "Just as with men who have freedom of choice as to both virtue and vice, so it is among the angels."

Theophilus of Antioch (second century)- "For God with power over himself, made man free, and now God vouchsafes to him as a gift through his own philanthropy and pity, when men obey him. For as man, disobeying, drew death to himself, so, obeying the will of God, he who desires is able to procure for himself life everlasting."

Tatian of Syria (late second century) – "Our freewill has destroyed us: we who were free have become slaves . . ."

Bardasian of Syria (c154-222)-"But God in his benignity, chose not so to make man: but by freedom he exalted him above many of his creatures."

Clement of Alexandria (c150-215) – "We, who have heard by the Scriptures that self–determining choice and refusal have been given by the Lord to men, rest in the infallible criterion of faith, manifesting a willing spirit, since we have chosen life and believe God through his voice."

Tertullian of Carthage (c155-225) – I find then that man was by God constituted free, master of his own will and power: indicating the presence of God's image and likeness in him by nothing so well as by this constitution of his nature... you will find that when he sets before men good and evil, life and death, that the entire course of discipline is arranged in precepts by God's calling men from sin, and threatening them or exhorting them; and this on no other ground than that man is free with a will either for obedience or resistance. . . . Since, therefore, both the goodness and purpose of God are discovered in the gift to man of freedom in his will . . .

Origen (c185-254) – "This is also clearly defined in the teaching of the church that every rational soul is possessed of freewill and volition"

Novation of Rome (c200-258) – "He also placed man at the head of the world, and man, too, made in the image of God, to whom he imparted mind, and reason, and foresight, that he might imitate God . . . And when he had given him all things for his service, he willed that he alone would be free."

Methodius of Olympus (C260, martyred 311) – "Now those who decide that man is not possessed of freewill, and affirm that he is governed by the unavoidable necessities of fate . . . are guilty of impiety toward God himself, making him out to be the cause and author of human evils."

Arnobius of Sicca (c253-327) – "Does he thrust back or repel anyone from the kindness of the Supreme who gives to all alike the power of coming to him? To all, he says, the fountain of life is open, and no one is hindered or kept back from drinking . . ."

Cyril of Jerusalem (c310-386) – "Thou hast a soul self–governed, the noblest work of God, made after the image of its creator, immortal, because of God that gives it immortality, a living being rational, imperishable, because of him that bestowed these gifts; having free power to do what it willeth."

Gregory of Nyssa (c355-395) – Being the image and the likeness . . . of the Power which rules all things, man kept also in the matter of a freewill this likeness to him whose will is over all." Jerome (c347-420) – It is in vain that you misrepresent me and try to convince the ignorant that I condemn free-will.

John Chrysostom (c347-407) – All is in God's power, but so that our freewill is not lost. It depends therefore on us and on him. We must first choose the good, and then he adds what belongs to him. He does not precede our willing, that our freewill may not suffer. But when we have chosen, then he affords us much help. . . It is ours to choose beforehand and to will, but God's to perfect and bring to the end."
(Adapted from Marston and Forster — pages 297-304)

> *"Previous to Augustine there was no serious development in Christianity of a theory of predestination." Before Augustine, earlier so–called "Church Fathers" such as Justin, Origen, and Irenaeus "know nothing of unconditional predestination; they teach free will." (Hastings' Encyclopaedia of Religion and Ethics, 1919, Vol. X, p. 231) In their refutation of Gnosticism, they are described as regularly expressing their belief in the free moral agency of man as "the distinguishing characteristic*

> *of human personality, the basis of moral responsibility, a divine gift whereby man might choose that which was well-pleasing to God," and as speaking of "the autonomy of man and the counsel of God who constraineth not."*
> The New Schaff-Herzog Encyclopedia of Religious Knowledge, edited by S. Jackson, 1957, Vol. IX, pp. 192, 193.

Before Augustine no important church father had written saying that God's choice of who would be saved was irresistible and was not a free choice of each man. Only with Augustine did this theology take root in the doctrines of the church and remain prominently there until the present day.

Search the writings of the early church fathers in the first 350 years after Christ and you will not find evidence of the predestination of salvation, of irresistible grace, of limited atonement, of the absolute foreknowledge of God concerning all things future, or many of the other doctrines that Augustine promoted. I don't doubt his sincerity, but I very strongly question his theological conclusions.

To have right theology, we must first base our studies on the Holy Scriptures. We can learn from others who have and are also studying to understand God and his purposes, but when the writings of those others disagree with the Scriptures, we must set them aside. A lot of Augustine's writings fit into this category.

Much of the theology of Luther and Calvin was based on the theology of Augustine –

Martin Luther, was born in Germany in 1483 and joined an <u>Augustinian</u> monastery at Erfurt in 1505. He was born–again when he understood that salvation was by faith alone and not through our works. He protested the selling of indulgences (forgiveness for money) and many other corrupt practices in the Roman church. He was excommunicated and had to hide in fear for his life. In early years, Luther was in favor of a free church, the priesthood of all believers, and toleration of theological differences. He was against persecution and the killing of other Christians, and helped to stem such violence on several occasions.

However, as time went on, he expressed antagonistic views toward Jews, writing that Jewish synagogues and homes should be destroyed, their money confiscated, and liberty curtailed. He believed that Jews should be completely driven out of the German territories. Who knows if Adolf Hitler didn't find support for his anti-Semitic policies in the teachings of Luther?

Once, during a tour of the city of Thuringia, he became enraged at the widespread burning of convents, monasteries, bishops' palaces, and libraries. He wrote at that time that these rebels who had resorted to violence should be put down like mad dogs.

> *Therefore let everyone who can, smite, slay, and stab, secretly or openly, remembering that nothing can be more poisonous, hurtful, or devilish than a rebel ... For baptism does not make men free in body and property, but in soul; and the gospel does not make goods common, except in the case of those who, of their own free will, do what the apostles and disciples did in Acts 4 [:32–37]. They did not demand, as do our insane peasants in their raging, that the goods of others—of Pilate and Herod—should be common, but only their own goods. Our peasants, however, want to make the goods of other men common,*

270 GOD IS WITH US

> *and keep their own for themselves. Fine Christians they*
> *are! I think there is not a devil left in hell; they have all*
> *gone into the peasants. Their raving has gone beyond all*
> *measure.*

Luther was more tolerant of theological differences than Calvin and Zwingli, but he nevertheless supported violence done to some Christians and Jews.

John Calvin (born *Jehan Cauvin*) was a Frenchman born in 1509 and raised in a staunch Roman Catholic family. He studied theology for five years at the University of Paris (1523-28) before diverting into law studies (This was mostly because his father had a falling out with the local bishop). By 1532 Calvin finished his law studies and also published his first book, a commentary on De Clementia by the Roman philosopher, Seneca. The colleges he attended were strongly influenced by the humanistic approach to learning. He broke from the Roman Catholic Church around 1530. He formed part of a movement to reform the church, and was branded a heretic. He fled France and roamed through several cities in Switzerland and Germany for many years eventually settling down in Geneva. Calvin was a tireless polemic and apologetic writer who generated much controversy. He was influenced by the Augustinian tradition, which led him to expound the doctrine of predestination and the absolute sovereignty of God in salvation of the human soul from death and eternal damnation.

Calvin wanted a city controlled by the clergy — a theocracy, though early on he favored the separation of church and state. It took Calvin fourteen years before he could fully impose his version of liturgy, doctrine, organization of the church and moral behavior on the city of Geneva. During this period,

Michael Servetus, a Spaniard regarded by both Catholics and Protestants as having heretical views regarding the Trinity, arrived in Geneva. He was denounced by Calvin and executed by the city council. While instituting many positive policies, Calvin's government also punished "impiety" and dissent against his particular version of Christianity with execution. In the first five years of his rule in Geneva, fifty–eight people were executed and seventy–six exiled for their religious beliefs.

Calvin has had a profound influence on Reformed Theology, and often Protestants are classified as Calvinists or non–Calvinists, or five–point Calvinist, or three–point Calvinist, etc. depending on how firmly one adheres to his teaching.

Calvin was a prolific reformer of the church of his day, but he was intolerant and viscously attacked those who disagreed with him. He was responsible for the death and persecution of many people who were guilty only of not seeing things his way. *(Compiled and adapted from several sources including Wikopedia and the Christian Classic Ethereal Library)*

I realize that these men and other reformers were under tremendous pressure for survival in a hostile environment. Life was not easy and they had to make some radical decisions just to stay alive and keep their reform in progress. But there were other reformers like Menno Simons who did not let their dire circumstances slow their practice of love toward other Christians, or let their theology succumb to the pressures of their time (except perhaps in their adherence to absolute pacifism, probably as a reaction to the other reformer's militarism).

We owe a great debt to the sixteenth century reformers, but we don't owe allegiance to all their practices or to the entirety

272 GOD IS WITH US

of their theology. There are some good things to imitate, and a number of things to shun. Augustine, Luther and Calvin were true believers and servants of God trying to serve him as best they knew how, but like Peter, they had feet of clay and were far from perfect.

Our allegiance must be to God and his Word, and not to any church structure, particular brand of theology, or to following the name of someone other than Christ. Even Luther was appalled and upset that others should call his church "Lutherans." He considered himself a miserable worm, certainly not worthy of having a movement inspired and carried along by God branded with his name.

It would do a lot of good for the Evangelical/Protestant church of our day to clean out the theological attic and rid it of many old relics that do not reconcile with God's written Word.

17. Conclusion

Congratulations! You have made it through. I hope that your desire to walk with God has grown. Even if you don't agree with all I have written, the exercise in studying the Scriptures should cause some growth in your understanding, and hopefully in your walk with the Lord. Perhaps the seeds that have been planted will grow and with time you will understand a lot more about these things.

The Christian life is a journey, not a stagnant stay in one place. As we travel along, we should be learning more and understanding more, but we especially should be becoming more like Jesus in our character.

It is not imperative for all Christians to believe the same in all the minor details. But it is imperative that we believe that God, our Creator, is a Rewarder of those who seek him (Hebrews 11:6), that Jesus of Bethlehem was God's eternal Son (John 8:24), and that he rose from the dead as a sign of victory over sin and death. We also should believe that we will rise with him some day when he returns for all of his flock.

I hope that while you were reading through these pages, you took off your theological glasses and approached the Scriptures with an open mind and heart. We can never grow if we distort the Scriptures so that we can maintain our previously formed doctrines. If in order to reconcile your viewpoints with the Word, you have to reinterpret what the Bible says in order to make it fit, then there is something wrong with your theology.

> *What knowledge can result from adapting the meaning of the Scriptures to suit one's own likes? The true sage discovers, through the Spirit's wisdom, the hidden mysteries to which the Scriptures bear witness.*
>
> Peter of Damaskos
> (Twelfth Century)

Our God and Creator is an awesome God. He is awesome in his goodness, his love, his kindness, and his mercy. He is also a powerful God, but his power and justice take a back seat to his glory that shows in his character. God punishes out of necessity, but he loves and forgives because that is really what he wants to do.

God is available 24/7, and though you may not audibly hear his voice or detect his presence, he is always listening and attentive to your cries for help and your prayers of thanksgiving. Not only does he hear, but he acts on your behalf on every occasion. God answers prayer, not always the way we would like, but always in a good and appropriate way.

He is not "there," far away and out of touch, but he is "here," attentive to your needs, working to bless your life, hoping for your faith to grow so that he might be able to give you more of the best things from his treasury. God has always been with and for his creation, especially after the Eternal Son became a man, but he is especially with those who have become part of his family.

> *Since He did not spare even His own Son but gave Him up for us all, won't He also give us everything else?*
> Romans 8:32 NLT

Never underestimate the depth of his love for you and his commitment to you as one of his beloved children. Don't mistake his discipline for rejection, and don't believe that because you don't get everything you want, God doesn't love you. All he asks is for you to trust him all the time and in every situation.

Biblical evidence for skeptics

If God knows everything that will ever happen, then nothing that will happen tomorrow or next year can be changed. In order for it to change, it would mean that God was wrong about what he knew. If the future is unchangeable, then no one, not even God can do anything to alter it. In that case, God would be as helpless as anyone else to have an influence in the outcome of things. To believe that the future is unalterable is a belief system known as fatalism, and it not only condemns us to a meaningless existence in which we are trapped like characters on a movie reel, but it also ties the hands of God.

Fatalism is the thesis that human acts occur by necessity and hence are unfree. Theological fatalism is the thesis that infallible foreknowledge of a human act makes the act necessary and hence unfree. If there is a being who knows the entire future infallibly, then no human act is free. ("Foreknowledge and Free Will" – Stanford Encyclopedia of Philosophy first published Tue Jul 6, 2004; substantive revision Thu Aug 25, 2011)

Most reformed theologians would deny that they are fatalists, but since they believe that the outcome of all of man's decisions is already decided, there can be no other conclusion. They are fatalists by the very definition of the word. The Bible does not support fatalism, but instead is a narrative about God's ongoing and changing love relationship with his creation. It is a live-action drama in which the characters write the script as they go along. God has a plan for how it will turn out, but he has not predetermined precisely what each character will say or do. Within the Bible, there is always a sense of uncertainty, with various possible choices to be made. As a result of those choices there are also varying consequences. There is <u>absolutely</u> no sign anywhere in any of the Bible books of a fatalistic belief where all future things are already determined and the characters have no say in how it will turn out. Many thousands of expressions of uncertainty and possible options for man's actions are expressed throughout the Bible and only in a small minority of cases is it stated that a future thing is already determined.

The subjunctive mood in grammar — While studying Spanish many years ago, having to learn how to speak in the subjunctive mood was the hardest thing of all. This verb mood is what drives language students crazy because they often don't even understand it in their own language. The subjunctive is all about the uncertain, the possible, the unknown, the undecided, the conditional. The subjunctive is a grammatical mood found in many languages. Subjunctive forms of verbs are typically used to express various states of events that have not yet happened such as a wish, an emotion, a possibility, a judgment, an opinion, a necessity, or an action.

The Bible is full of verbs in the subjunctive and conditional moods and tenses. Subjunctive verbs like "would" (581 times), "should" (338), "could" (268), and conditional words: "if" (1589), "might" (178), "may" (1055), "perhaps" (35), "lest" (9), "maybe" (3), "be careful" (77), "be on your guard" (12), and other words and phrases which express uncertainty about the future abound and predominate in God's interaction with men. Additional words like: "wish" (22), "bless you" (36), "hope that" (10), "wish that" (5), "believe that" (17) also express uncertainty about the future.

The word "but" (3804 times) is also conditional in many cases but not in all. In some uses, it is more of a prohibition, or an exception to a prior statement. For example:

But the LORD said to him, "Not so; if anyone kills Cain, he will suffer vengeance seven times over."
                                                Genesis 4:15 NIV

This use of "but" expresses a rebuttal or contradiction to a previous statement. But in the following case, it is part of a conditional statement involving choices that Cain must make. The outcome depends on the decisions and actions of Cain.

Then the LORD said to Cain, "Why are you angry? Why is your face downcast? If you do what is right, will you not be accepted? <u>But</u> if you do not do what is right, sin is crouching at your door; it desires to have you, <u>but</u> you must master it."

Genesis 4:6-7 NIV

Also, the word "because" (1590 times) may be a simple statement of explanation like:

And God blessed the seventh day and made it holy, <u>because</u> on it he rested from all the work of creating that he had done.

Genesis 2:3 NIV

But it is most often a statement of cause and effect like:

So the LORD God said to the serpent, "<u>Because</u> you have done this, "Cursed are you above all the livestock and all the wild animals! You will crawl on your belly and you will eat dust all the days of your life.

Genesis 3:14 NIV

Also:

The LORD then said to Noah, "Go into the ark, you and your whole family, <u>because</u> I have found you righteous in this generation.

Genesis 7:1 NIV

This key word often demonstrates the consequences of choices we make. In most of its biblical uses it expresses the result of an action by someone. A choice was made, and the word "because" expresses the consequences of that choice.

The Bible, especially the Old Testament, is full of subjunctive and conditional verb forms where the future is still to be determined. Therefore, it is not good interpretation if we ignore more than 4233 instances of subjunctive and conditional forms in which the future was clearly dependent on the actions of people. If we add the instances of "but" and "because" we have a total of 9627 cases in which uncertainly about the future or the consequence of man's actions are expressed. In the majority of these cases where uncertainty was expressed, it was God who was speaking personally or through his prophets. These thousands of word usages in the uncertain tenses should drive theologians who believe in the absolute foreknowledge of God crazy because they cannot come up with a reasonable explanation for them. If there is uncertainty about the future, and since it is most often expressed by God himself, then significant parts of our future are still to be decided. When we let the Bible speak for itself, we see the obvious: many details of the future are still being determined and are dependent on how men react to God's imploring work in their lives. In the face of all this Biblical evidence it is really absurd to believe that every detail of the future has already been decided and that no one, even God can change one part of it. I challenge anyone to find serious biblical evidence that supports such a doctrine, or to bring one biblical character forward as a witness to defend it.

In these next four chapters, I am probably going to overwhelm you with quotes from the Bible. The purpose is to show you that throughout the Bible God has not given any of his servants reason to believe that he always knew how everything would turn out.

Perhaps you don't need to read all of them to be convinced, but some people may need to see all the evidence before they will soften up and let go of their cherished but erroneous convictions. Even then, the skeptics will probable try to wiggle out of it because it destroys their prior theological formation. Read only as long as is necessary. If you get bogged down because of the weight of the evidence, remember you don't need to read it all.

18. Overwhelming biblical evidence that the future has not all been determined

Genesis — Deuteronomy

Let's look at just some of the instances where uncertainty is expressed from Genesis to Deuteronomy:

Genesis

> *God looked at everything he had made. And he saw that everything <u>was very good</u>. There was evening, and then there was morning. This was the sixth day.*
>
> Genesis 1:31

Ten times in Genesis, God saw what he had made, and said it was good. After he had made man he said it was "very good." Apparently, God was pleased with his work of creation as well he should have been. But, he could not have been <u>pleased</u> unless there could have been some other outcome. Pleasure represents hope fulfilled.

> *Out of the ground the LORD God formed every beast*
> *of the field and every bird of the sky, and brought them*
> *to the man <u>to see what he would call them; and whatever</u>*
> *<u>the man called a living creature, that was its name</u>.*
> Genesis 2:19 NASB

Did God know what names Adam was going to call each animal? The text does not support that interpretation. It says "whatever" name Adam came up with was the name God used. God does not desire or need to be a micromanager of every decision that his creatures make.

> *The LORD God said, "Look, the man <u>has become like</u>*
> *<u>us</u>—he knows about good and evil. And now the man*
> *<u>might take the fruit</u> from the tree of life. If the man eats*
> *that fruit, he will live forever."*   Genesis 3:22

God prevented man from making a choice that would have condemned him to eternal separation and death with no escape. In this prohibition God showed tremendous mercy. He put a fence around the choice that would have condemned all men to the "Lake of Fire." Why would God go to the trouble to give the impression that there was danger here, if in his foreknowledge he knew that there was absolutely no possibility that Adam could eat it? God did not believe that the future was already determined.

> *"Why are you so angry?" the LORD asked Cain. "Why*
> *do you look so dejected? You will be accepted if you do*
> *what is right. But if you refuse to do what is right, then*
> *watch out! Sin is crouching at the door, eager to control*
> *you. But <u>you must subdue it and be its master</u>."*
> Genesis 4:6-7 NLT

God tells Cain that he must make a choice. There is no evidence here that God already knew which way he would choose. Even after Cain's heinous crime, God was hoping that his life would turn out for good.

> The LORD observed the extent of human wickedness on the earth, and He <u>saw</u> that everything they thought or imagined was consistently and totally evil. So <u>the LORD was sorry He had ever made them and put them on the earth. It broke His heart.</u> And the LORD said, "I will wipe this human race I have created from the face of the earth. Yes, and I will destroy every living thing—all the people, the large animals, the small animals that scurry along the ground, and even the birds of the sky. <u>I am sorry I ever made them.</u>" Genesis 6:5-7 NLT

Why does it not say "foresaw" instead of "saw"? Obviously, the Lord was observing in the present what man did, and responded to it. And apparently he was disappointed in man; to be disappointed you have to have hope that things would have turned out better than they did. God is a God of hope – he desires good choices and good things for his creatures.

> But the LORD came down <u>to look</u> at the city and the tower the people were building. "Look!" He said. "The people are united, and they all speak the same language. After this, nothing they set out to do will be impossible for them! Come, let's go down and confuse the people with different languages. Then they won't be able to understand each other." Genesis 11:5-7 NLT

This statement is either "errant" or it means that God did not know from a distance everything that man was planning. If you believe in the inerrancy of the Bible, this statement must be accepted at face value in spite of it not agreeing with classical theology's understanding of God's omniscience. Instead of saying "this must mean something else because it doesn't fit my theology," we should say, "how should my theology conform to the Bible?"

> Then the LORD said, "I have heard many times that the people of Sodom and Gomorrah are very evil. I will go and see _if they are as bad as I have heard_. _Then I will know for sure._" Genesis 18:20-21

Unless he is lying (which is impossible), God is saying that he needs to investigate to find out the full truth about what is in men's hearts.

> The two men said to Lot, "Are there any other people from your family living in this city? Do you have any sons–in–law, sons, daughters, or any other people from your family here? If so, you should tell them to leave now. Genesis 19:12

If God knew everything about everything including the future, why didn't these angels know everyone who lived in the city, and who were Lot's relatives?

> In the dream God responded, "Yes, I know you are innocent. That's why _I kept you_ from sinning against Me, and why _I did not let you touch her_. Genesis 20:6 NLT

Why does he not say, "I <u>knew</u> that you would not sin against me?" Why would God have to <u>DO</u> anything to prevent it if he already knew how it was going to turn out? Wouldn't it automatically happen without God's present intervention?

> *At that moment the angel of the LORD called to him from heaven, "Abraham! Abraham!" "Yes," Abraham replied. "Here I am!" "Don't lay a hand on the boy!" the angel said. "Do not hurt him in any way, for <u>now I know</u> that you truly fear God. You have not withheld from Me even your son, your only son."*
>
> Genesis 22:11-12 NLT

Obviously, God wasn't one hundred percent sure that Abraham would follow through with the command to kill his son. Later, it says that Abraham believed that God could raise Isaac up from the dead (Hebrews 11:19). He believed in the possibility of killing Isaac and then seeing God bring him back to life again. Abraham did not believe that all his actions were already determined.

To say that God was only doing this to prove to Abraham what God already knew is a violation of the text and of sound interpretation. God himself says that he has learned something from the test. If God had already known how the test would turn out, he surely could have used different words to describe it.

> *Abraham said to him, "No, don't take my son to that place. The LORD, the God of heaven, brought me from my homeland to this place.*
> *That place was the home of my father and the home of my family, but he promised that this new land would belong to my family. May he send his angel before you so that you can choose a wife for my son. If the girl refuses to come with you, <u>you will be free from this promise</u>. But you must not take my son back to that place."*
>
> Genesis 24:6-8

Abraham was not sure that his servant would be successful on his mission to find a wife from his relatives. He believed in various possible outcomes. He didn't believe that the future was already known by God, and was therefore unchangeable.

> The LORD appeared to Isaac and said, "Do not go down to Egypt; live in the land where I tell you to live. Stay in this land for a while, and I will be with you and will bless you. For to you and your descendants I will give all these lands and will confirm the oath I swore to your father Abraham. Genesis 26:2-3 NIV

God promised to bless Isaac if he stayed in Canaan, but recognized that he might not.

> Then Jacob made a promise. He said, "If God will be with me, and if he will protect me on this trip, and if he gives me food to eat and clothes to wear, and if I return in peace to my father's house–if he does all these things–then the LORD will be my God. I am setting this stone up as a memorial stone. It will show that this is a holy place for God, and I will give God one-tenth of all he gives me." Genesis 28:20-22

Jacob did not believe that the future was already determined and absolutely foreknown by God.

Exodus

> So God was good to the midwives, and the Israelites continued to multiply, growing more and more powerful. And because the midwives feared God, He gave them families of their own. Exodus 1:20-21 NLT

If the midwives hadn't feared God, they would not have had their own families. God's blessings on their lives were dependent on their heart attitudes and their faith actions. God responded to the faith of the midwives, and changed their future situation.

> Then God said, "If the people don't believe you when you use your walking stick, _then_ they will believe you when you show them this sign. If they still refuse to believe after you show them both of these signs, _then_ take some water from the Nile River. Pour the water on the ground, and as soon as it touches the ground, it will become blood."
> Exodus 4:8-9

God expresses uncertainly about how the Egyptians will react to the miracles. The text clearly indicates that he did not know exactly how they would respond.

> Then the _LORD's anger_ burned against Moses and he said, "What about your brother, Aaron the Levite? I know he can speak well. He is already on his way to meet you, and his heart will be glad when he sees you. You shall speak to him and put words in his mouth; I will help both of you speak and will teach you what to do. He will speak to the people for you, and it will be as if he were your mouth and as if you were God to him. _But_ take this staff in your hand so you can perform miraculous signs with it."
> (NLT 1996 – _Be sure_ to take your shepherd's staff along)
> Exodus 4:14-17 NIV

Why would God caution Moses to take his staff if he already knew he would?

> *On the way to Egypt, Moses stopped at a place to spend the night. The LORD met Moses at that place <u>and tried to kill him</u>. But Zipporah took a flint knife and circumcised her son. She took the skin and touched his feet. Then she said to Moses, "You are a bridegroom of blood to me." Zipporah said this because she had to circumcise her son. So God let Moses live.*   Exodus 4:24-26

It doesn't say he "threatened" to kill him. It says that his intention was to kill him. The straightforward interpretation is that Zipporah believed that God would kill her husband unless she acted to save him.

> *Pharaoh made the people leave Egypt. God did not let the people take the road leading to the land of the Philistines. That road by the Mediterranean Sea is the shortest way, but God said, "<u>If</u> the people go that way they will have to fight. Then <u>they might change their minds and go back to Egypt</u>." So God led them another way through the desert by the Red Sea. The Israelites were dressed for war when they left Egypt.*   Exodus 13:17-18

Here, God limited the choices. He didn't allow the people to be tempted and make the wrong choice. This shows the sovereignty of God as well as the free will of man.

> *Now <u>if you obey me fully</u> and keep my covenant, <u>then</u> out of all nations you will be my treasured possession. Although the whole earth is mine, you will be for me a kingdom of priests and a holy nation.*   Exodus 19:5-6 NIV

> *The LORD said to Moses, "I have seen these people, and I know that they are very stubborn. They will always turn*

*against me. <u>So now let me destroy them in anger</u>. Then I
will make a great nation from you." But Moses begged
the LORD his God, "LORD, don't let your anger destroy
your people. You brought them out of Egypt with your
great power and strength. But if you destroy your people,
the Egyptians will say, 'God planned to do bad things
to his people. That is why he led them out of Egypt. He
wanted to kill them in the mountains. He wanted to wipe
them off the earth.' So don't be angry with your people.
Please change your mind! Don't destroy them. Remember
Abraham, Isaac, and Israel. These men served you, and
you used your name to make a promise to them. You said,
'I will make your people as many as the stars in the sky.
I will give your people all this land as I promised. This
land will be theirs forever.'" So the LORD felt sorry for
the people. He did not do what he said he might do–he
did not destroy them.*   Exodus 32:9-14

Was God toying with Moses and talking sheer nonsense, or
was this a real possibility? If it wasn't a possibility, why does
God lie to his most cherished servant? Moses apparently took
God's threat very seriously. Moses didn't believe that the future
was already decided.

*The next day Moses said to the people, "You have
committed a terrible sin, but I will go back up to the
LORD on the mountain. <u>Perhaps</u> I will be able to obtain
forgiveness for your sin." So Moses returned to the LORD
and said, "Oh, what a terrible sin these people have
committed. They have made gods of gold for themselves.
But now, if You will only forgive their sin–<u>but if not</u>, erase
my name from the record You have written!"*
     Exodus 32:30-33 NLT

Moses did not believe that the future was all set in concrete. He believed that it was a variable, that people's actions moved God's actions, and that's God's mercy trumped his judgment.

> Then the LORD said to Moses, "Leave this place, you and the people you brought up out of Egypt, and go up to the land I promised on oath to Abraham, Isaac and Jacob, saying, `I will give it to your descendants.' I will send an angel before you and drive out the Canaanites, Amorites, Hittites, Perizzites, Hivites and Jebusites. Go up to the land flowing with milk and honey. <u>But I will not go with you, because</u> you are a stiff–necked people and <u>I might destroy you on the way.</u>"   Exodus 33:1-3 NIV

> Then Moses said to him, "If you don't go with us, then don't make us leave this place. Also, how will we know if you are pleased with me and these people? If you go with us, we will know for sure. If you don't go with us, these people and I will be no different from any other <u>people on the earth." Then the LORD said to Moses</u>, "I will do what you ask. I will do this because I am pleased with you and because I know you very well."
>   Exodus 33:15-17

God said he would not go with them, but later he did. If his not going was not a possibility, why is God making idle threats? Is God an inveterate bluffer? Do you believe that God would say such things if they were not possible?

Leviticus

Here are twenty three tremendous blessings if Israel follows God and is faithful:

"If you follow my decrees and are careful to obey my commands, I will send you rain in its season, and the ground will yield its crops and the trees of the field their fruit. Your threshing will continue until grape harvest and the grape harvest will continue until planting, and you will eat all the food you want and live in safety in your land. "I will grant peace in the land, and you will lie down and no one will make you afraid. I will remove savage beasts from the land, and the sword will not pass through your country. You will pursue your enemies, and they will fall by the sword before you. Five of you will chase a hundred, and a hundred of you will chase ten thousand, and your enemies will fall by the sword before you. "I will look on you with favor and make you fruitful and increase your numbers, and I will keep my covenant with you. You will still be eating last year's harvest when you will have to move it out to make room for the new. I will put my dwelling place among you, and I will not abhor you. I will walk among you and be your God, and you will be my people. I am the LORD your God, who brought you out of Egypt so that you would no longer be slaves to the Egyptians; I broke the bars of your yoke and enabled you to walk with heads held high.

Leviticus 26:3-12 NIV

Here are thirty nine tremendous curses if they don't:

"`But if you will not listen to me and carry out all these commands, and if you reject my decrees and abhor my laws and fail to carry out all my commands and so violate my covenant, then I will do this to you: I will bring upon you sudden terror, wasting diseases and fever that will destroy your sight and drain away your life. You will

plant seed in vain, because your enemies will eat it. I will set my face against you so that you will be defeated by your enemies; those who hate you will rule over you, and you will flee even when no one is pursuing you." `If after all this you will not listen to me, I will punish you for your sins seven times over. I will break down your stubborn pride and make the sky above you like iron and the ground beneath you like bronze. Your strength will be spent in vain, because your soil will not yield its crops, nor will the trees of the land yield their fruit."`If you remain hostile toward me and refuse to listen to me, I will multiply your afflictions seven times over, as your sins deserve. I will send wild animals against you, and they will rob you of your children, destroy your cattle and make you so few in number that your roads will be deserted." `If in spite of these things you do not accept my correction but continue to be hostile toward me, I myself will be hostile toward you and will afflict you for your sins seven times over. And I will bring the sword upon you to avenge the breaking of the covenant. When you withdraw into your cities, I will send a plague among you, and you will be given into enemy hands. When I cut off your supply of bread, ten women will be able to bake your bread in one oven, and they will dole out the bread by weight. You will eat, but you will not be satisfied." `If in spite of this you still do not listen to me but continue to be hostile toward me, then in my anger I will be hostile toward you, and I myself will punish you for your sins seven times over. You will eat the flesh of your sons and the flesh of your daughters. I will destroy your high places, cut down your incense altars and pile your dead bodies on the lifeless forms of your idols, and I will abhor you. I will turn your cities into ruins and lay

> *waste your sanctuaries, and I will take no delight in the pleasing aroma of your offerings. I will lay waste the land, so that your enemies who live there will be appalled. I will scatter you among the nations and will draw out my sword and pursue you. Your land will be laid waste, and your cities will lie in ruins. Then the land will enjoy its sabbath years all the time that it lies desolate and you are in the country of your enemies; then the land will rest and enjoy its sabbaths. All the time that it lies desolate, the land will have the rest it did not have during the sabbaths you lived in it.* Leviticus 26:14-35 NIV

Many of God's actions depended on the choices the Israelites made. If they obeyed God, they would receive amazing blessings. If they disobeyed, they would receive curses in increasing severity. Was God only <u>pretending</u> that he didn't know how it was all going to turn out? The Israelites did not believe that their future was already known by God.

Numbers

> *Soon the people began to complain about their hardship, and the LORD heard everything they said. <u>Then the LORD's anger blazed against them</u>, and He sent a fire to rage among them, and He destroyed some of the people in the outskirts of the camp. Then the people screamed to Moses for help, and <u>when he prayed to the LORD, the fire stopped</u>.* Numbers 11:1-2 NLT

Anger is a response to something that you didn't know about previously. How could God react with anger if he already knew it was going to happen? Wouldn't he just stay angry all of the time if he already knew their actions?

> *Moses heard all the families standing in the doorways of*
> *their tents whining, and the LORD became extremely*
> *angry. Moses was also very aggravated. And Moses said*
> *to the LORD, "Why are You treating me, Your servant,*
> *so harshly? Have mercy on me! What did I do to deserve*
> *the burden of all these people? Did I give birth to them?*
> *Did I bring them into the world? Why did You tell me*
> *to carry them in my arms like a mother carries a nursing*
> *baby? How can I carry them to the land You swore to give*
> *their ancestors? Where am I supposed to get meat for all*
> *these people? They keep whining to me, saying, 'Give us*
> *meat to eat!' I can't carry all these people by myself! The*
> *load is far too heavy! If this is how You intend to treat*
> *me, just go ahead and kill me. Do me a favor and spare*
> *me this misery!"*   Numbers 11:10-15 NLT

Moses preferred to be put to death than to carry the burden of
complaints by all the people. He believed this was a real option.

> *Two of the men who had explored the land, Joshua son*
> *of Nun and Caleb son of Jephunneh, tore their clothing.*
> *They said to all the people of Israel, "The land we traveled*
> *through and explored is a wonderful land! And <u>if the</u>*
> *<u>LORD is pleased with us</u>, He will bring us safely into*
> *that land and give it to us. It is a rich land flowing with*
> *milk and honey. Do not rebel against the LORD, and*
> *don't be afraid of the people of the land. They are only*
> *helpless prey to us! They have no protection, but the*
> *LORD is with us! Don't be afraid of them!"*
>   Numbers 14:6-9 NLT

What Joshua and Caleb believed did not happen until forty
years later because of Israel's lack of faith. The text gives no

reason to believe that the time of Israel's entrance into Canaan was predetermined.

> *And the LORD said to Moses, "How long will these people treat Me with contempt? Will they never believe Me, even after all the miraculous signs I have done among them? I will disown them and destroy them with a plague. Then I will make you into a nation greater and mightier than they are!"* Numbers 14:11-12 NLT

God was going to keep his promise to Abraham, Isaac and Jacob, but he could have done it via plan B, or C, or D. What matters are God's intention, his sovereignty, and power: It is not predetermined how he will accomplish his purposes. God's hands are never tied concerning the future unless he has made a vow about things to come.

> *Meanwhile, Korah had stirred up the entire community against Moses and Aaron, and they all gathered at the Tabernacle entrance. Then the glorious presence of the LORD appeared to the whole community, and the LORD said to Moses and Aaron, "Get away from all these people <u>so that I may instantly destroy them!</u>" But Moses and Aaron fell face down on the ground. "O God," <u>they pleaded</u>, "You are the God who gives breath to all creatures. Must You be angry with all the people when only one man sins?"* Numbers 16:19-22 NLT

Moses and Aaron believed that it was possible to reason and negotiate with God, and that his response would change the future.

> *Then the LORD gave the donkey the ability to speak. "What have I done to you that deserves your beating me*

*three times?" it asked Balaam. "You have made me look
like a fool!" Balaam shouted. "If I had a sword with
me, I would kill you!" "But I am the same donkey you
have ridden all your life," the donkey answered. "Have
I ever done anything like this before?" "No," Balaam
admitted. Then the LORD opened Balaam's eyes, and
he saw the angel of the LORD standing in the roadway
with a drawn sword in his hand. Balaam bowed his head
and fell face down on the ground before him. "Why did
you beat your donkey those three times?" the angel of
the LORD demanded. "Look, I have come to block your
way because you are stubbornly resisting me. Three times
the donkey saw me and shied away; <u>otherwise, I would</u>
<u>certainly have killed you by now and spared the donkey.</u>"*

Numbers 22:28-33 NLT

In this case, Balaam's donkey was smarter than her master,
and she didn't believe that the future was already determined.
God declares that if it weren't for her, Balaam would be dead.

*The LORD said to Moses, "Phinehas son of Eleazar,
the son of Aaron, the priest, has turned my anger away
from the Israelites; for he was as zealous as I am for my
honor among them, so that in my zeal I did not put an
end to them. <u>Therefore</u> tell him I am making my covenant
of peace with him. He and his descendants will have a
covenant of a lasting priesthood, <u>because</u> he was zealous
for the honor of his God and made atonement for the
Israelites."*   Numbers 25:10-13 NIV
*(NLT – So I have stopped destroying all Israel as I intended
to do in my anger.)*

The actions of Phinehas changed God's plans.

"Do you intend to stay here while your brothers go across and do all the fighting?" Moses asked the men of Gad and Reuben. "Why do you want to discourage the rest of the people of Israel from going across to the land the LORD has given them? Your ancestors did the same thing when I sent them from Kadesh–barnea to explore the land. After they went up to the valley of Eshcol and explored the land, they discouraged the people of Israel from entering the land the LORD was giving them. Then the LORD was very angry with them, and He vowed, 'Of all those I rescued from Egypt, no one who is twenty years old or older will ever see the land I swore to give to Abraham, Isaac, and Jacob, for they have not obeyed Me wholeheartedly. The only exceptions are Caleb son of Jephunneh the Kenizzite and Joshua son of Nun, for they have wholeheartedly followed the LORD.' "The LORD was angry with Israel and made them wander in the wilderness for forty years until the entire generation that sinned in the LORD's sight had died.

Numbers 32:6-13 NLT

This is Plan B in action. There is no evidence here that this was his original intention, but God adjusted his plans according to the behavior of the people. God's relationship with his people is an on–going drama full of variables.

Then Moses said, "If you keep your word and arm yourselves for the LORD's battles, and if your troops cross the Jordan and keep fighting until the LORD has driven out His enemies, then you may return when the LORD has conquered the land. You will have fulfilled your duty to the LORD and to the rest of the people of Israel. And the land on the east side of the Jordan will be your property from the LORD.

Numbers 32:20-22 NLT

> *So Moses, Eleazar the priest, Joshua son of Nun, and*
> *all the leaders of the tribes of Israel heard them make*
> *that promise. Moses said to them, "The people of Gad*
> *and Reuben will cross the Jordan River. They will march*
> *before the LORD into battle. They will help you take the*
> *land. And you will give the land of Gilead as their part of*
> *the country. But if they do not cross the river with you*
> *ready to fight, they will not get any land on this side. They*
> *will get only a share of the land of Canaan with the rest*
> *of you."*   Numbers 32:28-30 NLT

It is stated as a possibility that the Gadites and the Reubenites
could have received their inheritance on the western side of the
Jordan River. Their inheritance was not predetermined, but was
affected by choices they made.

> *But if you fail to drive out the people who live in the land,*
> *those who remain will be like splinters in your eyes and*
> *thorns in your sides. They will harass you in the land*
> *where you live. And I will do to you what I had planned*
> *to do to them."*   Numbers 33:55-56 NLT

Deuteronomy

> *"In the future, when you have children and grandchildren*
> *and have lived in the land a long time, do not corrupt*
> *yourselves by making idols of any kind. This is evil in*
> *the sight of the LORD your God and will arouse His*
> *anger. "Today I call on heaven and earth as witnesses*
> *against you. If you break My covenant, you will quickly*
> *disappear from the land you are crossing the Jordan to*
> *occupy. You will live there only a short time; then you*

will be utterly destroyed. For the LORD will scatter you among the nations, where only a few of you will survive. There, in a foreign land, you will worship idols made from wood and stone–gods that neither see nor hear nor eat nor smell. But from there you will search again for the LORD your God. And if you search for Him with all your heart and soul, you will find Him. "In the distant future, when you are suffering all these things, you will finally return to the LORD your God and listen to what He tells you. For the LORD your God is a merciful God; He will not abandon you or destroy you or forget the solemn covenant He made with your ancestors.

Deuteronomy 4:25-31 NLT

God knew it was possible for the Israelites to become corrupt, but his words indicate that it was only a possibility, and not a certainty. We see again the sovereignty of God working his plan alongside the freedom of choice given to man.

"So remember this and keep it firmly in mind: The LORD is God both in heaven and on earth, and there is no other. If you obey all the decrees and commands I am giving you today, all will be well with you and your children. I am giving you these instructions so you will enjoy a long life in the land the LORD your God is giving you for all time."   Deuteronomy 4:39-40 NLT

God over and over warns Israel of the consequences of wrong behavior, and the blessings of seeking the Lord. Why waste all these words if the two different outcomes were not possible? If God had known how it would turn out, he needn't have said anything.

"The LORD heard the request you made to me. And He said, 'I have heard what the people said to you, and they are right. Oh, that they <u>would always have hearts like this</u>, that they might fear Me and obey all My commands! <u>If they did</u>, they and their descendants <u>would prosper forever</u>.

Deuteronomy 5:28-29 NLT

"The LORD did not set His heart on you and choose you because you were more numerous than other nations, for you were the smallest of all nations! Rather, it was simply that the LORD loves you, and He was keeping the oath He had sworn to your ancestors. That is why the LORD rescued you with such a strong hand from your slavery and from the oppressive hand of Pharaoh, king of Egypt. Understand, therefore, that the LORD your God is indeed God. He is the faithful God who keeps His covenant for a thousand generations and lavishes His unfailing love <u>on those who love Him and obey His commands</u>. But He does not hesitate <u>to punish and destroy those who reject Him</u>.

Deuteronomy 7:7-10 NLT

"If you listen to these regulations and faithfully obey them, the LORD your God will keep His covenant of unfailing love with you, as He promised with an oath to your ancestors. He will love you and bless you, and He will give you many children. He will give fertility to your land and your animals. When you arrive in the land He swore to give your ancestors, you will have large harvests of grain, new wine, and olive oil, and great herds of cattle, sheep, and goats. You will be blessed above all the nations of the earth. None of your men or women will be childless, and all your livestock will bear young. And the LORD will protect you from all sickness. He

will not let you suffer from the terrible diseases you knew in Egypt, but He will inflict them on all your enemies!

Deuteronomy 7:12-15 NLT

Remember how the LORD your God led you all the way in the desert these forty years, to humble you and to test you in order to know what was in your heart, whether or not you would keep his commands.

Deuteronomy 8:2 NIV

If God is "all knowing" about everything, why did he have to test them? This literally says that God wanted to know what was in their hearts because he didn't already know. You only perform tests to find out what you don't already know. Your doctor doesn't say, "I already know for certain that you have cancer in the pancreas, but we are going to run some tests to find out if you do."

"But I assure you of this: If you ever forget the LORD your God and follow other gods, worshiping and bowing down to them, you will certainly be destroyed. Just as the LORD has destroyed other nations in your path, you also will be destroyed if you refuse to obey the LORD your God.

Deuteronomy 8:19-20 NLT

And the LORD said to me, "I have seen this people, and they are a stiff-necked people indeed! Let me alone, so that I may destroy them and blot out their name from under heaven. And I will make you into a nation stronger and more numerous than they." Deuteronomy 9:13-14 NIV (NLT – *"been watching these people and they are extremely stubborn"*)

304 GOD IS WITH US

God was reacting to what he had <u>seen</u> in the hearts of the people. It does not refer in any way to his foreknowledge of events.

> *I was afraid of the LORD'S terrible anger. He was angry enough to destroy you, but <u>the LORD listened to me again</u>. The LORD was very angry with Aaron—<u>enough to destroy him</u>! So I also prayed for Aaron at that time.*
>
> Deuteronomy 9:19-20

Moses believed that his prayers kept the Israelites and Aaron from being destroyed by the Lord.

> *"The Lord says, 'You must listen carefully to the commands I give you today: You must love the LORD your God, and serve him with all your heart and all your soul. If you do that, <u>I will</u> send rain for your land at the right time. <u>I will</u> send the autumn rain and the spring rain. Then you can gather your grain, your new wine, and your oil. And <u>I will</u> make grass grow in your fields for your cattle. You will have plenty to eat.' "He says, 'Be careful! Don't be fooled. Don't turn away from me to serve other gods and to bow down to them.' If you do that, the LORD will <u>become very angry with you</u>. He will shut the skies, and there will be no rain. The land will not make a harvest, and you will soon die in the good land that the LORD is giving you.* Deuteronomy 11:13-17

> *"Today I am giving you <u>a choice</u>. <u>You may choose</u> the blessing or the curse. You will get the blessing <u>if you listen and obey</u> the commands of the LORD your God that I have told you today. But <u>you will get the curse if you refuse to listen and obey</u> the commands of the LORD*

> *your God. So don't stop living the way I command you*
> *today, and don't follow other gods that you don't know.*
>
> Deuteronomy 11:26-28

These are more warnings from the Lord about making wrong choices.

> *"A prophet or someone who explains dreams might come*
> *to you and tell you that they will show you a sign or a*
> *miracle. And the sign or miracle they told you about might*
> *come true. Then they might ask you to follow other gods*
> *(gods you don't know) and say to you, 'Let's serve these*
> *gods!' Don't listen to them, because the LORD your God*
> *is testing you. He wants to know if you love him with all*
> *your heart and all your soul.*   *Deuteronomy 13:1-3*

Why would God need to test us to find out what he has "known from eternity past?" Obviously, God does not know which path each man is going to take.

> *"The LORD your God promised your fathers that he*
> *would make your land larger. He will give you all the*
> *land that he promised to give to your ancestors. He will*
> *do this if you completely obey his commands that I give*
> *you today–if you love the LORD your God and always*
> *live the way he wants. Then, when he gives you more*
> *land, you should choose three more cities for safety. They*
> *should be added to the first three cities.*
>
> Deuteronomy 19:8-9

> *"Now, if you will be careful to obey the LORD your God*
> *and follow all his commands that I tell you today, the*
> *LORD your God will put you high above all the nations*

on earth. If you will obey the LORD your God, <u>all these blessings will come to you and be yours</u>: "He will bless you in the city and in the field. He will bless you and give you many children. He will bless your land and give you good crops. He will bless your animals and let them have many babies. He will bless you with calves and lambs. He will bless your baskets and pans and fill them with food. He will bless you at all times in everything you do. "The LORD will help you defeat your enemies who come to fight against you. Your enemies will come against you one way, but they will run away from you seven different ways! "The LORD will bless you and fill your barns. He will bless everything you do. The LORD your God will bless you in the land that he is giving you. The LORD will make you his own special people, as he promised. The Lord will do this <u>if</u> you follow the LORD your God and obey his commands. Then all the people in that land will see that you are called to be the LORD'S people, and they will be afraid of you. "And the LORD will give you many good things. He will give you many children. He will give your cows many calves. He will give you a good harvest in the land that the LORD promised your ancestors to give you. The LORD will open his storehouse where he keeps his rich blessings. He will send rain at the right time for your land. He will bless everything you do. You will have money to lend to many nations. And you will not need to borrow anything from them. The LORD will make you be like the head, not the tail. You will be on top, not on the bottom. This will happen <u>if you listen</u> to the commands of the LORD your God that I tell you today. You must carefully obey these commands. You must not turn away from any of the teachings that I give you today. You must not turn

> *away to the right or to the left. You must not follow*
> *other gods to serve them.* Deuteronomy 28:1-14

The fulfillment of God's promises to specific people had conditions attached. The promise was made to the forefathers, but the people who participated in those promises could vary depending on their faith and obedience. Not all of Abraham's, Isaac's, and Jacob's descendents lived to see the Promised Land – many died in the wilderness because of their unbelief.

> *But if you don't listen to what the LORD your God tells*
> *you–if you don't obey all his commands and laws that I*
> *tell you today–then all these bad things will happen to you:*
> Deuteronomy 28:15

> *All these curses will come on you. They will keep chasing*
> *you and catching you, until you are destroyed, <u>because</u>*
> *<u>you did not listen</u> to what the LORD your God told*
> *you. <u>You did not obey</u> the commands and laws that he*
> *gave you.* Deuteronomy 28:45

> *You might have as many people as the stars in the sky.*
> *But only a few of you will be left, <u>because you did not</u>*
> *<u>listen</u> to the LORD your God. "The LORD was happy*
> *to be good to you and to make your nation grow. In the*
> *same way the LORD will be happy to ruin and destroy*
> *you. You are going to take that land to be yours. But*
> *people will take you out of that land!*
> Deuteronomy 28:62-63

> *When all these blessings and curses I have set before you*
> *come upon you and you take them to heart wherever the*
> *LORD your God disperses you among the nations, <u>and</u>*

*when you and your children return to the LORD your
God and obey him with all your heart and with all your
soul according to everything I command you today, then
the LORD your God will restore your fortunes and have
compassion on you and gather you again from all the
nations where he scattered you.* Deuteronomy 30:1-3 NIV

*"Today I have given you a choice between life and death,
success and disaster. I command you today to love the
LORD your God. I command you to follow him and to
obey his commands, laws, and rules. Then you will live,
and your nation will grow larger. And the LORD your
God will bless you in the land that you are entering to
take for your own. But if you turn away from your God
and refuse to listen, if you are led away to worship and
serve other gods, you will be destroyed. I am warning you
today, if you turn away from God, you will not live long
in that land across the Jordan River that you are ready
to enter and take for your own. "Today I am giving you
a choice of two ways. And I ask heaven and earth to be
witnesses of your choice. You can choose life or death.
The first choice will bring a blessing. The other choice
will bring a curse. So choose life! Then you and your
children will live. You must love the LORD your God
and obey him. Never leave him, because he is your life.
And he will give you a long life in the land that he, the
LORD, promised to give to your ancestors--Abraham,
Isaac, and Jacob."* Deuteronomy 30:15-20

God gives us different options, and based on our choices, he
either blesses or curses us. There is no hint of predetermination
or foreknowledge of what each man will choose.

> *The LORD said to Moses, "You will die soon. And after*
> *you have gone to be with your ancestors, these people*
> *will not continue to be faithful to me. They will break*
> *the agreement I made with them. They will leave me and*
> *begin worshiping other gods–the false gods of the land*
> *where they are going. At that time I will become very*
> *angry with them, and I will leave them. I will refuse to*
> *help them, and they will be destroyed. Terrible things will*
> *happen to them, and they will have many troubles. Then*
> *they will say, 'These bad things happened to us because*
> *our God is not with us.' And I will refuse to help them,*
> *because they have done evil and worshiped other gods.*
> Deuteronomy 31:16-18

God knew the evil in the heart of these people and what they would decide to do once the restraint of Moses was taken away. But at the same time, it was not true of all of the people – some chose to continue to worship the true God.

Conclusion

If you believe in the absolute foreknowledge of God about all things future, how do you explain that God was making credible warnings about things whose outcome he supposedly "already knew?" You cannot legitimately argue that God's actions were anthropomorphisms (God acting as though he were a man). If this were true and he were only saying these things for the benefit of man, then how could it be of any benefit to man if God already knew what he would think, believe and do? What men believed or did would already have been pre–determined by God's foreknowledge, so God's play–acting could not have made any real difference in the outcome. If it was all foreknown, then God already knew what man was going to believe. There can be no education taking place either for man or for God if indeed God already knows everything.

Was God only pretending that these people had a choice? The ignorant "hillbillies" in those days believed that his threats and conditional promises were real. Apparently they did not have the theological knowledge that we do, or they wouldn't have fallen for God's theatrics.

In my theology, I would rather side with Abraham, Moses, David, Isaiah, and their like than with many Christians of our time. You cannot find one person in the first five books of the Bible (or any of the other books) who believed that the future was already determined. Page after page after page reveals that the future was determined first by the initiative of God, then by the actions of men, and at last by God's response to those actions. God's purpose never wavered, but his path on how to achieve his purposes was in constant change owing to the faithfulness or unfaithfulness of men.

19. More overwhelming evidence Joshua – Job

Joshua

Throughout the Old Testament, we see warning after warning about the consequences of disobeying God, and the blessings when we repent and obey.

> Joshua said, "Why have you brought this trouble on us? The LORD will bring trouble on you today." Then all Israel stoned him, and after they had stoned the rest, they burned them. Over Achan they heaped up a large pile of rocks, which remains to this day. <u>Then the LORD turned from his fierce anger</u>.
> Joshua 7:25-26 NIV

> Never stop following him. Don't become friends with those people who did not leave when you took the land. They are not part of Israel. Don't marry any of their people. <u>If</u> you become friends with those people, the LORD your God <u>will not help you</u> defeat your enemies. They will become like a trap for you. They will cause

you pain–like smoke and dust in your eyes. And you will be forced to leave this good land. The LORD your God gave you this land. <u>But you can lose it if you don't obey this command</u>.   Joshua 23:12-13

"It is almost time for me to die. You know and really believe that the Lord has done many great things for you. You know that the LORD your God has not failed in any of his promises. He has kept every promise that he has made to us. Every good promise that the LORD your God made to us has come true. But in the same way, the LORD will make his other promises come true: <u>If you do wrong, bad things will happen to you</u>. You will be forced to leave this good land that the LORD your God has given to you. This will happen <u>if you refuse to keep your agreement with the LORD your God</u>. You will lose this land if you go and serve other gods. You must not worship those other gods. <u>If you do</u>, the LORD will become very angry with you. <u>Then</u> you will quickly be forced to leave this good land that he gave you."
                                  Joshua 23:14-16

Moses, in his parting message, clearly shows that the future of Israel will be determined by their behavior. Moses did not believe that the future was already decided.

Judges

The angel of the LORD went up to the city of Bokim from the city of Gilgal. The angel spoke this message from the Lord to the Israelites: "I brought you out of Egypt and led you to the land that I promised to give to your ancestors. I *told you I would never break my agreement with you. But in return, <u>you must never</u> make any agreement with the people living in that land. You must destroy their altars. <u>I told you that, but you didn't obey me.</u> "<u>Now I will tell you this,</u> 'I will not force the other people to leave this land any longer. These people will become a problem for you. They will be like a trap to you. Their false gods will become like a net to trap you.'"* Judges 2:1-3

This was a change in God's original plan. At this point in Israel's history we are at plan J or K.

After that whole generation died, the next generation grew up. This new generation did not know about the LORD or what he had done for the Israelites. So the Israelites did something very evil before the LORD. They began serving the false god Baal. It was the LORD, the God their ancestors worshiped, who had brought the Israelites out of Egypt. But <u>they stopped following him</u> and began to worship the false gods of the people living around them. <u>This made the LORD angry.</u> The Israelites <u>stopped following</u> the LORD and began worshiping Baal and Ashtoreth. <u>The LORD was angry with the Israelites</u>, so he let enemies attack them and take their possessions. <u>He let their enemies who lived around them defeat them.</u> The Israelites could not protect themselves from their enemies. When the Israelites went out to fight, they always lost. They lost because the LORD was not on their side. He had already warned them that they would lose if they served the gods of the people living around them. The Israelites suffered very much. Judges 2:10-15

<u>So the LORD became angry</u> with the Israelites, and he said, "This nation has broken the agreement that I made

with their ancestors. They have not listened to me. So I will no longer defeat the nations and clear the way for the Israelites. Those nations were still in this land when Joshua died, and I will let them stay in this land. I will use them to test the Israelites. <u>I will see if the Israelites can keep the LORD'S commands as their ancestors did.</u>" The LORD allowed those nations to stay in the land. He did not quickly force them to leave the country. He did not help Joshua's army defeat them.

Judges 2:20-23

The LORD did not force all the other nations to leave Israel's land. <u>He wanted to test the Israelites</u>. None of the Israelites living at this time had fought in the wars to take the land of Canaan. So he let those other nations stay in their country. (He did this to teach the Israelites who had not fought in those wars.) Here are the names of the nations the Lord left in the land: the five rulers of the Philistines, all the Canaanites, the people of Sidon, and the Hivites who lived in the Lebanon mountains from Mount Baal Hermon to Lebo Hamath. <u>He left those nations in the land to test the Israelites. He wanted to see if the Israelites would obey the LORD'S commands</u> that he had given to their ancestors through Moses.

Judges 3:1-4

Again, why would God need to test the Israelites if he already knew everything that was in their heart and what they were going to do in the future? Don't say that this test was only to show the Israelites how they would react, or just to teach them warfare. That's not what the text says. It says that the purpose of the test was for God to find out how they would react.

The LORD <u>saw</u> that the Israelites did evil things. They forgot about the LORD their God and served the false gods Baal and Asherah. <u>The LORD was angry</u> with the Israelites, so he allowed King Cushan Rishathaim of Aram Naharaim to defeat the Israelites and to rule over them. The Israelites were under that king's rule for eight years.   Judges 3:7-8

Once again the Israelites did evil in the eyes of the LORD, and <u>because</u> they did this evil <u>the LORD gave</u> Eglon king of Moab power over Israel.   Judges 3:12 NIV

After Ehud died, the Israelites once again <u>did</u> evil in the eyes of the LORD. <u>So</u> the LORD sold them into the hands of Jabin, a king of Canaan, who reigned in Hazor.   Judges 4:1-2 NIV

Again the Israelites did evil in the eyes of the LORD, <u>and</u> for seven years he gave them into the hands of the Midianites.   Judges 6:1 NIV

Gideon said to God, "If you will save Israel by my hand as you have promised–look, I will place a wool fleece on the threshing floor. If there is dew only on the fleece and all the ground is dry, <u>then</u> I will know that you will save Israel by my hand, as you said." And that is what happened. Gideon rose early the next day; he squeezed the fleece and wrung out the dew–a bowlful of water. Then Gideon said to God, "Do not be angry with me. Let me make just one more request. Allow me one more test with the fleece. This time make the fleece dry and the ground covered with dew." That night God did so. Only the fleece was dry; all the ground was covered with dew.
                Judges 6:36-40 NIV

316 GOD IS WITH US

Again the Israelites did evil in the eyes of the LORD. They served the Baals and the Ashtoreths, and the gods of Aram, the gods of Sidon, the gods of Moab, the gods of the Ammonites and the gods of the Philistines. <u>And because</u> the Israelites forsook the LORD and no longer served him, <u>he became angry</u> with them. He sold them into the hands of the Philistines and the Ammonites, who that year shattered and crushed them.

Judges 10:6-8 NIV

The LORD replied, "When the Egyptians, the Amorites, the Ammonites, the Philistines, the Sidonians, the Amalekites and the Maonites oppressed you and you cried to me for help, did I not save you from their hands? <u>But</u> you have forsaken me and served other gods, <u>so</u> I will no longer save you. Go and cry out to the gods you have chosen. Let them save you when you are in trouble!" But the Israelites said to the LORD, "We have sinned. Do with us whatever you think best, but please rescue us now." Then they got rid of the foreign gods among them and served the LORD. <u>And he could bear Israel's misery no longer</u>. Judges 10:11-16 NIV

Again the Israelites did evil in the eyes of the LORD, <u>so</u> the LORD delivered them into the hands of the Philistines for forty years. Judges 13:1 NIV

The whole book of Judges relates Israel's straying from God to do evil and worship false gods, and his response to their cries when they were afflicted. If they had remained faithful to God, he would not have afflicted them and given them into the hands of their enemies. What happened to them was a consequence of their actions.

1 Samuel

> "*Therefore* the LORD, the God of Israel, declares: `I promised that your house and your father's house would minister before me forever.' But now the LORD declares: `Far be it from me! Those who honor me I will honor, but those who despise me will be disdained. The time is coming when I will cut short your strength and the strength of your father's house, so that there will not be an old man in your family line and you will see distress in my dwelling. Although good will be done to Israel, in your family line there will never be an old man. Every one of you that I do not cut off from my altar will be spared only to blind your eyes with tears and to grieve your heart, and all your descendants will die in the prime of life.* 1 Samuel 2:30-33 NIV

Here, God breaks a promise he had made to Eli the priest because of the unfaithfulness of his sons and his own unfaithfulness. After this dressing down from God, Eli did not believe that the future was already decided and couldn't be changed, because God changed it.

> *You must fear and respect the LORD. You must serve him and obey his commands. You must not turn against him. You and the king ruling over you must follow the LORD your God. If you do, God will save you. But if you don't listen to the LORD, if you refuse to do what the LORD says, he will be against you. The LORD will destroy you and your king.* 1 Samuel 12:14-15

> *But you must honor the LORD. You must serve him sincerely with all your heart. Remember the wonderful*

things he has done for you. But if you are stubborn and do evil, God will throw you and your king away, like dirt swept out with a broom. 1 Samuel 12:24-25

Samuel said, "You did a foolish thing. You did not obey the LORD your God. If you had done what he commanded, the LORD would have let your family rule Israel forever. But now your kingdom won't continue. The LORD was looking for a man who wants to obey him. He has found that man—and the LORD has chosen him to be the new leader of his people, because you didn't obey his command." 1 Samuel 13:13-14

Then the LORD said to Samuel, "I am sorry that I ever made Saul king, for he has not been loyal to Me and has refused to obey My command." Samuel was so deeply moved when he heard this that he cried out to the LORD all night. 1 Samuel 15:10-11NLT

For rebellion is like the sin of divination, and arrogance like the evil of idolatry. Because you have rejected the word of the LORD, he has rejected you as king." 1 Samuel 15:23 NIV

God reluctantly changed his plans because of the sinfulness of Saul.

When Samuel turned to leave, Saul caught Samuel's robe. The robe tore. Samuel said to Saul, "In this same way the LORD has torn the kingdom of Israel from you today. He has given the kingdom to one of your friends, a man who is a better person than you. The one who lives forever, the God of Israel, does not lie and will not

> *change his mind. He is not like a man who is always*
> *changing his mind. "*   1 Samuel 15:27-29

This is covered in detail in Chapter 10 *"Does God change his mind?"* I believe this statement refers to this specific decision by God to take the kingdom from Saul and give it to David. It is not a general declaration about all of God's plans and decisions, but refers to this plan to tear the kingdom from Saul. Samuel did change <u>his</u> mind and went with Saul to the sacrifices. But God did not change his mind. It is possible that God would have allowed Saul to continue as king after his first great offense if he had seriously repented. But after this new, greater offense, God decided that there was no hope for Saul to truly worship him. Saul turned away from God and toward his own ego, and he went downhill from there.

> *Until the day Samuel died, he did not go to see Saul again,*
> *though Samuel mourned for him. <u>And the LORD was</u>*
> <u>*grieved*</u> *that he had made Saul king over Israel.*
>   1 Samuel 15:35 NIV

When God, in his own words says "I am grieved," why don't we believe him? It's because our theological prejudice won't allow us to accept the Scripture for what it says. We condemn cults for doing this, and yet we are hypocrites because we often do the same thing ourselves.

2 Samuel

> *Then Nathan said to David, "You are that rich man! This*
> *is what the LORD, the God of Israel, says: 'I chose you*
> *to be the king of Israel. I saved you from Saul. I let you*

take his family and his wives, and I made you king of Israel and Judah. As if that had not been enough, I would have given you more and more. So why did you ignore my command? Why did you do what I say is wrong? You let the Ammonites kill Uriah the Hittite, and you took his wife. It is as if you yourself killed Uriah in war. So your family will never have peace! When you took Uriah's wife, you showed that you did not respect me.'

2 Samuel 12:7-10

It had not been God's plan for David to have continual warfare, but because of his sin, God changed his plan.

David said, "While the baby was still living, I cried and refused to eat because I thought, 'Who knows? <u>Maybe the LORD will feel sorry for me and let the baby live.</u>' But now the baby is dead, so why should I refuse to eat? Can I bring the baby back to life? No. Some day I will go to him, but he cannot come back to me."

2 Samuel 12:22-23

David believed that it was in God's power to change what happened to his Son. He did not believe that the decision was already a foregone conclusion.

1 Kings

Bathsheba answered, "Sir, you used the name of the LORD your God and made a promise to me. You said, 'Your son Solomon will be the next king after me. He will sit on my throne.' Now, you don't know this, but Adonijah is making himself king. He is giving a big fellowship meal. He has killed many cattle and the best sheep, and he has invited all of your sons to the meal. He also invited Abiathar the priest and Joab, the commander of your army, but he did not invite your faithful son Solomon. Now, my lord and king, all the Israelites are watching you. They are waiting for you to decide who will be the next king after you. If you don't decide, then after you are buried, these men will say that Solomon and I are criminals."   1 Kings 1:17-21

Bathsheba didn't believe in the absolute foreknowledge of God.

"I am about to die, like all men must. But you are growing stronger and becoming a man. Now, carefully obey all the commands of the LORD your God. Carefully obey all his laws, commands, decisions, and agreements. Obey everything that is written in the Law of Moses. If you do this, you will be successful at whatever you do and wherever you go. And if you obey the LORD, he will keep his promise about me. He said, 'If your sons carefully live the way I tell them, sincerely, with all their heart, the king of Israel will always be a man from your family.'"   1 Kings 2:2-4

David didn't believe that the future was a foregone conclusion.

The LORD said to Solomon, "If you obey all my laws and commands, I will do for you what I promised your father David. I will live among the children of Israel in this Temple that you are building, and I will never leave the people of Israel."   1 Kings 6:11-13

"When famine or plague comes to the land, or blight or mildew, locusts or grasshoppers, or when an enemy

besieges them in any of their cities, whatever disaster or disease may come, and <u>when</u> a prayer or plea is made by any of your people Israel–each one aware of the afflictions of his own heart, and spreading out his hands toward this temple – then hear from heaven, your dwelling place. Forgive and act; <u>deal with each man according to all he does, since you know his heart (for you alone know the hearts of all men)</u>, so that they will fear you all the time they live in the land you gave our fathers.

1 Kings 8:37-40 NIV

"As for you, if you walk before me in integrity of heart and uprightness, as David your father did, and <u>do all I command and observe my decrees and laws</u>, I will establish your royal throne over Israel forever, as I promised David your father when I said, `You shall never fail to have a man on the throne of Israel.' "<u>But if</u> you or your sons turn away from me and do not observe the commands and decrees I have given you and go off to serve other gods and worship them, <u>then</u> I will cut off Israel from the land I have given them and will reject this temple I have consecrated for my Name. Israel will then become a byword and an object of ridicule among all peoples. And though this temple is now imposing, all who pass by will be appalled and will scoff and say, `<u>Why</u> has the LORD done such a thing to this land and to this temple?' People will answer, `<u>Because</u> they have forsaken the LORD their God, who brought their fathers out of Egypt, and have embraced other gods, worshiping and serving them–<u>that is why</u> the LORD brought all this disaster on them.' "

1 Kings 9:4-9 NIV

The following are numerous clear promises and warnings, and also explanations of why God changes his plans:

*I will take the kingdom from Solomon <u>because he stopped
following me and began worshiping Ashtoreth</u>, the goddess
of Sidon; Chemosh, the god of Moab; and Milcom, the
god of the Ammonites. Solomon stopped following my
ways and doing what I say is right. <u>He does not obey</u> my
laws and commands as his father David did.*

1 Kings 11:33

*The LORD <u>became angry</u> with Solomon <u>because</u> his heart
had turned away from the LORD, the God of Israel, who
had appeared to him twice. Although he had forbidden
Solomon to follow other gods, Solomon did not keep
the LORD's command. So the LORD said to Solomon,
"<u>Since</u> this is your attitude and you have not kept my
covenant and my decrees, which I commanded you, <u>I will</u>
most certainly tear the kingdom away from you and give
it to one of your subordinates. Nevertheless, for the sake
of David your father, I will not do it during your lifetime.
I will tear it out of the hand of your son.*

1 Kings 11:9-12 NIV

*`See, I am going to tear the kingdom out of Solomon's
hand and give you ten tribes. But for the sake of my
servant David and the city of Jerusalem, which I have
chosen out of all the tribes of Israel, he will have one
tribe. <u>I will</u> do this because they have forsaken me and
worshiped Ashtoreth the goddess of the Sidonians,
Chemosh the god of the Moabites, and Molech the god
of the Ammonites, and have not walked in my ways, nor
done what is right in my eyes, nor kept my statutes and
laws as David, Solomon's father, did.*

1 Kings 11:31-33 NIV

324 GOD IS WITH US

However, as for you, I will take you, and you will rule over all that your heart desires; you will be king over Israel. If you do whatever I command you and walk in my ways and do what is right in my eyes by keeping my statutes and commands, as David my servant did, I will be with you. I will build you a dynasty as enduring as the one I built for David and will give Israel to you.

1 Kings 11:37-38 NIV

Even after this, Jeroboam did not change his evil ways, but once more appointed priests for the high places from all sorts of people. Anyone who wanted to become a priest he consecrated for the high places. This was the sin of the house of Jeroboam that led to its downfall and to its destruction from the face of the earth.

1 Kings 13:33-34 NIV

So when Ahijah heard the sound of her footsteps at the door, he said, "Come in, wife of Jeroboam. Why this pretense? I have been sent to you with bad news. Go, tell Jeroboam that this is what the LORD, the God of Israel, says: `I raised you up from among the people and made you a leader over my people Israel. I tore the kingdom away from the house of David and gave it to you, but you have not been like my servant David, who kept my commands and followed me with all his heart, doing only what was right in my eyes. You have done more evil than all who lived before you. You have made for yourself other gods, idols made of metal; you have provoked me to anger and thrust me behind your back.c "Because of this, I am going to bring disaster on the house of Jeroboam. I will cut off from Jeroboam every last male in Israel—slave or free. I will burn up the house of Jeroboam as one burns *dung, until it is all gone. Dogs will eat those belonging to Jeroboam who die in the city, and the birds of the air will feed on those who die in the country. The LORD has spoken!'*   1 Kings 14:6-11 NIV

"As for you, go back home. When you set foot in your city, the boy will die. All Israel will mourn for him and bury him. He is the only one belonging to Jeroboam who will be buried, because he is the only one in the house of Jeroboam in whom the LORD, the God of Israel, has found anything good.   1 Kings 14:12-13 NIV

And he will give Israel up <u>because</u> of the sins Jeroboam has committed and has caused Israel to commit."   1 Kings 14:16 NIV

Judah did evil in the eyes of the LORD. By the sins they committed <u>they stirred up</u> his jealous anger more than their fathers had done.   1 Kings 14:22 NIV

He committed all the sins his father had done before him; his heart was not fully devoted to the LORD his God, as the heart of David his forefather had been. Nevertheless, for David's sake the LORD his God gave him a lamp in Jerusalem by raising up a son to succeed him and by making Jerusalem strong. For David had done what was right in the eyes of the LORD and had not failed to keep any of the LORD's commands all the days of his life– except in the case of Uriah the Hittite.   1 Kings 15:3-5 NIV

As soon as he began to reign, he killed Jeroboam's whole family. He did not leave Jeroboam anyone that breathed,

326 GOD IS WITH US

but destroyed them all, according to the word of the LORD given through his servant Ahijah the Shilonite–because of the sins Jeroboam had committed and had caused Israel to commit, and because he provoked the LORD, the God of Israel, to anger.   1 Kings 15:29-30 NIV

As soon as he began to reign and was seated on the throne, he killed off Baasha's whole family. He did not spare a single male, whether relative or friend. So Zimri destroyed the whole family of Baasha, in accordance with the word of the LORD spoken against Baasha through the prophet Jehu– because of all the sins Baasha and his son Elah had committed and had caused Israel to commit, so that they provoked the LORD, the God of Israel, to anger by their worthless idols.   1 Kings 16:11-13 NIV

But Omri did evil in the eyes of the LORD and sinned more than all those before him. He walked in all the ways of Jeroboam son of Nebat and in his sin, which he had caused Israel to commit, so that they provoked the LORD, the God of Israel, to anger by their worthless idols.   1 Kings 16:25-26 NIV

When Ahab heard these words, he tore his clothes, put on sackcloth and fasted. He lay in sackcloth and went around meekly. Then the word of the LORD came to Elijah the Tishbite: "Have you noticed how Ahab has humbled himself before me? Because he has humbled himself, I will not bring this disaster in his day, but I will bring it on his house in the days of his son."   1 Kings 21:27-29 NIV

Elijah didn't believe that all of life's future events were already determined. God kept showing him that the future was being determined not only by God's desires, but also by the choices that men made.

2 Kings

> *But the LORD'S angel said to Elijah the Tishbite, "King Ahaziah has sent some messengers from Samaria. Go meet those men and ask them, 'There is a God in Israel, so why are you men going to ask questions of Baal Zebub, the god of Ekron? <u>Since you did this</u>, the LORD says, <u>You will not get up from your bed</u>. You will die!'" Then Elijah left.* 2 Kings 1:3-4

> *After they crossed the river, Elijah said to Elisha, "What do you want me to do for you before God takes me away from you?" Elisha said, "I ask you for a double share of your spirit on me." Elijah said, "<u>You have asked a hard thing</u>. If you see me when I am taken from you, <u>it will happen</u>. <u>But if you don't</u> see me when I am taken from you, <u>it will not happen</u>."* 2 Kings 2:9-10

Why would this have been hard if God already knew all of the future? It would have been either easy because it was foreknown or impossible because it wasn't. Elijah believed that God's decision concerning Elisha's request was still to be made, and was not already known.

> *Elisha said to him, "That is not true! My heart was with you when the man turned from his chariot to meet you. This is not the time to take money, clothes, olives, grapes, sheep, cattle, or men and women servants. <u>Now</u> you and your children will catch Naaman's disease. You will have*

leprosy forever!" When Gehazi left Elisha, his skin was as white as snow! He was sick with leprosy.
2 Kings 5:26-27
(NLT – Because you have done this, Naaman's leprosy will cling to you.)

These horses and chariots of fire came down to Elisha. He prayed to the LORD and said, "I pray that you will cause these people to become blind." So God did what Elisha asked. He caused the Aramean army to become blind.
2 Kings 6:18

There were four men sick with leprosy near the city gate. They said to each other, "Why are we sitting here waiting to die? There is no food in Samaria. If we go into the city, we will die there. If we stay here, we will also die. So let's go to the Aramean camp. If they let us live, we will live. If they kill us, we will just die." 2 Kings 7:3-4

The LORD said to Jehu, "You have done well. You have done what I say is good. You destroyed Ahab's family the way I wanted you to, so your descendants will rule Israel for four generations." 2 Kings 10:30

Jehoahaz son of Jehu became king over Israel in Samaria. This was during the 23rd year that Joash son of Ahaziah was king in Judah. Jehoahaz ruled 17 years. Jehoahaz did what the LORD considered wrong. Like Jeroboam son of Nebat, he committed sins that also caused the people of Israel to sin. And he never stopped doing those things. Then the LORD was angry with Israel. He let King Hazael of Aram and Hazael's son Ben-Hadad gain control of Israel. Then Jehoahaz begged the LORD to

help them. The LORD listened to him because he had seen the terrible troubles that the king of Aram had caused the Israelites. So the LORD sent a man to save Israel. The Israelites were free from the Arameans. So the Israelites went to their own homes, as they did before.
2 Kings 13:1-5

Elisha said to Jehoash, "Take a bow and some arrows." Jehoash took a bow and some arrows. Then Elisha said to the king of Israel, "Put your hand on the bow." Jehoash put his hand on the bow. Then Elisha put his hands on the king's hands. Elisha said, "Open the east window." Jehoash opened the window. Then Elisha said, "Shoot." Jehoash shot. Then Elisha said, "This is the LORD'S arrow of victory over Aram! You will defeat the Arameans at Aphek until you destroy them." Elisha said, "Take the arrows." Jehoash took the arrows. Then Elisha said to him, "Hit on the ground." Jehoash hit the ground three times. Then he stopped. The man of God was angry with Jehoash. Elisha said, "You should have hit five or six times! Then you would have defeated Aram until you destroyed it! But now, you will defeat Aram only three times."
2 Kings 13:15-19

Elisha did not believe that the future was already determined, but that it depended on how many times the king struck the ground. The future was open and was not foreknown or predetermined by God. The future changed because of what the king had done.

These things happened because the Israelites had sinned against the LORD their God. And it was the Lord who brought the Israelites out of the land of Egypt! He saved them from the power of Pharaoh, the king of Egypt. But the Israelites began worshiping other gods. They began doing the same things that other people did. And the LORD had forced those people to leave their land when the Israelites came. The Israelites also chose to be ruled by kings. The Israelites secretly did things against the LORD their God, and those things were wrong! The Israelites built high places in all their cities--from the smallest town to the largest city. They put up memorial stones and Asherah poles on every high hill and under every green tree. They burned incense there in all those places for worship. They did these things like the nations that the LORD forced out of the land before them. The Israelites did evil things that made the LORD angry. They served idols, and the LORD had said to them, "You must not do this." The LORD used every prophet and every seer to warn Israel and Judah. He said, "Turn away from the evil things you do. Obey my commands and laws. Follow all the law that I gave to your ancestors. I used my servants the prophets to give this law to you." But the people would not listen. They were very stubborn like their ancestors. Their ancestors did not believe the LORD their God. They refused to follow his laws and the agreement he made with their ancestors. They would not listen to his warnings. They worshiped idols that were worth nothing and they themselves became worth nothing. The LORD had warned them not to do the evil things that the people in the nations around them did. But they lived the same way those people lived. The people stopped following the commands of the LORD their God. They made two gold statues of calves. They made Asherah poles. They worshiped all the stars of heaven and served Baal. They sacrificed their sons and daughters in the fire.

They used magic and witchcraft to try to learn the future.
They sold themselves to do what the LORD said was evil.
They did this to make him angry. So the LORD became
very angry with Israel and removed them from his sight.
There were no Israelites left, except the tribe of Judah.

2 Kings 17:7-18

This account shows very clearly "cause and effect" of man's choices. Our decisions have consequences for what happens in the future. What happened is clearly not what God desired to do. He wanted to bless Israel, but they rebelled against him and he was left no recourse but to punish them. This doesn't sound like fatalism where everything was already known beforehand.

At that time Hezekiah became sick and almost died. The
prophet Isaiah son of Amoz went to see him and told
him, "The LORD says, 'You will die soon, so you should
tell your family what they should do when you die. You
will not get well.'" Hezekiah turned his face to the wall
that faced the Temple and began praying to the LORD.
"LORD, remember that I have sincerely served you with
all my heart. I have done what you say is good." Then
Hezekiah cried very hard. Before Isaiah had left the middle
courtyard, he received this message from the LORD, "Go
back and speak to Hezekiah, the leader of my people. Tell
him, 'This is what the LORD, the God of your ancestor
David, says: I heard your prayer and I saw your tears,
so I will heal you. On the third day you will go up to the
Temple of the LORD. I will add 15 years to your life. I
will save you and this city from the king of Assyria. I will
protect this city. I will do this for myself and because of
the promise I made to my servant David.'"

2 Kings 20:1-6

Isaiah said, "Which do you want? Should the shadow go forward ten steps or go back ten steps? This is the sign for you from the LORD to show that the LORD will do what he said he would do." Hezekiah answered, "It is an easy thing for the shadow to go down ten steps. No, make the shadow go back ten steps." Then Isaiah prayed, and the LORD made the shadow move back ten steps. It went back up the steps that it had already been on.

2 Kings 20:9-11

Hezekiah and Isaiah knew that life's events could be changed through the behavior of people. If it can be changed, then it cannot be foreknown.

"King Josiah of Judah sent you to ask advice from the LORD. Tell Josiah that this is what the LORD, the God of Israel, says: 'You heard the words I spoke against this place and those who live here. And when you heard those things, your heart was soft, and you showed your sorrow before the LORD. I said that terrible things would happen to this place. So you tore your clothes to show your sadness, and you began to cry. That is why I heard you.' This is what the LORD says. 'I will bring you to be with your ancestors. You will die and go to your grave in peace. So your eyes will not see all the trouble that I am bringing on this place.'" Then Hilkiah the priest, Ahikam, Acbor, Shaphan, and Asaiah gave that message to the king.

2 Kings 22:18-20

The LORD became so angry with Jerusalem and Judah that he threw them away. Zedekiah rebelled and refused to obey the king of Babylon.

2 Kings 24:20

1 Chronicles

Saul died <u>because</u> he was not faithful to the LORD. He did not obey the LORD'S word. Saul also went to a medium and asked her for advice instead of asking the LORD. <u>That is why the Lord killed Saul and gave the kingdom to Jesse's son David</u>.   1 Chronicles 10:13-14

Gad was David's seer. The LORD said to Gad, "Go and tell David: 'This is what the LORD says: I am going to give you three choices. <u>You must choose one of them. Then I will punish you the way you choose.</u>'" Then Gad went to David. He said to David, "The LORD says, 'David, choose which punishment you want: three years without enough food, or three months of running away from your enemies while they use their swords to chase you, or three days of punishment from the LORD. Terrible sicknesses will spread through the country, and the LORD'S angel will go through Israel destroying the people.' David, God sent me. Now, you must decide which answer I will give to him." David said to Gad, "I am in trouble! I don't want some man to decide my punishment. The LORD is very merciful, so let him decide how to punish me." So the LORD sent terrible sicknesses to Israel, and 70,000 people died. God sent an angel to destroy Jerusalem. But when the angel started to destroy Jerusalem, the LORD saw it and felt sorry for all the suffering. So he said to the angel who was destroying the people, "Stop! That is enough!" This happened when the angel of the LORD was standing at the threshing floor of Araunah the Jebusite.   1 Chronicles 21:9-15

Both Gad and David believed that God gave David a legitimate choice and it was not a predetermined out–come.

"And you, my son Solomon, acknowledge the God of your father, and serve him with wholehearted devotion and with a willing mind, for the LORD <u>searches every heart and understands every motive behind the thoughts</u>. If you seek him, <u>he will be found</u> by you; <u>but if</u> you forsake him, he will reject you forever. Consider now, for the LORD has chosen you to build a temple as a sanctuary. Be strong and do the work." 1 Chronicles 28:9-10 NIV

I know, my God, that <u>You examine our hearts and rejoice when You find integrity there</u>. You know I have done all this with good motives, and I have watched Your people offer their gifts willingly and joyously.
1 Chronicles 29:17 NLT

2 Chronicles

God said to Solomon, "<u>Because</u> your greatest desire is to help your people, and you did not ask for wealth, riches, fame, or even the death of your enemies or a long life, but rather you asked for wisdom and knowledge to properly govern My people–<u>I will</u> certainly give you the wisdom and knowledge you requested. But I will also give you wealth, riches, and fame such as no other king has had before you or will ever have in the future!"
2 Chronicles 1:11-12 NLT

"<u>But if you</u> or your descendants abandon Me and <u>disobey</u> the decrees and commands I have given you, and if you serve and worship other gods, <u>then I</u> will uproot the people from this land that I have given them. I will reject this Temple that I have made holy to honor My name.

*I will make it an object of mockery and ridicule among
the nations. And though this Temple is impressive now,
all who pass by will be appalled. They will ask, 'Why did
the LORD do such terrible things to this land and to this
Temple?' "And the answer will be, 'Because His people
abandoned the LORD, the God of their ancestors, who
brought them out of Egypt, and they worshiped other
gods instead and bowed down to them. That is why He
has brought all these disasters on them.'"*

2 Chronicles 7:19-22 NLT

*But when Rehoboam was firmly established and strong,
he abandoned the Law of the LORD, and all Israel
followed him in this sin. Because they were unfaithful to
the LORD, King Shishak of Egypt came up and attacked
Jerusalem in the fifth year of King Rehoboam's reign.*

2 Chronicles 12:1-2

*The prophet Shemaiah then met with Rehoboam and
Judah's leaders, who had all fled to Jerusalem because of
Shishak. Shemaiah told them, "This is what the LORD
says: You have abandoned Me, so I am abandoning you
to Shishak."*   2 Chronicles 12:5 NLT

*Then the leaders of Israel and the king humbled themselves
and said, "The LORD is right in doing this to us!" When
the LORD saw their change of heart, he gave this message
to Shemaiah: "Since the people have humbled themselves,
I will not completely destroy them and will soon give
them some relief. I will not use Shishak to pour out My
anger on Jerusalem.*   2 Chronicles 12:6-7 NLT

*At that time Hanani the seer came to King Asa and told
him, "Because you have put your trust in the king of*

Aram instead of in the LORD your God, you missed your chance to destroy the army of the king of Aram. Don't you remember what happened to the Ethiopians and Libyans and their vast army, with all of their chariots and charioteers? At that time you relied on the LORD, and He handed them over to you. <u>**The eyes of the LORD search the whole earth in order to strengthen those whose hearts are fully committed to Him**</u>. What a fool you have been! From now on you will be at war."

2 Chronicles 16:7-9 NLT

Some time later King Jehoshaphat of Judah made an alliance with King Ahaziah of Israel, who was very wicked. Together they built a fleet of trading ships at the port of Ezion–geber. Then Eliezer son of Dodavahu from Mareshah prophesied against Jehoshaphat. He said, "<u>Because</u> you have allied yourself with King Ahaziah, <u>the LORD will destroy your work.</u>" So the ships met with disaster and never put out to sea.

2 Chronicles 20:35-37 NLT

But after Jehoiada's death, the leaders of Judah came and bowed before King Joash and persuaded him to listen to their advice. They decided to abandon the Temple of the LORD, the God of their ancestors, and they worshiped Asherah poles and idols instead! <u>Because of this sin, divine anger fell on Judah and Jerusalem</u>. Yet the LORD sent prophets to bring them back to Him. The prophets warned them, but still the people would not listen. Then the Spirit of God came upon Zechariah son of Jehoiada the priest. He stood before the people and said, "This is what God says: Why do you disobey the LORD's commands and *keep yourselves from prospering? You have abandoned the LORD, and now He has abandoned you!"*

2 Chronicles 24:17-20 NLT

Uzziah was sixteen years old when he became king, and he reigned in Jerusalem fifty–two years. His mother was Jecoliah from Jerusalem. He did what was pleasing in the LORD's sight, just as his father, Amaziah, had done. Uzziah sought God during the days of Zechariah, who taught him to fear God. And as long as the king sought guidance from the LORD, God gave him success.

2 Chronicles 26:3-5 NLT

But when he had become powerful, he also became proud, which led to his downfall. He sinned against the LORD his God by entering the sanctuary of the LORD's Temple and personally burning incense on the incense altar. Azariah the high priest went in after him with eighty other priests of the LORD, all brave men. They confronted King Uzziah and said, "It is not for you, Uzziah, to burn incense to the LORD. That is the work of the priests alone, the descendants of Aaron who are set apart for this work. Get out of the sanctuary, for you have sinned. The LORD God will not honor you for this!"

2 Chronicles 26:16-18

Ahaz was 20 years old when he became king. He ruled 16 years in Jerusalem. He did not live right, as David his ancestor had done. Ahaz did not do what the LORD wanted him to do. He followed the bad example of the kings of Israel. He used molds to make idols to worship the Baal gods. He burned incense in the Valley of Ben Hinnom and sacrificed his own sons by burning them in the fire. He did the same terrible sins that the peoples living in that land did. The LORD had forced them out when the Israelites entered that land. Ahaz offered sacrifices and burned incense in the high places, on the hills, and under every green tree. Because Ahaz did these things, the LORD his God let the king of Aram defeat him. The king and his army defeated Ahaz and took many people of Judah as prisoners to the city of Damascus. Ahaz also suffered a terrible defeat by the king of Israel, Pekah son of Remaliah. Pekah and his army killed 120,000 of the bravest soldiers in Judah in one day. All this happened because the people of Judah had turned away from the LORD, the God their ancestors worshiped.

2 Chronicles 28:1-5

The LORD <u>gave troubles to Judah because</u> King Ahaz of Judah encouraged the people of Judah to sin. <u>He was very unfaithful to the LORD</u>.   2 Chronicles 28:19

Our ancestors <u>were not faithful and did what the LORD says is evil</u>. They stopped following him. They no longer paid any attention to the LORD'S house and turned their backs on him. They shut the doors of the porch of the Temple and let the fire go out in the lamps. They stopped burning incense and offering burnt offerings in the Holy Place to the God of Israel. <u>So the LORD became very angry</u> with the people of Judah and Jerusalem. <u>He punished</u> them so badly that it shocks and scares people to hear about it. But then they just laugh and shout their own insults against Judah. You know this is true. You have seen it happen. That is why our ancestors were killed in battle. Our sons, daughters, and wives were made prisoners. So now I, Hezekiah, have decided to make an agreement

with the LORD, the God of Israel. <u>Then he will not be</u>
<u>angry with us anymore</u>.   2 Chronicles 29:6-11

So the messengers took the king's letters all through Israel
and Judah. This is what the letters said: "Children of
Israel, <u>turn back to the LORD</u>, the God who Abraham,
Isaac, and Israel obeyed. <u>Then</u> God will come back to
you who are still alive and have escaped from the kings
of Assyria. Don't be like your fathers or your brothers.
The LORD was their God, but <u>they turned against him</u>.
<u>So</u> he made people hate them and speak evil about them.
You can see with your own eyes that this is true. Don't
be stubborn as your ancestors were. But <u>obey</u> the LORD
with a willing heart. <u>Come</u> to the Temple that he has made
to be holy forever. Serve the LORD your God. <u>Then</u> his
fearful anger will turn away from you. <u>If</u> you come back
and obey the LORD, your relatives and your children
will find mercy from the people who captured them. And
your relatives and your children will come back to this
land. The LORD your God is kind and merciful. <u>He</u>
<u>will not turn away from you if you come back to him</u>."
                                    2 Chronicles 30:6-9

So King Hezekiah did those good things in all Judah.
<u>He did what was good and right and faithful before the</u>
<u>LORD his God</u>. <u>He had success</u> in every work he began—
the service of God's Temple and in obeying the law and
commands, and in following his God. Hezekiah did all
these things with all his heart.   2 Chronicles 31:20-21

It was in those days that Hezekiah became very sick and
near death. He prayed to the LORD, and he spoke to
Hezekiah and gave him a sign. But <u>Hezekiah's heart was</u>

proud, so he did not give God thanks for his kindness. _This is why God was angry with Hezekiah_ and with the people of Judah and Jerusalem. But Hezekiah and the people living in Jerusalem _changed their hearts and lives._ _They became humble and stopped being proud._ So the LORD'S anger didn't come on them while Hezekiah was alive.   2 Chronicles 32:24-26

It was Hezekiah who stopped up the upper source of the waters of the Gihon Spring in Jerusalem and made the waters flow straight down on the west side of the City of David. And he was successful in everything he did. One time the leaders of Babylon sent messengers to Hezekiah. The messengers asked about a strange sign that had happened in the nations. When they came, _God left Hezekiah alone to test him and to know everything that was in Hezekiah's heart._   2 Chronicles 32:30-31

The LORD spoke to Manasseh and to his people, but _they refused to listen._ So the LORD brought commanders from the king of Assyria's army to attack Judah. These commanders captured Manasseh and made him their prisoner. They put hooks in him and brass chains on his hands and took him to the country of Babylon. When these troubles came to him, Manasseh _begged for help_ from the LORD his God. _He humbled himself_ before the God of his ancestors. Manasseh _prayed to God and begged him for help. God heard his begging and felt sorry for him, so he let Manasseh return to Jerusalem and to his throne._ Then Manasseh knew that the LORD was the true God.   2 Chronicles 33:10-13

When King Josiah heard the words of the law being read, he tore his clothes. Then the king gave a command to

Hilkiah, Ahikam son of Shaphan, Abdon son of Micah, Shaphan the secretary, and Asaiah the servant. The king said, "Go, ask the LORD for me and for the people who are left in Israel and in Judah. Ask about the words in the book that was found. <u>The LORD is very angry with us because our ancestors did not obey the LORD'S word</u>. They did not do everything this book says to do."

2 Chronicles 34:19-21

Huldah said to them, "This is what the LORD, the God of Israel, says: Tell King Josiah that the LORD says, 'I will bring trouble to this place and to the people living here. I will bring all the terrible things that are written in the book that was read in front of the king of Judah. I will do this <u>because the people left me</u> and burned incense to other gods. <u>They made me angry because of all the bad things they have done</u>. <u>So I will pour out my anger on this place</u>. Like a hot burning fire, my anger will not be put out!' "Go back to King Josiah of Judah, who sent you to ask what the LORD wants. Tell him, 'This is what the LORD, the God of Israel, says about the words you heard being read: Josiah, you repented and humbled yourself. In your sorrow you tore your clothes and cried before me. <u>So because your heart was tender</u>, I will take you to be with your ancestors. You will go to your grave in peace. You will not have to see any of the trouble that I will bring on this place and on the people living here.'" Hilkiah and the king's servants brought back this message to King Josiah.

2 Chronicles 34:23-28

The LORD, the God of their ancestors, sent prophets again and again to warn his people. He did this because <u>he felt sorry for them</u> and for his Temple. <u>He didn't</u>

want to destroy them or his Temple. But they made fun of God's prophets and _refused to listen_ to them. They hated God's messages. Finally, _the LORD could not hold his anger any longer_. He became angry with his people and there was nothing that could be done to stop it. _So God brought the king of Babylon to attack the people of Judah and Jerusalem_. The king of Babylon killed the young men even when they were in the Temple. He didn't have mercy on the people of Judah and Jerusalem. The king of Babylon killed young and old people. He killed men and women. He killed sick and healthy people. _God permitted Nebuchadnezzar to punish the people of Judah and Jerusalem_.   2 Chronicles 36:15-17

Ezra

There near the Ahava River, I announced that we all should fast. We should fast to make ourselves humble before our God. We wanted to ask God for a safe trip for ourselves, our children, and for everything we owned. I was embarrassed to ask King Artaxerxes for soldiers and horsemen to protect us as we traveled. There were enemies on the road. The reason I was embarrassed to ask for protection was because of what we had told the king. We had said to King Artaxerxes, "_Our God is with everyone who trusts him, but he is very angry with everyone who turns away from him._" So we fasted and prayed to our God about our trip. _He answered our prayers_.
                    Ezra 8:21-23

Then, when it was time for the evening sacrifice, I got up. I had made myself look shameful while I was sitting *there. My robe and coat were torn, and I fell on my knees with my hands spread out to the LORD my God. Then I prayed this prayer: "My God, I am too ashamed and embarrassed to look at you. I am ashamed because our sins are higher than our heads. Our guilt has reached all the way up to the heavens. We have been guilty of many sins from the days of our ancestors until now. We sinned so our kings and priests were punished. Foreign kings attacked us and took our people away. They took away our wealth and made us ashamed. It is the same even today.* Ezra 9:5-7

Nehemiah

When I heard this about the people of Jerusalem and about the wall, I sat down and cried. I was very sad. I fasted and prayed to the God of heaven for several days. Then I prayed this prayer: "LORD, God of heaven, you are the great and powerful God. You are the God who keeps his agreement of love with <u>people who love you and obey your commands</u>. "Please open your eyes and ears and listen to the prayer your servant is praying before you day and night. I am praying for your servants, the Israelites. I confess the sins we Israelites have done against you. I am confessing that I have sinned against you and that the other people in my father's family have sinned against you. We Israelites have been very bad to you. We have not obeyed the commands, rules, and laws you gave your servant Moses. Nehemiah 1:4-7

"Remember the instruction you gave your servant Moses, saying, `<u>If you are unfaithful, I will scatter you among the</u>

> *nations, but if you return to me and obey my commands,*
> *then even if your exiled people are at the farthest horizon,*
> *I will gather them from there and bring them to the place*
> *I have chosen as a dwelling for my Name.'*
>
> Nehemiah 1:8-9 NIV

Esther

> *Then Esther's message was given to Mordecai. When he*
> *got her message, Mordecai sent his answer back: "Esther,*
> *don't think that just because you live in the king's palace*
> *you will be the only Jew to escape. If you keep quiet now,*
> *help and freedom for the Jews will come from another*
> *place. But you and your father's family will all die. And*
> *who knows, maybe you have been chosen to be the queen*
> *for such a time as this."*   Esther 4:12-14

Mordecai believed that God had different options for saving
his people, and that the way he would do it was not foreknown
or predetermined.

> *Then Esther sent this answer to Mordecai: "Mordecai,*
> *go and get all the Jews in Susa together, and fast for me.*
> *Don't eat or drink for three days and nights. I and my*
> *women servants will fast too. After we fast, I will go to*
> *the king. I know it is against the law to go to the king if*
> *he didn't call me, but I will do it anyway. If I die, I die."*
>
> Esther 4:15-16

Esther knew that she could very well lose her life if the king
chose not to recognize her.

Job

> *Satan answered the LORD, "But Job has a good reason to respect you. You always protect him, his family, and everything he has. You have blessed him and made him successful in everything he does. He is so wealthy that his herds and flocks are all over the country. <u>But if you were to destroy everything he has, I promise you that he would curse you to your face.</u>"*   Job 1:9-11

> *Then another day came for the angels to meet with the LORD. Satan joined them for this meeting with the LORD. The LORD said to Satan, "Where have you been?" Satan answered the LORD, "I have been roaming around the earth, going from place to place." Then the LORD said to Satan, "Have you noticed my servant Job? There is no one on earth like him. He is a good, faithful man. He respects God and refuses to do evil. He is still faithful, even though you asked me to let you destroy, without reason, everything he has." Satan answered, "Skin for skin! A man will give everything he has to protect himself. I swear, <u>if you attack his flesh and bones, he will curse you to your face!</u>" So the LORD said to Satan, "All right, <u>Job is in your hands</u>, but you are not allowed to kill him."*   Job 2:1-6

Satan did not believe in God's foreknowledge of the future. God did not trust in his "foreknowledge" to tell him how the test of job would turn out. He trusted in his personal knowledge of Job's heart. He knew him, and knew where his love and loyalties lay. God did not initiate Job's suffering, but only responded to Satan's accusations against him.

346 GOD IS WITH US

Conclusion

You cannot find one person in these books of the Bible who believed that the future was already determined. These references show that God was inter-acting with men, and the way things turned out was a product of both God's initiative and man's response to him. Life was being lived by the participants and not being dictated by an invariable manuscript from the future.

20. Still more evidence
Psalms–Zechariah

You will probably grow tired of reading this chapter, because you will be reading evidence that says the same thing we have already seen, over and over – the future is not yet known by God but is a work in progress. You only need to read as far as it takes to convince you that all the future is not yet determined, and that your choices make a difference in how your life will turn out.

God does not know nor need to know every choice you will ever make. He will rejoice if you make good ones, and grieve if you make poor ones. He will eventually accomplish all his purposes, but the way he will do it is partly dependent on you, and certainly your individual benefits and rewards will depend on how you respond to God.

Psalm

> *Test me, O LORD, and try me, examine my heart and my mind;* Psalm 26:2 NIV

Why would David ask God to examine him if he already knew a millennium ago everything there was to know about him?

> I will instruct you and teach you in the way you should go; I will counsel you and watch over you.
> Psalm 32:8 NIV

David would not have needed this counsel since there was only one way he could go – the way that was predetermined by God's prior knowledge.

> How long, O LORD? Will you be angry forever? How long will your jealousy burn like fire?
> Psalm 79:5 NIV

David was appealing to God to stop being angry and come to Israel's rescue. He did not believe that the length of time that God would be angry was already determined, but that God's attitude could be changed.

> The LORD has sworn and will not change his mind: "You are a priest forever, in the order of Melchizedek."
> Psalm 110:4 NIV

Why would God need to swear on this issue that he would never change his mind, if he never changed his mind about anything? If God never changed his plans, then making this statement is superfluous. It would have been much easier to just state in the first chapter of Genesis that God never changes his mind about anything, and then save the paper and the ink used to write the rest of the Bible.

> A song for going up to the Temple. I look up to the hills, but where will my help really come from? My help will

come from the LORD, the Creator of heaven and earth.
He will not let you fall. Your Protector will not fall asleep.
Israel's Protector does not get tired. He never sleeps. The
LORD is your Protector. The LORD stands by your side,
shading and protecting you. The sun cannot harm you
during the day, and the moon cannot harm you at night.
The LORD will protect you from every danger. He will
protect your soul. The LORD will protect you as you
come and go, both now and forever!
Psalm 121:1-7

What harm could possibly come to the Psalmist if the course
of his life was already all laid out? Why would God bother to
watch over something for which he already knew the outcome?
If God already knew the future, the Psalmist was in no danger
and God could not have helped him anyway.

The LORD made a promise to David, an oath of loyalty
to him: "I will always put one of your descendants on your
throne. If your descendants obey my agreement and the
laws I teach them, then the king will always be someone
from your family."   Psalm 132:11-12

O LORD, you have searched me and you know me.
Psalm 139:1 NIV

This doesn't say "you have always known me from before the
beginning of time." Rather, it shows that God's knowledge
of the person is based on his present day examination of him.

God, examine me and know my mind. Test me and know
all my worries. Make sure that I am not going the wrong
way. Lead me on the path that has always been right.
Psalm 139:23-24

Why would David ask for this if he believed that God already knew everything about him and his future? This would be a meaningless, frivolous plea if David believed in God's omniscience of the future.

Proverbs

> *Wisdom begins with fear and respect for the LORD. Knowledge of the Holy One leads to understanding. Wisdom will <u>help you live longer; she will add years to your life</u>.*　　　　　Proverbs 9:10-11

This says that wisdom will add years to your life. How is this possible if God already knows how many days I will live as many theologians believe?

> *People might throw lots to make a decision, but the answer <u>always comes from the LORD</u>.*
> 　　　　　　　　　　　　　　　　Proverbs 16:33

We may throw the dice, but the Lord determines how they fall. Why does it say he determines it (present tense) rather than he already knows (past tense) how they will fall?

> *Fire tests the purity of silver and gold, but <u>the LORD tests the heart</u>.*　　　　　Proverbs 17:3

Why does the Lord test men's hearts? Usually a test exists in order to discover something unknown. Why would he bother to do this if he already knew what was in our hearts from eternity

STILL MORE EVIDENCE PSALMS-ZECHARIAH 351

past? Does he doubt what he already knows and try to get a second opinion? How do you explain the need for him to test us?

Isaiah

> *What more could have been done for my vineyard than I have done for it? <u>When I looked</u> for good grapes, why did it yield only bad?*   Isaiah 5:4 NIV

God expected something different than what he found.

> *The one who rescued you is the LORD, the one who formed you in your mother's womb. He says, "I, the LORD, made everything. I put the skies there myself. I spread out the earth before me." False prophets tell lies, but the Lord shows that their lies are false. He makes fools of those who do magic. He confuses even the wise. They think they know a lot, but he makes them look foolish. The Lord sends his servants to tell his messages to the people, and <u>he makes those messages</u> come true. He sends messengers to tell the people what they should do, and he proves that the advice is good. The Lord says to Jerusalem, "People will live in you again." He says to the cities of Judah, "You will be rebuilt." He says to them, "I will repair your ruins."* Isaiah 44:24-26

Here we see a God who once created in the past, but who now <u>continues</u> to act in the present. He did not create the future when he made the world. The future is being written each day as God works among his creatures.

> *I make known the end from the beginning, from ancient times, what is still to come. I say: My purpose will stand,*

and I will do all that I please. From the east I summon a bird of prey; from a far-off land, a man to fulfill my purpose. What I have said, that will I bring about; what I have planned, that will I do. Isaiah 46:10-11 NIV

God is declaring that he is in control and can do whatever pleases him. Since we know that God is 100% good, we can be assured that he is not going to do evil because that would never please him. He never says that what is written will happen by itself, but rather that **he** will make all things happen. The future is in his hands; he is not in the hands of the future.

Let the wicked change their ways and banish the very thought of doing wrong. Let them turn to the LORD that He may have mercy on them. Yes, turn to our God, for He will forgive generously. Isaiah 55:7 NLT

God responds to the actions of men. The door to the mercy seat is always open, and he desires to abundantly pardon.

Then you will call to the LORD, and he will answer you. You will cry out to him, and he will say, "Here I am." Stop causing trouble and putting burdens on people. Stop saying things to hurt people or accusing them of things they didn't do. Feel sorry for hungry people and give them food. Help those who are troubled and satisfy their needs. Then your light will shine in the darkness. You will be like the bright sunshine at noon. The LORD will always lead you and satisfy your needs in dry lands. He will give strength to your bones. You will be like a garden that has plenty of water, like a spring that never goes dry.
Isaiah 58:9-11

Promises, promises, promises! God gives many warnings not to do evil, but he also gives many promises of what will happen if we do good. Both promises and warnings are of no consequence if the outcome is already known. There would be no incentive to try to do good or to avoid evil because in the end, no one could do anything differently from what has been foreknown. If God already knows every detail of how things will turn out, he wasted a lot of his and our time working with the people in the Bible and having us read it. It would all be for nothing in the end because nothing whatsoever could be changed from what is already known by God.

> But _they turned against him_ and made his Holy Spirit very sad. _So the Lord became their enemy and fought against them_.   Isaiah 63:10

God reacts to the behavior of men.

Jeremiah

> "I knew you before I formed you in your mother's womb. Before you were born I set you apart and appointed you as My prophet to the nations."   Jeremiah 1:5 NLT

A very probable interpretation is that God knew him as an embryo in the fallopian tube, or even knew him as the sperm and egg which came together. There is no textual reason to say that God knew him from eternity, especially when God himself uses the term "before you were born." God, who knows all that is happening, knew Jeremiah before he made it to the womb, and before he was born. If he had known Jeremiah from all eternity, he would have said, "I have always known you." God could not "know" Jeremiah until he existed as a person. And the emphasis here is on the action of God in choosing Jeremiah, not on his foreknowledge of future things.

> *I thought, 'After she has done all this, she will return to Me.' But she did not return, and her faithless sister Judah saw this. She saw that I divorced faithless Israel because of her adultery. But that treacherous sister Judah had no fear, and now she, too, has left Me and given herself to prostitution.* Jeremiah 3:7-8 NLT

God was disappointed by the actions of Judah. It says that he expected better.

> "*I thought to Myself, 'I would love to treat you as My own children!' I wanted nothing more than to give you this beautiful land—the finest possession in the world. I looked forward to your calling Me 'Father,' and I wanted you never to turn from Me.* Jeremiah 3:19 NLT

God had high hopes, but his hopes were disappointed by the evil actions and spiritual adultery of his people.

> *The LORD All–Powerful, the God of Israel, says: Change your lives and do good things. If you do this, I will let you live in this place. Don't trust the lies that some people say. They say, "This is the Temple of the LORD, the Temple of the LORD, the Temple of the LORD!" If you change your lives and do good things, I will let you live in this place. You must be fair to each other. You must be fair to strangers. You must help widows and orphans. Don't kill innocent people! And don't follow other gods, because they will only ruin your lives. If you obey me, I will let*

you live in this place. I gave this land to your ancestors for them to keep forever.   Jeremiah 7:3-7

But, O LORD Almighty, you who judge righteously and <u>test the heart and mind</u>, let me see your vengeance upon them, for to you I have committed my cause.
Jeremiah 11:20 NIV

Why would testing be necessary if he already knows everything?

Then the LORD said, "Jeremiah, <u>if you change</u> and come back to me, <u>I</u> will not punish you. <u>If</u> you change and come back to me, <u>then</u> you may serve me. <u>If</u> you speak important things, not worthless words, <u>then</u> you may speak for me. The people of Judah should change and come back to you. But don't you change and be like them.
Jeremiah 15:19

Jeremiah's continued role in prophesying depended on his faithfulness.

I <u>see</u> everything they do. The people of Judah <u>cannot hide</u> the things they do. Their sin is not hidden from me.
Jeremiah 16:17

This verse clearly states that God is seeing what is going on and that men cannot hide anything from him. Why does God need to watch if he already knows by his foreknowledge? It would be a waste of his time and energy.

But I, the LORD, <u>search</u> all hearts and <u>examine</u> secret motives. I give all people their due rewards, <u>according to what their actions deserve</u>."   Jeremiah 17:10 NLT

What would be the purpose of making such a statement if God already knew what man was thinking and what his motives were ahead of time? God himself says that he examines men to see whether they deserve reward or punishment depending on what they do. There is no idea implied that God already knows what this will be, in fact the statement proves the opposite.

> *But you must <u>be careful to obey me</u>, says the LORD. You must not bring a load through the gates of Jerusalem on the Sabbath. You must make the Sabbath day a holy day. You will do this by not doing any work on that day. "'<u>If you obey this command</u>, the kings and leaders will be from David's family. It will be the kings who sit on David's throne and the leaders from Judah and Jerusalem who come through the gates of Jerusalem riding on chariots and on horses. And Jerusalem will have people living in it forever. People will come to Jerusalem from the towns and villages of Judah, from the land where the tribe of Benjamin lives, from the western foothills, from the hill country, and from the Negev. All these people will bring burnt offerings, sacrifices, grain offerings, incense, and thank offerings to the Temple of the LORD in Jerusalem. "'<u>But if you don't listen</u> to me and obey me, <u>bad things will happen</u>. If you carry loads into Jerusalem on the Sabbath day, you are not keeping it as a holy day. So I will start a fire that cannot be put out. That fire will start at the gates of Jerusalem, and it will burn until it burns even the palaces.'"* Jeremiah 17:24-27

Here we see clear choices and clear consequences of those choices. God's response or action depended on the action of his people. If his action had already been determined by his foreknowledge, then we might as well tear these pages from the

Bible. If the future was already decided, then God was cruel to even imply that it depended on what his people did.

> Then this message from the LORD came to me: "Family of Israel, you know that I can do the same thing with you. _You are_ like the clay in the potter's hands, and _I am_ like the potter." This message is from the LORD. "There may come a time when I will speak about a nation or a kingdom that I will pull up by its roots. Or maybe I will say that I will pull that nation or kingdom down and destroy it. _But if_ the people of that nation change their hearts and lives and stop doing evil things, _I will change my mind_ and not follow my plans to bring disaster to them. There may come another time when I speak about a nation that I will build up or plant. _But if_ I see that nation doing evil things and not obeying me, _I will think again_ about the good I had planned to do for that nation.
>
> Jeremiah 18:5-10

God could not do this if the decisions and the outcome were already determined. God keeps saying that the outcomes are in his hands. He is omnipotent and sovereign and can do as he pleases.

> They have built pagan shrines to Baal, and there they burn their sons as sacrifices to Baal. I have never commanded such a horrible deed; _it never even crossed My mind_ to command such a thing!   Jeremiah 19:5

God himself says that it did not even occur to him that men would do such evil things. He says that he was surprised by the level of corruption that existed in Israel. Why do we doubt his word? Aren't we being just like Eve in the Garden of Eden when she doubted what God told her?

358 GOD IS WITH US

> O LORD of Heaven's Armies, <u>You test</u> those who are righteous, and <u>You examine the deepest thoughts and secrets</u>. Let me see Your vengeance against them, for I have committed my cause to You.   Jeremiah 20:12 NLT

> The LORD said, "Jeremiah, go down to the king's palace. Go to the king of Judah and tell this message there: 'Listen to this message from the LORD, King of Judah. You rule from David's throne, so listen. King, you and your officials must listen well. All of your people who come through the gates of Jerusalem must listen to the message from the Lord. This is what the LORD says: Do what is right and fair. Protect those who have been robbed from the ones who robbed them. Don't hurt or do anything wrong to orphans or widows. Don't kill innocent people. <u>If you obey</u> these commands, kings who sit on David's throne will continue to come through the gates into the city of Jerusalem. They will come through the gates with their officials. The kings, their officials, and their people will come riding in chariots and on horses. But I, the LORD, tell you that <u>if you don't obey</u> these commands, <u>then</u> I promise with an oath in my own name that this king's palace will be destroyed—it will become a pile of rocks.'"   Jeremiah 22:1-5

After proclaiming his intention of destroying Jerusalem completely, God gives them one last chance.

> But <u>you would not</u> listen to Me," says the LORD. "You <u>made Me furious</u> by worshiping idols you made with your own hands, <u>bringing on yourselves all the disasters you now suffer</u>.   Jeremiah 25:7 NLT

Our actions are the key to determining what God does in our lives – will we listen to him or not?

And now the LORD of Heaven's Armies says: <u>Because you have not listened to Me</u>, <u>I will</u> gather together all the armies of the north under King Nebuchadnezzar of Babylon, whom I have appointed as My deputy. <u>I will</u> bring them all against this land and its people and against the surrounding nations. <u>I will completely destroy you</u> and make you an object of horror and contempt and a ruin forever.   Jeremiah 25:8-9 NLT

They themselves will be enslaved by many nations and great kings; I will repay them <u>according to their deeds</u> and the work of their hands."   Jeremiah 25:14 NIV

God is not reading from a scroll about the future. He is declaring what he is going to do.

He is like <u>an angry</u> lion that has left his cave. And <u>because of his terrible anger</u> and by the attacks of the enemy army, their land will become an empty desert.
                Jeremiah 25:38

Why would God get so angry if he knew from the beginning of time how it would turn out? God is a living person who relates, reacts and responds to other living persons. This is shown over and over and over again in the Scriptures.

The LORD said, "Jeremiah, stand in the Temple yard of the LORD. Give this message to all the people of Judah who are coming to worship at the Temple of the LORD. Tell them everything that I tell you to speak. Don't leave out any part of my message. <u>Maybe</u> they will listen and obey my message. <u>Maybe</u> they will stop living such evil lives. <u>If they change, I will change my mind about my</u>

plans to punish them. I am planning this punishment because of the many evil things they have done.
                                    Jeremiah 26:2-3

You people, change your lives! You must start doing good! You must obey the LORD your God. If you do that, he will change his mind. He will not do the bad things he told you about. As for me, I am in your power. Do to me what you think is good and right. But if you kill me, be sure of one thing. You will be guilty of killing an innocent person. You will make this city and everyone living in it guilty too. The LORD really did send me to you. The message you heard really is from the Lord.
                                    Jeremiah 26:13-15

Jeremiah did not believe that the future was already decided. These statements by God could only be lies if God already knew what they were going to do.

"King Hezekiah of Judah and the people of Judah did not kill Micah. You know that Hezekiah respected the LORD and wanted to please him. So the LORD changed his mind and didn't do the bad things to Judah that he said he would do. If we hurt Jeremiah, we will bring many troubles on ourselves. And those troubles will be our own fault."
                                    Jeremiah 26:19

You plan and do great things. You see everything that people do. You give a reward to those who do good things, and you punish those who do bad things—you give them what they deserve.
                                    Jeremiah 32:19

"You gave the Israelites this land that you promised to give to their ancestors long ago. It is a very good land

filled with many good things. They came into this land and took it for their own. <u>But they didn't obey you. They didn't follow</u> your teachings or do what you commanded. <u>So you made all these terrible things happen to them.</u>
Jeremiah 32:22-23

<u>*I have watched*</u> *the people of Israel and the people of Judah. Everything they do is evil. They have done evil things since they were young. The people of Israel have* <u>made me very angry</u> *because they worship idols that they made with their own hands." This message is from the LORD. "From the time that Jerusalem was built until now,* <u>the people of this city have made me angry. This city has made me very angry,</u> *so I must remove it from my sight. I will destroy Jerusalem because of all the evil things the people of Israel and Judah have done. The people, their kings, leaders, their priests and prophets, the people of Judah, and the people of Jerusalem* <u>have all made me angry.</u> *"They should have come to me for help, but they turned their backs to me. <u>I tried to teach them again and again, but they would not listen to me. I tried to correct them, but they would not listen.</u> They have made their idols, and I hate those idols. They put their idols in the Temple that is called by my name, so they made my Temple 'dirty.' "In the Valley of Ben Hinnom, they built high places to the false god Baal. They built those worship places so that they could burn their sons and daughters as sacrifices. I never commanded them to do such a terrible thing. <u>I never even thought the people of Judah would do such a terrible thing</u>.*
Jeremiah 32:30-35

Again, God says that he was surprised by the intensely evil deeds of these people. (Here, some readers will be trying to find a way out because these Scripture do not fit their theology. God himself declares that he did not know what these people would do. It's time for those readers to change their view of God and make it conform to God's Word).

> *"So this is what the LORD God All–Powerful, the God of Israel, says: 'I said that many bad things would happen to Judah and Jerusalem. I will soon make all those bad things happen. I spoke to the people, but <u>they refused to listen</u>. I called out to them, but they didn't answer me.'"*
> Jeremiah 35:17

> *<u>Maybe</u> the people of Judah will hear what I am planning to do to them and will stop doing bad things. <u>If they will do that, I will forgive them</u> for the terrible sins they have committed.*
> Jeremiah 36:3

This clearly shows that there were different possibilities for the future.

> *So I want you to go to the Temple of the LORD. Go there on a day of fasting and read to the people from the scroll. Read to the people the messages from the LORD that you wrote on the scroll as I spoke them to you. Read them to all the people of Judah who come into Jerusalem from the towns where they live. Perhaps they will ask the LORD to help them. Perhaps each person will stop doing bad things. The LORD has announced that he is very angry with them."*
> Jeremiah 36:6-7

Jeremiah believed that repentance was still possible and that the future was not set in concrete.

I will punish Jehoiakim and his children, and I will punish
his officials. I will do this because they are wicked. I will
bring terrible disasters on them and on all those who live
in Jerusalem and on the people from Judah. I will bring all
these bad things on them, just as I warned them, because
they have not listened to me. Jeremiah 36:31

Then Jeremiah said to King Zedekiah, "The LORD God
All–Powerful is the God of Israel. This is what he says,
'If you surrender to the officials of the king of Babylon,
your life will be saved, and Jerusalem will not be burned
down. And you and your family will live. But if you refuse
to surrender, Jerusalem will be given to the Babylonian
army. They will burn Jerusalem down, and you will not
escape from them. Jeremiah 38:17-18

If you will stay in Judah, I will make you strong–I will not
destroy you. I will plant you, and I will not pull you up.
I will do this because I am sad about the terrible things
that I made happen to you. Now you are afraid of the
king of Babylon. But don't be afraid of him. Don't be
afraid of the king of Babylon,' says the LORD, 'because
I am with you. I will save you. I will rescue you. He will
not get his hands on you. I will be kind to you, and the
king of Babylon will also treat you with mercy. He will
bring you back to your land. Jeremiah 42:10-12

This blessing God offered never happened because they went
to Egypt instead.

But you might say, 'We will not stay in Judah.' If you
say that, you will disobey the LORD your God. And you
might say, 'No, we will go and live in Egypt. We will not

be bothered with war there. We will not hear the trumpets of war, and in Egypt we will not be hungry.' If you say that, listen to this message from the LORD, you survivors from Judah. This is what the LORD All–Powerful, the God of the people of Israel, says: 'If you decide to go and live in Egypt, this will happen: You are afraid of the sword of war, but it will defeat you there. And you are worried about hunger, but you will be hungry in Egypt. You will die there. Everyone who decides to go live in Egypt will die by war, hunger, or disease. Not one person who goes to Egypt will survive. Not one of them will escape the terrible things that I will bring to them.' "This is what the LORD All–Powerful, the God of the people of Israel, says: 'I showed my anger against Jerusalem. I punished the people who lived there. In the same way I will show my anger against everyone who goes to Egypt. People will use you as an example when they ask for bad things to happen to other people. You will become like a curse word. People will be ashamed of you, and they will insult you. And you will never see Judah again.'

Jeremiah 42:13-18

They did not believe and obey God's promise, and they suffered the terrible consequences.

Jeremiah received a message from the Lord for all the people of Judah living in Egypt. The message was for the people of Judah living in the towns of Migdol, Tahpanhes, Memphis, and southern Egypt. This was the message: "This is what the LORD All-Powerful, the God of Israel, says: 'You people saw the disasters that I brought on the city of Jerusalem and on all the towns of Judah. The towns are empty piles of stones today. They were destroyed because the people living in them did evil. They gave sacrifices to other gods, and that made me angry! Your people and your ancestors did not worship those gods in the past. I sent my servants, the prophets, to those people again and again. They spoke my message and said to the people, "Don't do this terrible thing. I hate for you to worship idols." But they didn't listen to the prophets or pay attention to them. They didn't stop doing wicked things. They didn't stop making sacrifices to other gods. So I showed my anger against them. I punished the towns of Judah and the streets of Jerusalem. My anger made Jerusalem and the towns of Judah the empty piles of stone they are today.'   Jeremiah 44:1-6

The LORD hated the terrible things you did, and he could not be patient with you any longer. So he made your country an empty desert. No one lives there now. Other people say bad things about that country. The reason all those bad things happened to you is that you made sacrifices to other gods. You sinned against the LORD. You didn't obey him or follow his teachings or the laws he gave you. You didn't keep your part of the agreement."   Jeremiah 44:22-23

God did what he did because people did what they did. God's response or treatment of us is often dependent on the choices we make. It is not known ahead of time.

These things happened because of the LORD's anger against the people of Jerusalem and Judah, until He finally banished them from His presence and sent them into exile. Zedekiah rebelled against the king of Babylon.
                                Jeremiah 52:3 NLT

Ezekiel

Son of man, I have appointed you as a watchman for Israel. Whenever you receive a message from Me, warn people immediately. If I warn the wicked, saying, 'You are under the penalty of death,' but you fail to deliver the warning, they will die in their sins. And I will hold you responsible for their deaths. If you warn them and they refuse to repent and keep on sinning, they will die in their sins. But you will have saved yourself because you obeyed Me. Ezekiel 3:17-19

Therefore, I Myself, the Sovereign LORD, am now your enemy. I will punish you publicly while all the nations watch. Because of your detestable idols, I will punish you like I have never punished anyone before or ever will again. Ezekiel 5:8-9

Very soon now, I will show you how angry I am. I will show all of my anger against you. I will punish you for the evil things you did. I will make you pay for all the terrible things you did. I will not show you any mercy or feel sorry for you. I am punishing you for the evil things you did. You have done such terrible things. Now, you will know that I am the LORD. Ezekiel 7:8-9

So now, son of man, pretend you are being sent into exile. Pack the few items an exile could carry, and leave your home to go somewhere else. Do this right in front of the people so they can see you. For perhaps they will pay attention to this, even though they are such rebels. Ezekiel 12:3 NLT

Why would God deceive Ezekiel by telling him a lie that there was still hope for Israel to repent if indeed the future was already known by God?

> *Now, if evil people change their lives, they will live and not die. They might stop doing all the bad things they did and begin to carefully obey all my laws. They might become fair and good. God will not remember all the bad things they did. He will remember only their goodness, so they will live!" The Lord GOD says, "I don't want evil people to die. I want them to change their lives so that they can live!*   Ezekiel 18:21-23

God is always hoping for the best from people.

> *Why? Because, family of Israel, I will judge each of you only for what you do!" This is what the Lord GOD said. "So come back to me! Stop committing those crimes and do away with those things that cause you to sin! Throw away all the terrible idols with which you committed your crimes! Change your heart and spirit. People of Israel, why should you do things that will cost you your life? I don't want to kill you! Please come back and live!" This is what the Lord GOD said.*   Ezekiel 18:30-32

> *Therefore this is what the Sovereign LORD says: `Because you people have brought to mind your guilt by your open rebellion, revealing your sins in all that you do–because you have done this, you will be taken captive.'*   Ezekiel 21:24 NIV

> *I looked for someone who might rebuild the wall of righteousness that guards the land. I searched for someone*

*to stand in the gap in the wall so I wouldn't have to
destroy the land, but I found no one. So now I will pour
out My fury on them, consuming them with the fire of
My anger. I will heap on their heads the full penalty for
all their sins. I, the Sovereign LORD, have spoken!*
                                              Ezekiel 22:30-31

Why would God look for something that he knew he would
never find?

Daniel

*He changes the times and seasons. He gives power to
kings, and he takes their power away. He gives wisdom to
people, so they become wise. He lets people learn things
and become wise.*   Daniel 2:21

God is in control. By his own will, he determines the course of
world events. He removes kings and sets others on the throne
according to his will and in response to the actions of men, not
based on a written script which would allow God no freedom.

*Shadrach, Meshach, and Abednego replied, "O Nebuchad-
nezzar, we do not need to defend ourselves before you. If
we are thrown into the blazing furnace, the God whom
we serve is able to save us. He will rescue us from your
power, Your Majesty. But even if He doesn't, we want to
make it clear to you, Your Majesty, that we will never serve
your gods or worship the gold statue you have set up."*
                                          Daniel 3:16-18 NLT

They didn't believe that the decision to save them was
already made.

For this has been decreed by the messengers; it is commanded by the holy ones, so that everyone may know that the Most High rules over the kingdoms of the world. He gives them to anyone He chooses—even to the lowliest of people." Daniel 4:17

God does not have to obey the future: he has every right to make any changes he wishes at any time he wishes.

King Nebuchadnezzar, please accept my advice. Stop sinning and do what is right. Break from your wicked past and be merciful to the poor. Perhaps then you will continue to prosper. Daniel 4:27

Daniel believed that the choice the king made would affect the future. You may say that God already knew how it would turn out: but I say that if so, Daniel did not know, and he believed there was still hope. I trust Daniel's judgment.

All the people of the earth are nothing compared to Him. He does as He pleases among the angels of heaven and among the people of the earth. No one can stop Him or say to Him, 'What do you mean by doing these things?' Daniel 4:35 NLT

God has the freedom and power to change rules and rulers whenever he decides.

Then the man in the vision started talking again. He said, "Daniel, do not be afraid. From the very first day you decided to get wisdom and to be humble in front of God, he has been listening to your prayers. I came to you because you have been praying. But the prince (angel) of Persia has

> *been fighting against me for 21 days. Then Michael, one of the most important princes (angels), came to help me because I was stuck there with the king of Persia. Now I have come to you, Daniel, to explain to you what will happen to your people in the future. The vision is about a time in the future."*   Daniel 10:12-14

The decision was made immediately to answer Daniel's prayer, but because of a battle in the heavens, the arrival was delayed.

Hosea

> *The prophet says, "Israel, learn this: The time of punishment has come. The time has come for you <u>to pay for the evil things you did.</u>" But the people of Israel say, "The prophet is a fool. This man with God's Spirit is crazy." The prophet says, "<u>You will be punished for your terrible sins. You will be punished for your hate.</u>"*   Hosea 9:7

All of the prophetic warnings about the destruction to come are a result of man's sin. There is no evidence anywhere that God would have brought them if mankind had not sinned. Over and over again we see cause and effect.

> *My God will reject them <u>because</u> they have not obeyed him; they will be wanderers among the nations.*
> Hosea 9:17 NIV

> *The people of Samaria must bear the <u>consequences</u> of their guilt <u>because they rebelled against their God.</u> They will be killed by an invading army, their little ones dashed to death against the ground, their pregnant women ripped open by swords.*   Hosea 13:16 NLT

The end results were dependent on men's choices. The judgments coming on Israel were because of their sins – because of their choices of idolatry, sexual immorality, and oppression of the defenseless.

Joel

> This is the LORD'S message: "Now come back to me with all your heart. Cry and mourn, and don't eat anything! Show that you are sad for doing wrong. Tear your hearts, not your clothes." Come back to the LORD your God. He is kind and merciful. He does not become angry quickly. He has great love. _Maybe_ he will change his mind about the bad punishment he planned. _Who knows, maybe he will change his mind_ and leave behind a blessing for you. Then you can give grain and drink offerings to the LORD your God.   Joel 2:12-14

"_Who knows?_" _Perhaps_ God may change his mind and have pity.

> And _everyone who calls on the name of the LORD will be saved_; for on Mount Zion and in Jerusalem there will be deliverance, as the LORD has said, among the survivors whom the LORD calls.   Joel 2:32 NIV

Amos

> Hate evil and love goodness. Bring justice back into the courts. _Maybe_ then the LORD God All–Powerful will be kind to the survivors from Joseph's family.
>   Amos 5:15

This is what the Lord GOD showed me: He was <u>making</u> locusts. This was at the time the second crop began to grow, after the king's people had cut the first crop. Before the locusts could eat all the grass in the country, I said, "Lord GOD, I beg you, forgive us! Jacob cannot survive! He is too small!" <u>Then the LORD changed his mind about this</u>. The LORD said, "It will not happen." This is what the Lord GOD showed me: I saw the Lord GOD calling for judgment by fire. The fire destroyed the ocean and was beginning to eat up the land. But I said, "Lord GOD, stop, I beg you! Jacob cannot survive! He is too small!" <u>Then the LORD changed his mind about this</u>. The Lord GOD said, "It will not happen either."

Amos 7:1-6

Apparently Amos did not believe that God's actions were already determined, for he pleaded with God to change them and he did. Either God is the greatest play actor of all time, or he has the freedom to change his mind. He had Amos fully convinced that the future wasn't already determined.

Jonah

When the king of Nineveh heard about this, he left his throne, removed his robe, put on special clothes to show that he was sorry, and sat in ashes. The king wrote a special message and sent it throughout the city: A command from the king and his great rulers: For a short time no person or animal should eat anything. No herd or flock will be allowed in the fields. Nothing living in Nineveh will eat or drink water. But every person and every animal must be covered with a special cloth to show they are sad. People must cry loudly to God. Everyone must change their life and stop doing bad things.

> *<u>Who knows? Maybe God will stop being angry and change</u> <u>his mind</u>, and we will not be punished. God saw what the people did. He saw that they stopped doing evil. <u>So God</u> <u>changed his mind and did not do what he planned</u>. He did not punish the people.* Jonah 3:6-10

The King of Nineveh had better theology than many of today's theologians and pastors, because God did what the king hoped for, and did not destroy the city as he had threatened to do. (By the way, Jonah was the most successful evangelist ever; all the inhabitants of a whole world–class city repented and turned to God. But Jonah went into a snit because he didn't like these people. He was a great evangelist but a terrible missionary. Jonah was a good theologian, because he knew God's true nature, but he was a poor imitation as a lover of their souls.)

> *Jonah was not happy that God saved the city. Jonah became angry. He complained to the LORD and said, "LORD, I knew this would happen! I was in my own country, and you told me to come here. At that time I knew that you would forgive the people of this evil city, so I decided to run away to Tarshish. I knew that you are a kind God. I knew that you show mercy and don't want to punish people. I knew that you are kind, and if these people stopped sinning, <u>you would change your plans to</u> <u>destroy them</u>. So now, LORD, just kill me. It is better for me to die than to live."* Jonah 4:1-3

Jonah apparently didn't believe in the absolute foreknowledge of God.

> *And the LORD said, "You did nothing for that plant. You did not make it grow. It grew up in the night, and the next day it died. And now you are sad about it. If you can get*

> upset over a plant, <u>surely I can feel sorry</u> for a big city like
> Nineveh. There are many people and animals in that city.
> There are more than 120,000 people there who did not
> know they were doing wrong."   Jonah 4:10-11

We see here how God is absolutely concerned about the salvation
of the people in Nineveh. He feels for these people. He is a
compassionate God, meaning that he identifies with them and
puts himself into their shoes.

Nahum

> The LORD is a jealous God. The LORD punishes the
> guilty, and he is very angry. The LORD punishes his
> enemies, and he stays angry with them. The LORD is
> patient, but he is also very powerful! The LORD will
> punish the guilty; he will not let them go free. He will use
> whirlwinds and storms to show his power. People walk
> on the dusty ground, but he walks on the clouds.
>
> Nahum 1:2-3

Why would God get angry when somebody does something
if he already knew he was going to do it? Also, was his anger
absolutely foreknown? Did God know he was going to get
angry, but he couldn't stop himself in time?

Zephaniah

> All you humble people, come to the LORD! Obey his
> laws. Learn to do good things. Learn to be humble. <u>Maybe</u>
> then you will be safe when the LORD shows his anger.
>
> Zephaniah 2:3

Haggai

> *"Go up to the mountains, get the wood, and build the Temple. Then I will be pleased with the Temple, and I will be honored." This is what the LORD said. The LORD All-Powerful said, "You people look for a big harvest, but when you go to gather the crop, there is only a little grain. So you bring that grain home, and then I send a wind that blows it all away. Why is this happening? Because my house is still in ruins while each of you runs home to take care of your own house. That is why the sky holds back its dew and why the earth holds back its crops. "I gave the command for the land and the mountains to be dry. The grain, the new wine, the olive oil, and everything the earth produces will be ruined. All the people and all the animals will become weak."* Haggai 1:8-11

God's actions and even the weather which he controls were strongly influenced by man's actions.

Zechariah

> *The LORD <u>became very angry</u> with your ancestors. So you must tell the people what the LORD All–Powerful says, "Come back to me, says the LORD All–Powerful, and I will come back to you." This is what the LORD All–Powerful said. "Don't be like your ancestors. In the past the prophets spoke to them and said, 'The LORD All-Powerful wants you to change your evil way of living. Stop doing evil things!' But your ancestors did not listen to me." This is what the LORD said.*
> *Zechariah 1:2-4*

But they refused to listen and refused to do what he wanted. They closed their ears so that they could not hear what God said. They were very stubborn and would not obey the law. The LORD All–Powerful used his Spirit and sent messages to his people through the prophets. But the people would not listen, so the LORD All–Powerful became very angry. So the LORD All–Powerful said, "I called to them, and they did not answer. So now, if they call to me, I will not answer. I will bring the other nations against them like a storm. They didn't know those nations, but the country will be destroyed after those nations pass through. This pleasant country will be destroyed."
Zechariah 7:11-14

The LORD All–Powerful says, "Your ancestors made me angry, so I decided to destroy them. I decided not to change my mind." This is what the LORD All–Powerful said. "But now I have changed my mind. And in the same way I have decided to be good to Jerusalem and to the people of Judah. So don't be afraid! But you must do this: Tell the truth to your neighbors. When you make decisions in your cities, be fair and do what is right. Do what brings peace. Don't make secret plans to hurt your neighbors. Don't make false promises. You must not enjoy doing these things, because I hate them!" This is what the LORD said.
Zechariah 8:14-17

Conclusion

If you made it this far, you should be more than convinced that no one in these Bible books believed that the future was already known by God. The evidence is overwhelming that

God had and has freedom to do what he pleases, and that he is not a slave to any foreknowledge of the future. God makes his decisions in the present even though he is following a general plan for how the big picture will turn out.

21. New Testament evidence Matthew – Revelation

Evidence from the gospels

> *But after Joseph thought about this, an angel from the Lord came to him in a dream. The angel said, "Joseph, son of David, don't be afraid to accept Mary to be your wife. The baby inside her is from the Holy Spirit. She will give birth to a son. You will name him Jesus. Give him that name because he will save his people from their sins."*
> Matthew 1:20-21

Old Testament believers did not know the name of the Messiah, but they knew and believed what he would do for them. They looked forward in hope to the promise of God to deliver them from their sins. Here, for the first time, the name of the Deliverer is given.

Why was it necessary for God to "instruct" Joseph what the baby's name should be if God knew he couldn't get it wrong?

> *After the wise men left, an angel from the Lord came to Joseph in a dream. The angel said, "Get up! Take the child with his mother and escape to Egypt. Herod wants to kill the child and will soon start looking for him. Stay in Egypt until I tell you to come back."*
>
> Matthew 2:13

Why did God need to be concerned about what Herod would try to do to Jesus if he foreknew that he would not be killed? The Angel warns Joseph to flee to Egypt. Why did God have to intervene in history to prevent the premature death of his Son? What if Joseph hadn't gone? We know that God was not going to let his Son die prematurely because his life and death and resurrection were all part of God's plan to rescue sinners. However, it appears that he had to take a hand in the matter instead of leaving it to be determined by his foreknowledge.

> *So Jesus was baptized. As soon as he came up out of the water, the sky opened, and he saw God's Spirit coming down on him like a dove. A voice from heaven said, "This is my Son, the one I love. <u>I am very pleased with him.</u>"*
>
> Matthew 3:16-17

How could the Father be "pleased" with his son? There must have been something that Christ, in his human form as Jesus, did that pleased the Father. The Father's pleasure in his Son could not date to eternity or be based on his foreknowledge, but had to be based on something that Jesus had done in his short life of thirty years. "Pleased" is an expression of acceptance, contentment, and emotion.

> *We pray that your kingdom will come– that what you want will be done here on earth, the same as in heaven.*
>
> Matthew 6:10

Why would Jesus teach us to pray for God's kingdom to come if its coming was inevitable? Does the fact that we pray this prayer change the timing of the kingdom in the least? If so, did God know this beforehand? If he did, then our prayer did not change anything.

> Forgive our sins, just as we have forgiven those who did wrong to us. Don't let us be tempted, but save us from the Evil One.' Yes, _if you_ forgive others for the wrongs they do to you, _then your Father_ in heaven will also forgive your wrongs. But _if you don't_ forgive others, _then your Father_ in heaven will not forgive the wrongs you do.
> Matthew 6:12-15

Our on–going forgiveness is contingent on our willingness to forgive others. If our forgiveness was foreknown before time began, how could it be conditioned on our forgiving others?

> "When you fast, don't make yourselves look sad like the hypocrites. They put a look of suffering on their faces so that people will see they are fasting. The truth is, that's all the reward they will get. So when you fast, wash your face and make yourself look nice. Then no one will know you are fasting, except your Father, who is with you even in private. _He can_ see what is done in private, and he will reward you.
> Matthew 6:16-18

It doesn't says, Father who "already knows" what is done in secret, but who "sees" what is done. The clear emphasis is that God is watching to see what we will do. There is no hint that he already knows.

> Jesus did not do many miracles there, because the people did not believe in him.
> Matthew 13:58

This reading might allow that he chose not to do the miracles, but the same occasion in Mark 6:46 makes it very clear that he <u>could not</u> do them. What Jesus did was partially dependent on people's faith in him.

> *Then the followers came to Jesus alone. They said, "We tried to force the demon out of the boy, but we could not. Why were we not able to make the demon go out?" Jesus answered, "You were not able to make the demon go out, because your faith is too small. Believe me when I tell you, if your faith is only as big as a mustard seed you can say to this mountain, 'Move from here to there,' and it will move. You will be able to do anything."*
>
> Matthew 17:19-20

> *Jesus answered, "The truth is, <u>if</u> you have faith and no doubts, you will be able to do the same as I did to this tree. And you will be able to do more. You will be able to say to this mountain, 'Go, mountain, fall into the sea.' And if you have faith, it will happen. <u>If you believe, you will get anything you ask for in prayer.</u>"*
>
> Matthew 21:21-22

These teachings indicate that the works that God can do through a person are dependent on how much faith he has. God is limited or empowered by our faith to advance his kingdom. This is not an empty, impossible promise. It is open–ended: it cannot depend on what God already knows.

> *His master replied, "<u>Well done</u>, good and faithful servant! You have been faithful with a few things; I will put you in charge of many things. Come and share your master's happiness!"*
>
> Matthew 25:21 NIV

The faithfulness of the servant as well as the reward were uncertain until the servant proved his faithfulness by his actions. Both he and God were happy at how it turned out. Happiness expresses joy about an event that was uncertain, but turned out well.

> *Then Jesus went on a little farther away from them. He fell to the ground and prayed, "My Father, <u>if it is possible</u>, don't make me drink from this cup. But do what you want, not what I want." Then he went back to his followers and found them sleeping. He said to Peter, "Could you men not stay awake with me for one hour? Stay awake and pray for strength against temptation. Your spirit wants to do what is right, but your body is weak." Then Jesus went away a second time and prayed, "My Father, if I must do this and <u>it is not possible</u> for me to escape it, then I pray that what you want will be done."*
> Matthew 26:39-42

Didn't Jesus already know exactly what was going to happen? Why make this useless appeal to his Father when it could change nothing?

> *So he came to them and said, "All authority in heaven and on earth is given to me. So go and make followers of all people in the world. Baptize them in the name of the Father and the Son and the Holy Spirit. Teach them to obey everything that I have told you to do. You can be sure that I will be with you always. I will continue with you until the end of time."*
> Matthew 28:18-20

Why go to the trouble to tell them to make disciples as if it depended on them, knowing that it would not make one iota of difference in the end? Why instruct the disciples to do something for which Jesus already knew the outcome?

> Then Jesus said to them, "People everywhere give honor to a prophet, except in his own town, with his own people, or in his home." Jesus <u>was not able</u> to do any miracles there except the healing of some sick people by laying his hands on them. <u>He was surprised</u> that the people there had no faith. Then he went to other villages in that area and taught.　　　Mark 6:4-6

Their lack of faith limited his ability to perform miracles. His actions were dependent to some degree on the actions of men. On other occasions, both Jesus and the disciples "saw that a person had faith to be healed," and they were healed.

> Jesus said to the father, "Why did you say 'if you can'? All things are possible for the one who believes."
> 　　　Mark 9:23

Of course, we know that not everything is possible for God. It is not possible for God to die, it is not possible for him to stop loving, it is not possible for him to lose control of the universe, it is not possible for Jesus to not be Lord of all creation, etc. Jesus is saying that everything <u>within the will of God</u> is possible for those who have faith to ask for it.

> Jesus went on a little farther away from them, fell to the ground, and prayed. He asked that, if possible, he would not have this time of suffering. He said, "Abba, Father! You can do all things. Don't make me drink from this cup. But do what you want, not what I want."
> 　　　Mark 14:35-36

Was the prayer answered? In Hebrews it says that when he prayed to be saved from some suffering in *"this cup"*, his prayer was answered. *(During the days of Jesus' life on earth, he offered up prayers and petitions with loud cries and tears to the one who could save him from death, and he was heard because of his reverent submission.* Hebrews 5:7 NIV). We don't know in what way his prayer was answered, but we know that it was, even though he suffered on the cross and died for a period of three days.

> *In the same way, I tell you, heaven is a happy place when one sinner decides to change. There is more joy for that one sinner than for 99 good people who don't need to change . . . In the same way, it's a happy time for the angels of God when one sinner decides to change.*
> Luke 15:7, 10

Why would Heaven have a celebration over something that they already knew was going to happen? Does God rejoice when a sinner repents? Or do only the angels rejoice because God hasn't revealed to them what he already knew? If God knew it would happen, why didn't he rejoice the day before or a year earlier?

> *Jesus was doing all this on the Sabbath day. So these Jews began trying to make him stop. But he said to them, "My Father never stops working, and so I work too."*
> John 5:16-17

What work is God doing if everything is already predetermined? What if he stopped working? Would things still turn out the same? Genesis says that he finished his work of creation in six days, but it does not mean that he never worked again. He is still the provider and sustainer of all that he has made.

But Jesus answered, "I assure you that the Son can do nothing alone. He does only what he sees his Father doing. The Son does the same things that the Father does. The Father loves the Son and shows him everything he does. This man was healed. But the Father will show the Son greater things than this to do. Then you will all be amazed. John 5:19-20

What is the Father doing if everything has already been done and it is known in the future?

"I can do nothing alone. I judge <u>only the way I am told</u>. And my judgment is right, because I am not trying to please myself. I want only to please the one who sent me. John 5:30

The miracles and the teaching were assigned to Jesus by the Father. There was an ongoing spiritual dialogue between the two to assure that Jesus understood what the Father wanted him to do.

Jesus looked up and saw a crowd of people coming toward him. He said to Philip, "Where can we buy enough bread for all these people to eat?" He asked Philip this question to test him. <u>Jesus already knew what he planned to do</u>. John 6:5-6

Why would John make this statement if he believed that Jesus **always** knew what he was going to do? This statement shows that it was an anomaly and not the normal way things worked. It does not prove that Jesus had absolute foreknowledge (omniscience of the future), but rather disproves it.

Evidence from Paul's epistles

> *Is Apollos so important? Is Paul so important? We are only servants of God who helped you believe. Each one of us did the work God gave us to do. I planted the seed and Apollos watered it. But God is the one who made the seed grow. So the one who plants is not important, and the one who waters is not important. Only God is important, because he is the one who makes things grow. The one who plants and the one who waters have the same purpose. And <u>each one will be rewarded for his own work</u>.*   1 Corinthians 3:5-8

Our future rewards have not been predetermined and are not already known by God. They will depend on how well each servant performs his task in his lifetime.

> *I am free. I belong to no other person, but I make myself a slave to everyone. I do this <u>to help save as many people as I can</u>. To the Jews I became like a Jew so that I could help save Jews. I myself am not ruled by the law, but to those who are ruled by the law I became like someone who is ruled by the law. <u>I did this to help save</u> those who are ruled by the law. To those who are without the law I became like someone who is without the law. <u>I did this to help save</u> those who are without the law. (But really, I am not without God's law–I am ruled by the law of Christ.) To those who are weak, I became weak so that I could help save them. I have become all things to all people. <u>I did this so that I could save people in any way possible</u>.*   1 Corinthians 9:19-22

Paul had not read the writings of Augustine, Calvin's *Institutes*, or the doctrinal statements of many churches. He believed that his actions could lead to the salvation of more people.

Evidence from other New Testament writers

> *Some of the sailors wanted to leave the ship, and they lowered the lifeboat to the water. They wanted the other men to think that they were throwing more anchors from the front of the ship. But Paul told the army officer and the other soldiers, "If these men do not stay in the ship, you will lose all hope of survival." So the soldiers cut the ropes and let the lifeboat fall into the water.*
>
> Acts 27:30-32

Paul did not believe that all would be saved from the sea no matter what they did. The salvation of the soldiers and the prisoners depended on their taking action. The outcome was not predetermined. Even though God had shown Paul his intention of saving all souls on board, Paul's statement makes it obvious that the salvation of all was conditional.

> *Our fathers on earth disciplined us for a short time in the way they thought was best. But God disciplines us to help us so that we can be holy like him. We don't enjoy discipline when we get it. It is painful. But later, after we have learned our lesson from it, we will enjoy the peace that comes from doing what is right.*
>
> Hebrews 12:10-11

Discipline is an ongoing work in the life of the believer. The discipline changes according to the need of the person. What parent would say to his child, "Tomorrow you are going to get a spanking no matter what you do?", or "Starting Saturday you will be grounded for a month just in case you think about doing something wrong." God, as a loving and wise Father, is attentive to our thoughts and actions and adjusts his discipline (correction) according to what it takes to straighten us out.

Do you know where your fights and arguments come from? They come from the selfish desires that make war inside you. You want things, but you don't get them. So you kill and are jealous of others. But you still cannot get what you want. So you argue and fight. You don't get what you want because you don't ask God. Or when you ask, you don't receive anything, because the reason you ask is wrong. You only want to use it for your own pleasure. James 4:1-3

Does this sound like the decisions are already made? James didn't believe that every outcome was already decided.

Conclusion

There are hundreds of Bible references that demonstrate this truth, and scores of Bible servants who believed that the future was and is being determined partly by the actions of men.

Is it reasonable to believe that the future is already established and can't be changed based on any of these scriptures? Has God anywhere given reason for us to believe that our faith and our actions won't make any difference in the way things turn out? Is there a reasonable amount of biblical evidence to support the belief that God already knows everything in the future? The clear answer to these questions is "no."

The doctrine of the absolute foreknowledge of God is not derived from the Bible but rather injected into our theology from some other source. If you insist on believing it, you must look for some other holy book to support it.

A critique of Frame's "No Other God"[1]

While in the process of editing the manuscript that you now have before you, I asked several friends to read it and give me their responses. One old friend, who is a Bible translator, responded in great detail and not only gave his critique but also made many corrections to my abundant grammatical errors. He now considers me his heretical friend. He said that I had to read John Frame's book, "No Other God," and that that would straighten me out. So, I obtained a copy and carefully studied it. However, after reading it, it only strengthened my resolve to publish my own manuscript.

Disagreements

Frame obviously starts out from a reformed theological position and attempts to prove it superior to the positions of those he

---

1   Frame, John M. *No Other God*. Phillipsburg, NJ, P&R (Presbyterian and Reformed) Publishing, 2001.

categorizes as "open theists." Unfortunately, Frame has done what people on both sides of the issue often do: set up straw men that purportedly represent what the other side believes and then proceed to tear these straw men to shreds and go away thinking that they have conquered the enemy.

One of Frame's biggest straw men is to state that open theists all believe in absolute libertarian freedom. He then dedicates at least one wasted chapter and many other statements inserted throughout the text to show how man does not have absolute freedom to act. The error is that no one in his right mind after reading the Bible would say that man lives in a vacuum and is not influenced by his surroundings or is completely free from some intervention and influence on God's part. No one I have read (and I admit that my theological reading is very limited, mostly on purpose) is saying that man has "libertarian" freedom.

The whole discussion about God's sovereignty and man's freedom boils down to whether or not God controls (manipulates) every detail of everything in his creation and whether or not man has any influence whatsoever in the outcome, and therefore any moral responsibility. Open theism does not deny that God has ultimate control over everything. But in its reasonable version it declares that God, by his own volition, has created some space for men and other creatures to make choices. This in no way refutes the doctrine of his sovereignty.

Frame, like most reformed theologians defends the absolute sovereignty of God, and accuses open theists of denying it. However, I would say that it is the reformed theologians who deny God's sovereignty. They say that the future is already determined and is therefore unchangeable. The obvious conclusion is that God cannot change it, and therefore is not sovereign over everything. The Bible states often that "God does whatever he pleases," and yet they say that he doesn't have freedom to adjust anything in the future. To conclude that God cannot change the future is to effectively put him out of business.

In my understanding, God's sovereignty and man's limited free will are easily reconcilable without losing either. First, we must understand what free will means and also what is sovereignty. I have tried to explain that in chapter eleven. However, God's absolute foreknowledge of all things future is not reconcilable with either limited free will or God's sovereignty.

Frame makes open theists guilty by association because the Socianists of the sixteenth century denied the exhaustive foreknowledge of God. *"They also denied the full diety of Christ, his substitutionary atonement, and justification by the imputed righteousness of Christ"* (page 33). If I agree with the Roman Catholic Church that God is trinity, does that make me guilty of believing in the Assumption of Mary or the infallibility of the Pope? Just because I agree with the heretic Socianist on some point doesn't make me agree with everything he believes. In fact, open theism as I have been exposed to it believes strongly in most of the things that the Socianists denied.

Reformed or classical theologians believe in many of the tenets taught by Augustine and the sixteenth-century reformers, but hopefully they don't share in their practice of persecuting and even killing good Christians whose only fault is to disagree with them on some theological issue. In my book in chapter sixteen, I share a lot about Augustine and the reformers only to demonstrate that they were not inerrant and that we cannot swallow all of their doctrines without careful examination.

On page 39, Frame states, *"The open theists claim to be evangelicals, but they reject doctrines (such as God's exhaustive foreknowledge) that have never before been controversial in evangelical circles."* To my knowledge, this is the only doctrine that we are completely rejecting, unless perhaps Calvin's version of the doctrine of predestination. The truth is that some of these reformed doctrines have been questioned time and again throughout church history. The Moravians, the Wesleys, Charles Finney, the early church fathers, and the Scriptures themselves throw this doctrine into doubt. In 431, a group of Italian bishops, led by Julian, defended the Pelagian view against the Augustinian concept of predestination. The only available history of the writings of Pelagius is found in the writings of his opponents Augustine and Jerome. The conquerors write the history books, and they often don't tell the whole story. Knowing human nature as we do, can we trust them to say concisely what Pelagius was really teaching, or were they also destroying straw men?

Church history is full of discussion about these topics. To say that no one who is evangelical ever questioned these things before is to deny history altogether. What is probably new is the term "evangelical" as we use it in our generation, though it is a term derived from the Gospels themselves. For Frame to say that the doctrines we are discussing have been settled in the Evangelical church throughout most of history flies in the face of the historical evidence. At the Second Council of Orange (529), the bishops concluded, *"We not only do not believe that any are foreordained to evil by the power of God, but even state with utter abhorrence that if there are those who want to believe so evil a thing, they are anathema."* Frame's reformed theology and his statement on page 68 (*"For now it is important to see that God does in fact bring about the sinful behavior of human beings, whatever problems that may create in our understanding")* would not have fared well at this synod. For him to say that reformed theology was always the norm shows his ignorance of important elements in church history.

Frame states in chapter thirteen, page 205 that open theists deny the inspiration and inerrancy of Scripture. Nothing could be further from the truth. I, for one, hold Scripture above tradition, doctrinal statements, theology, and even history. There are no more faithful witnesses than the Scriptures themselves and the people who are revealed to us in the Scriptures. My contention with reformed theologians is that they go to great lengths to explain away the plain and simple statements of the Bible, and so I would accuse them of a sense of disbelief in inerrancy. I believe that God revealed to us exactly what he wanted to reveal and that he revealed it in a way that we could understand it and therefore understand him. Frame, like many church leaders, goes into long explanations at times to reinterpret the words of the Bible and explain why they do not mean what they say.

Frame makes the proverbial mistake in several places of jumping from a specific case into drawing a general conclusion about every case. On page 62, he states, *"God's foreknowledge of one individual implies comprehensive control over the entire human family."* Once he makes this quantum leap, he runs with it throughout the book believing that his conclusion is proven. Another example is that since God gave messages to his prophets that came true exactly as he told them, this proves that God knows all the future, or at least controls every detail of everything that is going to happen. That is like saying that my neighbor bought a Ford Mustang and it's a lemon; therefore all Ford Mustangs are lemons. It is extremely poor logic and reasoning to jump to such conclusions. The veracity of a certain instance of God's foreknowledge or foreordination is no proof of absolute foreknowledge of all things.

"Frame states on page 65 that *"Scripture teaches directly that God brings about our free decisions. He does not foreordain merely what happens to us, but also what we choose to do."* I think he attempts to prove this statement from Scripture, but I confess that I missed all of the proof. He normally points to an instance in which God took full control of a situation and caused something to happen, and concludes that this is always the case. I have already pointed out that this is terrible logic. The evidence that God can control a situation is no proof that he always does.

Frame cites Scripture saying that "God does not change," but then later proves that he does. Much to his credit, he does distinguish between God's nature and morality, which never change, and his actions and responses which do.

Frame is loath to use the word "repent' in any of his statements. He keeps substituting the word "relent" every chance he gets. This is a common result of holding to the belief that God never changes his mind about anything because then he would not be sovereign. I have treated this in chapter ten, so will not speak about this in detail. The word used in the Hebrew text means "to change one's mind," which literally means to rethink something previous. The word "relent" means to give in to some kind of pressure to make a change. It suggests that God didn't really want to do it, but that he was obliged to change. Repent leans more toward his making his own decision to change. So, the choice of the word relent is a poor one if trying to prove that God doesn't ever change and that man has no influence on him.

With Frame and reformed theologians, they believe that the question of divine control over the affairs of men is a question of either/or. Either he controls it all, or he controls nothing. They are afraid that by believing that God does not control everything, he loses his ability to control anything. They say that every thought and act and step a man takes is foreordained and caused by God and yet man is morally responsible. I cannot comprehend how a person can be responsible for something over which he has absolutely no control. My translator friend says that it is because of my pea brain – of which condition he also claims to suffer. But it is the only brain I have, and I don't have the luxury of a brain transplant to get a better one. This is all God gave me and I am stuck with it for the time being. I never held my children responsible for things that happened to them and over which they themselves had absolutely no control.

To say that man is responsible though he cannot control anything is like saying it was my rook's fault that I made the stupid move in chess, or to blame it for my losing the game. Therefore, I am going to put it down the garbage disposal to punish it (similar to what people do with their golf clubs). That kind of inanimate object has no life and when the game is over it just goes back in the box unless I decided to punish it. It neither knows nor cares what is happening or what happens next, whereas man does both.

Apparently Frame has never seen a dog on a leash. The master has ultimate control, and the dog's freedom is limited. The master says, "Let's take a walk around the block," and the dog has no choice but to follow. He may prefer to go somewhere else and thus strain at the leash, but he does not have libertarian freedom. However, his master does not control his steps to the side or back and forth. If he bites a passing pedestrian, he will probably get a kick in the ribs because that wasn't the master's fault, and the dog knows better.

Many theologians are afraid that if we admit that God doesn't control absolutely everything it makes him a lesser God. I believe that the fact that he delegates some authority makes him a greater God who is not at all threatened with sharing some of his control. In the final analysis, what we believe doesn't change God's nature one iota. I am reminded of Gideon's father's response when the village wanted to kill Gideon for tearing down the idol of their god Baal. *"Are you going to plead Baal's cause? Are you trying to save him? Whoever fights for him shall be put to death by morning! If Baal really is a god, he can defend himself when someone breaks down his altar"* Judges 6:31. God is never in any real danger and doesn't need anyone to defend him.

We who subscribe to a certain degree of freedom for man have never said that God doesn't have a plan, a pattern, or a fabric for history. Don't accuse us of believing the absurd. The Bible clearly reveals God at work shaping, molding, guiding and fulfilling his purposes in his creation. What we are saying is that man is a co-actor in the fulfillment of God's purposes. His purpose will be fulfilled, but the degree to which it is fulfilled in each individual man depends in some part on his response to God's prompting. We see ourselves as made in his image, and in growing toward being like him in his character. Our Father is not an autocratic dictator who allows his children no choice between chocolate and vanilla. Life and history are a dynamic interaction between the Creator and his creation.

Frame has managed to exterminate a whole army of straw men, but he has not refuted the truth of what open theists in general are saying.

I have noticed that in the first half of his book he sets out to defend the reformed theological position, but to a great degree in the second half, particularly chapters ten and eleven he contradicts it. He acknowledges that God changes his plans based on man's actions, that God has feelings that change with time and that God "relents" and changes what he said he was going to do.

One of my problems with reformed theology and the doctrine of predestination as it is taught in their schools is that it says that certain persons were chosen from before the beginning of creation to be saved and others were chosen to stay lost. If this were so, then the ones destined for salvation were never lost in any true sense of the word. If salvation is predetermined for some and impossible for others, then it is senseless to talk about salvation because some cannot be saved and the others never were in danger of condemnation. Christ's death on the cross never really saved anyone since it was already predetermined who would be saved and who would not. It is useless to talk about being saved if I was never really lost, but only misplaced for a while.

Agreements

I appreciate the times when Frame admits that he struggles with interpretation. He says that he is still in process, and that he has learned some good things from the open theists. He comments on page 211 that, as a result of the open theists writings, *"I have concluded that there is indeed more 'give-and-take' between God and his creatures than traditional theology has generally acknowledged."* Also, *"If traditional theology would put more emphasis (as Scripture certainly does) on the temporal interaction between God and the world, it would become less abstract, more practical, and more conducive to piety and obedience."* That would make a good foreword to my book.

I suspect that one of the main reasons for the Charismatic movement in the last fifty years is that they were feeling the need for a more personal God to whom they could relate. They were tired of the wooden god of classical theology. This does not condone what errors they might have, but at least they were looking for the real God.

I also agree with him when he says that God is above time but also in time, and he implies that there is a sequence of events in Heaven. I believe that this is consistent with the overall biblical message.

I agree with him that what is today called "open theism" is not a new doctrine or new theology. In fact, as he himself says, it is much older than reformed theology, which basically had its birth in the early fifth century. His bibliography on open–theist writings dates to as early as 1882. He could probably go back much farther than that if he expanded his search to include other descriptions of open theism–type writings. Chapter sixteen in my book shows clearly that the concept of man's free will was an integral part of the early church fathers' understanding of God's workings. I have also tried to show convincingly that it was an indispensable part of the theology of all Bible characters.

I agree with him when he says that Arminians and some open theists are not consistent with the Scriptures when they say that God knows everything in the present including the motives of a man's heart, but that he doesn't know the future. I point out in several places that God reveals that he does not always know every motive or intention in the heart of man. I do believe that he knows every action, every thought, every idea, etc., because those things become manifest to God before they are manifest to man. But I don't believe that he knows my thoughts before I think them. He knows the general condition of my heart, but because man is a partially free agent, he may make choices that either please or disappoint God. I am sure that somewhere, someone who reads my book is preparing a cross for me since I deny that God knows everything in the heart of man in the present. However, a Christian dying of crucifixion is probably a better way to go than Alzheimer's or cancer, so bring it on.

Conclusions

Why is the Westminster Confession considered the highwater mark of sound doctrine? This convocation of the divines in 1647 to elaborate sound doctrine for the Anglican Church was called for by the British parliament. Once this document was published did that mean that there could never be a better understanding of the works of God? Is the Westminster Confession the new last book of the Bible, or is it possibly wrong in some aspects? Every generation needs to shape its understanding of God based on the Scriptures, and not rely too heavily on tradition.

I do not wish Frame or other like–minded theologians ill. I believe that they are simply misguided by their tradition, and by faulty hermeneutics in some areas. I believe that they are not as devoted to inerrancy as they claim, and allow their theological preconceptions to influence the way they read and interpret the Bible. I do not claim to be exempt from this condition, though I have tried as hard as I know to not let my theological preparation dictate how I read and interpret God's word. There is nothing wrong with every once in a while throwing caution to the wind and reading the Bible again with no theological straightjacket to guide or misguide me. That way, I have no proverbial axe to grind or school of thought to defend. In fact, what I believe today is a good distance from some of the things I believed in my early ignorance. I hope I can still say the same in a few years when I come to the end of the road. If I don't grow, I might as well be dead and head on home to my Father's house where we will finally understand it all.

I could say much more about Frame's many other inconsistencies, but having better things to do I will end this critique.